Valerie Maher
WALLS
of
GLASS

First published in 1995 by Pretani Press
17 Main Street, Conlig, Newtownards BT23 3PT

This book has received support from the Cultural Traditions Programme of the Community
Relations Council, which aims to encourage acceptance and understanding of cultural diversity.

Printed in Northern Ireland by The Universities Press (Belfast) Limited

ISBN 0 948868 22 8

If I Can Dream

There must be lights burning brighter, somewhere.
Got to be birds flying higher in the sky, more blue.
If I can dream of a better land, where all my brothers walk hand in
    hand,
Tell me why! oh why, oh why can't my dreams come true – oh
    why?

There must be peace and understanding, sometime.
Strong winds of promise, that will blow away all the doubt and
    fear.
If I can dream of a warmer sun, where hope keeps shining on
    everyone,
Tell me why! oh why, oh why won't that sun appear?

We're lost in a cloud with too much rain,
We're trapped in a world that's troubled with pain.
But as long as a man has the strength to dream,
He can redeem his souls and fly – he can fly.

Deep in my heart there's a trembling question.
Still I am sure that the answer's going to come someday.
Up there in the dark, there's a beckoning candle.
While I can dream, while I can walk, while I can stand, while I can
    talk,
While I can dream, please let my dream come true.

Let it come true right now – Lord, let it come true right now!

Words and music by W Earl Brown
Recorded by Elvis Aron Presley (1968)

I dedicate this book to my husband John, and children Kevin, Stephen, Heather, Peter and Shauna, and also to the memory of a dear friend, Graeme Lowry.

Contents

Acknowledgements

Special thanks to:

Joe Fernandez
Tom Mahony
Frank Chisum
Brenden Bowyer
Patsy Anderson
George Klein
Charlie Hodge
Richard Davis
George Twamley

Chapter 1

HOW THE WEB WAS WOVEN

In the beginning God created the world and all its creatures. Why He decided to fashion Man, and then allow this particular creature to spawn havoc among all the others, is a complete mystery. His head has most likely been thumping with the stress of it ever since, as He has been blamed for all the damage Man has done. Not content with a male specimen of the human race, God went and created a female to keep the male company.

Well, it was only a matter of time before 'sex' reared its ugly head, an activity which resulted in the males having all the pleasure while the females were left to suffer agony whilst in the throes of childbirth. God also decided to play little jokes along the way, throwing in the occasional 'odd ball', two prime examples being my parents Charlotte and William. In His infinite wisdom God decided that these two people should somehow cross each other's paths. I was going to say 'fall madly in love and settle down in matrimonial bliss', only this would be quite erroneous, as love had little to do with it. Their meeting proved that God *can* make mistakes, as a more mismatched couple would be extremely difficult to find. Indeed, their relationship proved to be an unmitigated disaster.

My mother was born in 1912, the same year the *Titanic* sank. To this day I have often wondered which was the bigger catastrophe – the sinking of the *Titanic* or the arrival of Charlotte Russell (to use my mother's maiden name). She was born into a working-class family who lived in a small two-up, two-down terraced house in the Donegall Road area of Belfast.

These little houses, which were huddled together in a warren of narrow streets, were all made to the same design – two small bedrooms upstairs, and a minute living area downstairs which led to a scullery barely large enough for the family cat to turn full circle in, never mind find itself being swung round by the tail. A jawbox, cooker and a small cupboard holding cooking utensils, were the scullery's only fixtures. A Lilliputian-size bedroom, which also served as quarters for the laying out of the dead, was most unhygienically situated just off this excuse for a kitchen.

Sanitation was provided by a small brick outhouse in the back yard, attached to the scullery wall. The lavatory was a hole surmounted by a wooden bench. In the winter one's arse was frozen to the point of turning blue if one had to spend more than two minutes waiting for nature to take its course. In the hot summer months the bloody thing stank to high heaven as it only flushed when it took the headstaggers – about once a day. My grandfather laid down the law for its usage: 'Only one square of newspaper to be used by each person to wipe their backside, as any more will clog up the pot.' This exercise was to make sure that all the contents disappeared in one fell swoop, thus saving my grandfather the trouble of having to un-clog the accursed thing with the bent rod he used to get round the S-bend.

The area reeked of unemployment and poverty, while the undertakers were kept busy and well fed with their takings from the poor, who were forever mourning the death of some family member who had died of consumption or diphtheria, two ailments prevalent at the beginning of the century in poorer areas of the country. However, my grandfather Russell was one of the lucky few who held down a job of work. He worked as a master baker, and this enabled him to keep his family well provided for with food. He also fed a few local waifs with leftovers that were somewhat on the stale side but nevertheless eatable – a treat that was much appreciated and earned him the name 'the soda bread man'.

He was a tall, thin man of gaunt appearance, who sported a dew drop on the end of his nose in all weathers, summer or winter. A hypochondriac of the first degree who spent the best part of his leisure time reading medical books to find out which disease he could expound upon during his next meeting with his cronies. He would scare them witless by suggesting that their ailments had all the symptoms of the malady he had just read about. They would then be duly informed of their impending doom – which he invariably predicted would probably take place a few weeks hence. He was a man to avoid if you didn't feel too well, for if you felt ill before you met him it was nothing to the way you felt after you left him.

Grandmother Russell was the opposite. She was small, fat and ruddy-cheeked, a very good-looking woman in her time who could have had her pick of men. But alas, this was not to be, for John Russell came aknocking on her door and hung on to the knocker until she could take no more, making her give in to him with resignation rather than love. She spent the rest of her life voicing her hatred for men whenever my Granda Russell's name was mentioned. In fact, she never even called him by his Christian name as it stuck in her craw to do so. So called him 'the aule buck', as in 'here comes the aule buck for his tea'. She was not on her own in this attitude, for many of the women in the street held their men at arm's length, the lack of birth control options being a constant worry to those of child-bearing age. Any sign of endearment toward one's husband too often resulted in one more mouth to feed.

Her stoic disregard for any possible romance in a relationship obviously rubbed off on my mother, who was solely intent on finding a man with money, and to hell with love. Sure didn't love soon fly out the window, whereas a man with money was a long-term investment. When love died one could at least buy whatever one desired to fill the void. This was a miscalculation which was to bring my mother much misery in later life. The inability to express love verbally has also been handed down through the family, including to myself. Those three little words 'I love you' do not slide easily off my tongue, even when my heart is hurting to the point of breaking. I tend to express my love in giving – not always a good way to be.

My father, William Linton, on the other hand was born with a silver spoon in his mouth, a large silver spoon that overflowed with home-made preserves, roast beef and Yorkshire pudding. The Lintons were an upper-class family who originated from St Helen's in Liverpool, a family who were able to hire a maid to set the dinner table with silver cutlery, crystal glasses and the best of china on a tablecloth of linen. A striking contrast to the soup bowls and mugs that rested on the daily newspaper (usually the *News Letter*) that graced the table in the Russell household. My paternal grandmother's neck was always adorned with the finest pearls and jet beads money could buy, while my maternal grandmother's neck was bedecked with beads of sweat from a life of hardship. Her ruddy cheeks were often stained with the tears of grief occasioned by the loss of her first child Billy, who died at the age of three with diphtheria.

Billy was a beautiful child who had hair the colour of corn and the brightest blue eyes which would have made the finest sapphires look dull in comparison. Grandma Russell often said he looked like an angel, and when he died what little happiness she had died with him. My grandfather was just as devastated – his hair actually turned white with the shock, making him appear far older than his years. He had stood behind a wall of glass separating him from his young son and helplessly watched him choke to death. The hospitals in those days did not allow parents into the ward with their children – especially those dying from diptheria, it being so contagious – hence the glass partition. Only twenty-four hours earlier the child had refused a sweet from a neighbour and my grandfather had chastised him for being ungrateful. Now the words of 'my throat's sore, Daddy' haunted him. He had to control the urge to smash the glass in his anguish. When the child died my grandfather's nerves were shattered, depression set in and he lost all pride in his appearance. He would stand at his front door for hours on end, his head bent in despair. From then on 'the soda bread man' became known as 'the grumpy aule lad', a label he did not deserve, especially from people with short memories – those who might have starved to death if he had not had the kindness of heart to feed them at the end of his day's work.

Yet, death was commonplace then. Many an old woman used to stand at the front door wringing her hands in despair, crying: "Ach anee and anee, my wee grandchil' would be alive the day if he [or she] had been fed right. The wee angel is away to meet his maker for the sake of a bite to eat." They would watch with sunken eyes as the horse-drawn hearse carried away a grandchild who had been crippled with rickets caused by malnourishment.

Those were hungry times, compared to the present day when no-one in the British Isles can honestly say they have to go without food. In the early part of this century, if one had no money to buy food, then anything that wasn't nailed to the floor was sold. That is, after the wife's wedding ring had been pawned and replaced with a curtain ring for the sake of one's dignity. The table was of no use if there was no food to put on it; neither was the food cabinet if there was no food to store in it. When you were down to your uppers the 'outdoor relief', a poor equivalent of today's dole, came to the rescue. When starvation reared its ugly head the 'People's Palace' or the 'Cripples' Institute' on the Donegall Road would not refuse a bowl of soup or a roll and cup of hot tea. But by God you had to be in a bad way – ready to collapse with malnutrition. Many young lads joined the Army or Navy just to be properly fed. Some of the poor beggars paid a high price for this when they lost their lives fighting for King and Country in the First World War.

My mother was only a year old when her brother Billy died and she was shunted between aunts and other relatives while her parents grieved for their lost son. In the meantime a second daughter was born; this child was lavished with love, probably by way of substitute for Billy, which only served to harden my mother as she felt left out in the cold. To compensate for the lack of affection, she was given dolls and whatever else she wanted by her relatives, but nothing compensates for the lack of a parent's love. It turned her into a material person unable to express love for the greater part of her life. Even as a child her tongue was sharper than a knife. The rest of the children in her street turned to shivering wrecks when Charlotte joined them for a game. They knew she would take over the whole shebang. A wallop from Charlotte usually left them with a red ear if they did not jump to attention when she decided one game should

10

end and be replaced by another. One of her friends who had a stutter was petrified to the point of being struck immobile whenever our Lottie joined their childish frolics.

She had a penchant for acting. Christmas meant pantomime, and pantomime meant Cinderella being acted out to Charlotte's specifications. The Fairy Godmother was not the gentle creature we all knew and loved. Her name was changed to Fairy Nettle-Sting, while her wand was replaced with a long thin stick, pilfered from one of the prickly bushes that grew in the playground at the bottom of the street. Charlotte commandeered the backyard of Agnes the stutterer and woe betide anyone foolish enough not to have learned their lines to perfection. Agnes – or 'Aggie' as her friends called her – had perfected her lines to a 'T'. Yet as soon as Fairy Nettle-Sting made her entrance with prickly stick in hand, Aggie froze on the spot, and all she had learnt went out the yard door. Her rickety thin legs knocked at the knees and the blood drained from her already sickly complexion.

"Do ye know yer lines?" Charlotte would hiss in her face. "Ask Fairy Nettle-Sting for a wish or I'll beat the bake off ye!" For good measure she hit Aggie round her frail legs with the stick. Aggie's mouth opened and closed but no sound came forth, apart from "F...f...fai..." Wallop! Agnes felt the wrath of Charlotte's short temper and that was the end of the pantomime.

Poor Agnes, apart from the three pennies and an orange which Father Christmas left in her stocking, Christmas was not a happy time. It was bad enough that her father got drunk on cheap whisky prior to dinner and then proceeded to beat up his wife, without the added indignity of being confronted by Charlotte Russell armed with the dreaded wand and a face that shone with health – for sickness was another thing our Charlotte did not suffer from, as even germs were afraid to come too close to her.

Granny Linton, even though she didn't lack financially, nevertheless had her worries with regard to maternal matters. Her first child Elsie was born on 16 September 1895 without much difficulty, but this was followed by thirteen miscarriages (all boys) before William, my father, made his debut into the world in 1908, also on 16 September, exactly thirteen years to the day after his sister's arrival. Elsie died of consumption, more commonly known as tuberculosis, when my father was thirteen years of age, leaving him an only child. This tragedy made him more precious and he became a 'mother's boy', effectively tying him to my grandmother's apron strings until she died. He was not permitted to indulge in normal boyish behaviour, for my grandmother believed in children being seen but not heard. To her, a child was to stay in its proper place – in the garden and playing hoop and stick or croquet.

My Grandfather Linton, a robust and jovial individual – who I have always thought resembled a ginger-haired walrus in any family photographs – had the appetite of a horse and could have downed a leg of lamb in the time it took an ordinary individual to eat a leg of chicken. He tried to make his only son more self-assured, but lost the battle to his wife, who, although she appeared fragile from the outside, was mentally strong on the inside. The money he lost gambling on horses was a constant source of embarrassment to the family, which led to my father's hatred of gambling. My grandfather was not, in my opinion, a match for my grandmother, who resembled a tall, thin, witchlike schoolmarm, with eyes as grey as smoke with dark circles underneath. She had a Lancashire accent as broad as your boot, and the appetite of a mouse on a diet.

They had moved to Ireland in the early 1900s when my grandfather was offered a good position with one of the best organ building companies in Belfast. Their first priority was to find a place to lay their heads, and after much deliberation purchased a house on the Stranmillis Road. It was in this house that they first experienced the hostility of the natives with regard to matters of religion, proof that it hasn't simply been the events of the past twenty five years which have spawned our present pathetic hatreds and bigotries.

My father's parents were financially able to acquire the services of a maid when the need arose. They were Protestants, but being quite unaware of the depth of the religious divide in Belfast, employed a Catholic girl to take care of their domestic tasks. They failed to see any connection between this act and the sudden aloofness of the neighbours. However, one day the front door was almost blattered up the hallway. On responding to the commotion, which seemingly sounded like a barn door being kicked by a horse, my grandfather was confronted by a woman so hysterical she literally foamed at the mouth. The conversation went something like this:

"Yes, what can I do for you, my good woman?" my grandfather asked in his clear English voice.

"Dae yousens have a woman that kicks wi' the wrong fut workin' fer yous?" enquired the irate female in a not so clear Ulster voice. My grandfather, being English and not used to Ulster idiom, thought she meant someone who played football or some other game.

"I'm afraid I don't know what you mean, my dear lady," he answered, at the same time surveying her appearance, since she no more resembled a lady than Sammy Davis Jnr had the look of Elvis.

"I mean a Fenian, ye stupid git! An' wut the hell are ye afeard aff, anyway?" By this time she was poking his ribs with her middle finger. He pondered on her remarks for a few minutes before replying.

"Oh, you mean a Catholic. Why didn't you say so? And, by the way, I'm afraid of nobody – if that's what you mean by afeard." He was most probably quite bewildered by her and no doubt assumed she had escaped from a lunatic asylum.

"There's nay diff'rence, git ridda her! Dae ye hear me? Or by Jaysus I'll git the men on ye!" (The 'men' probably being some unruly thugs who frequented a pub in some other district of the town.) At this juncture she turned on her heels and stomped off into the night, never to be seen again by my grandfather. The incident left him even more bemused by the mentality of the Irish.

As far as he was concerned Ireland meant one was Irish, full stop – he had not as yet been 'educated' by those who insisted the northern part was only for the Protestant population. Catholicism, to them, was the religion of a minority who had been cursed with the mentality of sex maniacs and whose only interest was to turn out babies at a rate of knots.

My father followed in my grandfather's footsteps and went into carpentry. He worked for the same organ builders, and, low and behold, the factory was situated in the Donegall Road where my mother lived. God help the Russells and the Lintons – life was never to be the same again!

Charlotte Russell was standing on the corner of her street when William Linton swept by on his motorbike. A sight seldom seen in the 1930s, as most men couldn't afford a pushbike never mind a motorbike. A pot of soup plus a soda farl for the dinner was more important than cavorting up and down the road on a piece of metal on wheels, for money was hard to come by in that particular end of town.

Charlotte's eyes popped out like organ stops at the sight of William on his machine. To her it must have seemed the next best thing to a mobile bank. If he could afford a motorbike surely to God he must have money somewhere – her prayers for a man with money were not going unheeded after all. William – 'Bill' as he was more commonly known – roared up the Donegall Road with all the style of Billy the Kid on his trusted steed, weapons at the ready, only *his* weapons were the tools of his trade – hammers, chisels and screwdrivers.

The sight must have been more than Charlotte could bear, because her agitated state was taken out on the poor fellow she had to meet that same night for a date. He turned up in his duncher cap, his suit frayed at the edges, and with down-at-the-heel shoes. She took one look at this poor unfortunate soul – who, after all, was out of work and couldn't afford the grandeur expected of Charlotte, especially after she had just witnessed a meal ticket for life – and promptly ate the gob off him. She gave him such a berating for daring to turn up for a lady like herself in such tatty disarray he ended up doffing his cap and backing down the road like a menial servant.

Charlotte could not content herself now, and all the males within a ten-mile radius were looked upon as nothing other than the scum of the earth – out of work, out of pocket, and the further out of her sight the better! She hunted every picture house and dance hall in her search for Bill. She even started to attend church on Sundays in the hope that her prayers for a second sighting of the vision on wheels would be answered. These prayers seemed to be falling on deaf ears when fate at last intervened. As she preened herself in the ladies' room at a dance in St Aiden's church hall, putting the finishing touches to her finger-waved nut brown hair with saliva-wetted fingers, and dabbing her lips with a touch more lip rouge to accentuate her Clara Bow smile, she perchanced to hear the plaintive cry of bagpipes coming from an upstairs room.

Being of a curious nature, she followed in the direction from which this wailing sound was emanating. On reaching the room she was astounded to find it full of kilted males practising for the St Aiden's pipe band. Low and behold, at the front stood a six-foot blonde-haired wallet draped in tartan, beating the snare drum with the deftness of a tattoo artist – it was Bill. Little did he know the fate that was about to befall him or he would have scarpered there and then and joined the Foreign Legion at the first opportunity.

With the cunning of a fox Charlotte lurked behind the door that separated her from her prey, just in case her ticket to a wealthy future slipped away in an unguarded moment. As soon as the band practice ended, she flounced across the room like a prima ballerina. With one hand on her heart and the other busy patting her hair and smoothing her eyebrows, she pinched her cheeks between thumb and forefinger to give herself a flushed look, making her appear coy and innocent. Then she deftly weaved her way through the dispersing bandsmen, grabbed Bill by the elbow just as he was in the process of removing his tartan beret, pulled him towards her and stared him straight in the eyes.

"Don't I know you from somewhere?" she asked.

Bill, surprised at being thus accosted, replied: "I don't think so, madam, not to my knowledge anyway."

I imagine Charlotte very nearly fainted when he addressed her as 'madam', and her heart now beat faster than the snare drum Bill had been playing earlier.

"Don't you ride a motorbike?" She must have been sweating blood by this time.

"I'iee..." stammered Bill.

She didn't give him time to reply for fear he would tell her to get lost. "Indeed you do, for I've seen you ride up the Donegall Road on quite a few occasions!" I'm sure she must have been in a panic by now, worried he was going to give her the old heave-ho.

"Ah yes, I work up there in an organ works." Bill's winning smile coupled with his boyish good looks left Charlotte in a state of bliss.

"I just knew it was you!" she gasped. She had found her Prince Charming at last and collapsed on the seat beside the bandstand in a heap.

Lord only knows what happened after that fateful night but Bill didn't get away. The unlucky sod was caught hook, line and sinker. Fairy Nettle-Sting threw away her wand, she no longer felt the need for it – she could weave her own brand of magic now that she had caught her prey. Charlotte was her own worst enemy from then on. No-one was good enough to cross her path and she alienated herself from her neighbours and family by sticking to Bill like glue, fearful he would find fresh pickings.

Bill lived in a bungalow in Stockman's Lane with his parents. It was located not far from the Malone Road, where the crème de la crème of society lived. Charlotte had delusions of grandeur – a husband with money plus the chance to mix with the upper classes. If she was lucky enough to catch him in her trap she would be made for life. Little did she know what lay in store.

The bungalow was small compared to today's standards, with only two bedrooms, but it did have two reception rooms, a relatively large scullery and, the most important luxury of all, a bathroom where the lavatory flushed with the greatest of ease. All this plus gardens front and rear planted with rose bushes and fruit trees, and situated within throwing distance of parkland and meadows. It held no comparison to the bleak kitchen house which was rapidly disappearing into the furthest corners of my mother's mind.

My grandmother was to treat her with disdain from day one. She had plans for her son, and Charlotte Russell was not one of them. Granny Linton had another girl in mind for my father, a girl of good stock, one he would be proud to be seen with. Not a backstreet factory worker who, in her opinion, was only fit for washing floors and scrubbing steps. On hearing that her beloved son had befriended a girl from a lower-class background, her reaction must have been similar to Lady Bracknal's in *The Importance of Being Earnest* when she heard her grand-daughter was to marry a man who had been found in a handbag when he was a baby. Only my grandmother's reaction was not to cry in alarm, "A hannndbaag!" but "The Donegall Road! How on earth could you drag yourself so low as to cavort with a hussy from an area so downmarket?" Or should I say 'harea', as her Lancashire accent made her inclined to pronounce every other word with an 'h' in front. May I take this opportunity to make my apologies to those people who come from the Donegall Road. I am not trying in any way to demean them. It's just that some people have a deficiency in their mental outlook, and my grandmother was one such person. Granda Linton was more tolerant than his wife; he was down-to-earth and had a more understanding nature.

Needless to say, love conquered all, or, to be more accurate, determination conquered all. I don't think my mother knew what love for a man really meant, it was simply a means to an end. Anyway, an affair of the heart could well be replaced by an affair with the wallet. Little did she know that access to the heart cost nothing, whereas it would have taken the skill of an expert magician to gain access to Bill's wallet without his knowledge.

In due course mother managed to wangle her way into the Linton household. She was made to feel a total outcast by my Granny Linton on her very first visit to the bungalow in Stockman's Lane. But Charlotte, determined not to let 'the toffy-nosed bitch', as she called her, stand in the way of her plans, she took all cuts as compliments.

Granda Linton, on the other hand, took a liking to her and made her feel welcome. Quite probably he was fed up to the back teeth with his stuffy wife and the chinless wonders she called friends. His son also got up his nose with his excessive mother-fixation. Perhaps he had hopes Charlotte could untangle my father from his mother's apron strings and turn him into a real man. So to Granda Linton Charlotte was like a breath of fresh air. She was down-to-earth and called a spade a flamin' shovel. She didn't object to my granda's gambling or his more than occasional tipple. Where she came from it was a way of life for most of the married men and not a mortal sin which threw you "hinto the harms hof the devil hin the here hafter", as Granny Linton would claim.

Unfortunately this friendship was short-lived, for he died in 1934 of heart failure, brought on by an allergy to bee stings, an allergy that was to be passed on to one of my own children. On his death bed he sent my father on a mission of mercy behind my granny's back to the betting shop for a last gamble. Luck didn't even shine on the bloody horse – it lost. A few hours later my granda died, and now Charlotte was left to stand up for herself – to try and prove her worth. It was to be a task that often left her frustrated to the point of courting madness.

A woman has one usually reliable trick up her sleeve in her bid to entrap a man – sex. Lottie was no lover of the aule sex games, but she relented and let Bill have his wicked way while she lay back and thought of the bungalow and her escape from the side streets of the Donegall Road and winter nights on an outside lavatory. The shirt factory where she worked as a trouser-presser would also be history, for work outside the home was unheard of if one lived in a bungalow in Stockman's Lane married to a man with a trade. Bill must have thought he'd died and gone to heaven, though it would be among the few times he would get his oats without having to plead for hours on end. I know this because I had to lie in the bedroom beside theirs and listen to him whine "Ah, comon, Lottie, it will only take a minute", while my mother told him to "bugger off!" She probably thought it was fifty-nine seconds too long! As there were six of us born to Lottie and Bill she must have relented on occasion. It also proves one thing – sex need have little to do with love!

In March 1935 my mother and father married. She was five months pregnant. This must have been how she trapped my father into marriage. However, it takes two to tango, and my father was not the paragon of virtue his mother believed him to be. His real fault was not being as worldly-wise as my mother. She knew perfectly well what she was doing, whereas he obviously didn't think too carefully about the consequences of his flutter with mother nature.

My parents never ever celebrated their wedding anniversary, perhaps because they never wanted to let their children know of my mother's pre-marital condition. In the 1930s being pregnant before marriage had a far greater stigma attached to it than today. Or maybe it was because they did not want us to think they did things like that in those days. To be honest, I would have respected them more if they had been up front about the whole situation, for in later years they where to make my life hell on earth because of their attitude towards sex. If my mother had not been pregnant I personally don't think my father would have married her, for he never showed her love in any shape or form other than as father to her children. Their life together was one continuous argument. I am convinced that two more mismatched people have yet to be found.

Chapter 2

THAT'S WHEN YOUR HEARTACHES BEGIN

My mother's parents were quite fond of their daughter's fiancé. They were impressed by his white silk scarf, gloves and motorbike, three outward signs of unashamed wealth. Lottie became the talk of the area, with the neighbours conversing in hushed tones as they huddled in groups at their front doors.

"That one thinks she's the cat's whiskers, hangin' on tae that maun like grim death on the back aff that contraption aff his. Does she nat know she cud be goin' till her death on that thing."

Lottie would retort defiantly: "No, I'm not, I'm only going to Helen's Bay, so stop your gossiping", then fling her head back and let her chestnut-brown hair blow in the wind as if she hadn't a care in the world.

She tried her best to lose her Belfast accent by pronouncing '...ing', 'and' and 'the' properly. When asked if she wanted anything she did not reply "aye, a do", she made sure she said "yes, I do, thank you", in preparation for her life among the upper crust.

"She'll come a cropper, mark my words. It's only a matter of time afor her gaurd slips an' her Belfast tongue claps about in'er jowls, fer she's jis' like the rest aff us here in the street – Belfast born and bred," the neighbours would mutter as she swanned round the bend and up the road.

Charlotte's parents welcomed Bill into the Russell household, however modest it may have been. Surprisingly, Bill felt comfortable in his wife-to-be's humble abode. His future in-laws fed him home-made vegetable soup in a large bowl, with doorsteps of fresh bread to dip in it. He gobbled Ulster fry-ups of bacon, sausage, fried eggs and, of course, lots of Granda Russell's soda farls and potato bread, while the family gazed in amazement and wondered if his pallor was the result of anaemia rather than upper-class breeding. His blonde looks were a contrast to the dark, moody look of the Russells.

In return Bill entertained them with a tune on his ukulele and his rendition of the popular song, 'Ain't she sweet, as she waltzes down the street; now I ask you very confidentially, ain't she sweet?' His own mother detested this instrument because it had overtones of the lower classes, but the Russells would be transfixed by his dexterity and artistic flair and Lottie would go into raptures. He was a bright star and a refreshing breeze in their dull kitchen house.

Lottie tired to hide her pregnancy from her parents. Bill's mother was not long in letting the cat out of the bag. She tried to get the wedding stopped and Lottie put into a home for unmarried mothers. The Russells, however, stuck by their daughter and bought her a wedding dress that could be let out at the seams. Lottie's main concern was to make it up the aisle to hear Bill say those two precious words "I do", convincing herself – quite mistakenly as it turned out – that she could then mould him to fall in with her own plans.

Lottie was neither bright nor refreshing in her mother-in-law's eyes. My grandmother Linton openly called my mother a whore. It was Lottie's fault completely she was in 'that condition'. Bill, being such a paragon of virtue, was incapable of perpetrating such an act of indecency. Sure, by God, he was a gentleman and gentlemen just don't do such things. If that was the case, then thought transmission is a powerful force, and not to be toyed with!

The first family symposium to be held concerned the wedding reception, and it was decided to hold it in the bungalow in Stockman's Lane. This would mean that my grandmother Linton could take care of the culinary delights. She would bake the wedding cake, just to make sure the dew drop on the end of my grandfather Russell's nose didn't end up as part of the ingredients. Many family arguments soon ensued, but none bad enough to prevent my parents eventually making it up the aisle. I have one photograph of their wedding and I swear to God someone must have had a shotgun trained on my father's head. He bears the expression of a man about to face the gallows. Perhaps he had a premonition of the future – a lifetime with Charlotte, a fate worse than death itself.

They even spent their honeymoon in the bungalow. Seeing as they were going to live there anyway it didn't make much difference. So on their first night together as man and wife they were duly tucked into bed by my grandmother as if they were brother and sister. Can you imagine the effect this must have had on them? They probably lay like a pair of pickled herrings the rest of the night in case she came back to make sure they hadn't fallen out of bed. My father wasn't even allowed to give his wages to my mother. He had to hand his hard-earned money to my grandmother who doled out whatever she deemed necessary to keep my mother in clothes. This yearly allowance could have been counted on the fingers of one hand. My grandmother then took care of the rest – housekeeping and my father's requirements. Her disdain of my mother knew no bounds. She considered her totally useless as well as classless.

In July 1935 my mother gave birth to their first child, Elizabeth, a beautiful baby, but also a noisy little mite who cried incessantly. My mother need not have worried, for my grandmother took Elizabeth under her wing in the hope of turning her into a future lady, just to prove to my mother that the Linton breeding was stronger than that of the Russells.

[My sister Elizabeth's birth might have been one small event in the town of Belfast. The same year, 1935, on 8 January in the little town of Tupelo, Tennessee, a mother gave birth to twin boys in a tiny wooden shack. One of the twins survived. That, too, was a small, bittersweet event in a hick town in a southern state of America where poverty was a way of life. The boy's mother, Gladys Presley, named him Elvis Aron in the typical style of double-barrelled names common in the deep South, and cradled him in her arms and cried as she watched his twin brother Jesse Garon being buried in an unmarked grave. Little did she know then of the joy he would bring to the world through his singing – not least to one of the Lintons' children.]

A second child, Dorothy, was born in August of the following year, so my parents must have managed to fit in a little bit more of 'the other' after being tucked into bed by my grandmother. Dorothy was highly obstreperous, and wailed her flaming head off if you so much as looked at her sideways. Dorothy's childhood days were spent trying to make up her mind whether or not she wanted something. If you gave her sweets, she didn't want them; if you didn't give her sweets, she wanted them. In fact, most of the time she didn't know what the hell she wanted. My mother, however, was firmly convinced that all she wanted was a good hiding. Dorothy too was nurtured by grandma for a short while, that is until my mother fell pregnant again. Enough was enough – my grandmother was now sick to the gills with grandchildren, and informed my mother she would have to look after this child herself.

My brother Charles made his debut into the world in June of 1938. He reminded my mother of the brother she had lost when she was a child. Her brother's photograph had hung in the living room of their home in the Donegall Road and she had often remarked on his angelic beauty, with his blonde hair and big blue eyes. She decided to leave the pleasures of preening and moulding her two daughters to her mother-in-law and devoted what little motherly instincts she had on her son. She transformed him into the image of her brother by letting his blonde hair cascade in ringlets, and dressing him in blue to enhance the colour of his eyes. There is no denying he was a beautiful child, and she used this to best advantage, taking him wherever she went, boasting that he had inherited the good looks of the Russells rather than the insipid looks of the Linton clan.

By this time my mother was well and truly confirmed in my grandmother Linton's eyes as a sex maniac, slut and whore. Of course my father was still held to be completely blameless – mummy's boy must have been molested in his sleep by the worldly-wise backstreet scrubber. During all this time, my mother hardly ever visited her own parents. Indeed, she rarely went back to that area of town except on those occasions when she needed credit in the shop at the end of her parents' street. (This was all unknown to my father – he would have had a fit at the thought of his affluent friends finding out.) I can't blame her for going to this extreme seeing as she was kept so short of money. It must have been very demeaning to have to ask for every penny from your mother-in-law. Her dreams of a life of grandeur were in tatters by now and it was turning her into a very bitter woman, a bitterness that would increase as the years rolled on.

Her acrimonious manner had begun to permeate into her whole being, turning her into a most hateful person. She was her own worst enemy and shunned everybody she had grown up with. In turn, they treated her with the greatest of contempt. When I look back I can't help but feel great pity for her. Perhaps if my father had not perchanced to enter her life she would not have become a victim of her own making.

It was on one of her credit-seeking expeditions, when she had no other option than to pass her parents' home in order to get to the shop, that she hurt her father to the bone. My grandfather Russell suffered from bronchitis and would often sit at the front door for a breath of fresh air. He wheezed and spluttered but got no sympathy from his wife who was disgusted by his habit of spitting through smoke-stained dentures onto the pavement, in between moans of, "This bronkatus will git the better aff me yit, but sure nat a wan gives a fiddler's damn." Anyone brave enough to stand and talk about health problems in his presence was always reminded that their state of health could never be as bad as his. God help him, it was to be this very ailment that would carry him off in the end. Maybe if my mother had been capable of understanding other people's feelings, she would not have been so unfeeling on this occasion. Then again, how could she understand other people's feelings when she was incapable of understanding her own.

On this particular afternoon, my mother was undoubtedly feeling a trifle guilty yet again about having to demean herself by seeking credit, especially after having boasted so much about her life of imagined luxury. To accompany her to the shop she had brought Charles, who was then about three years of age. She was making a hasty retreat out of the street, in case she should be caught in the act of buying groceries in this way, when she spied her father sitting outside his front door. She had no choice but to pass by him. She knew that he knew what she had been up to, which only made matters worse. But no way was she going to admit to him that her life was not going to plan, she was much too proud for that.

He put his hand out to greet his little grandson and asked him for a kiss. My mother grabbed Charles by the arm and trailed him past his grandfather with such vehemence the child's arm was almost torn from its socket. Her only remark was a warning to him not to talk to such a silly, sick-looking old man who would only cough germs all over him. My grandfather was so devastated he cried in disbelief that a daughter could be so cruel, especially to a man in ill-health.

In her clumsy attempts to make herself into a lady, not only did she make a fool of herself, she turned her whole family against her. They laughed at her behind her back, even at her pathetic attempts to sell them tomatoes from my father's greenhouse. She had this stupid notion she was better than the rest of her family now that she was living in Stockman's Lane; this marital move, according to her, entitled her to call herself a lady. She didn't realise she was making a complete ass of herself. She did not try to bring herself up to the level of the upper class in the Lane, she tried in vain to bring the residents of the Lane down to her level, and in no way was this going to happen. Indeed, it would have been easier to pass the proverbial camel through the eye of a needle than to turn my mother into a lady.

The Second World War was well under way when I made my entrance into the world. I was born on 17 June 1943 in a private nursing home, this being a feather in my mother's cap, for it gave her a little bit of status. She boasted continuously of her luxurious confinement to her neighbours, and of the day I was accidentally taken to a doctor's wife in mistake for her baby, while my mother was handed the doctor's baby. This mistake was quickly rectified at the doctor's wife insistence, when she observed the tatty gown my mother had dressed me in. Of course, this observation was prudently changed to "their hair was a different colour" so as not to detract from my mother's story – a story I have had to listen to endlessly over the years. Sometimes I wish to God the mistake had not been rectified, as the story of my birth has now become an irritant to the eardrums. Charles, my brother, was disgusted with my mother on her return from hospital when he was informed that he had acquired another sister. He wanted a brother for company and enquired of my mother when she arrived home: "Has Hitler rationed the birth of boys as well as food and sweets?"

Right from day one I was made feel as welcome as a Rottweiler in a poodle parlour. From all accounts I was a quiet little mite; had I not woken up to be fed, I might well have been ignored completely. Charles, or 'Chuck' as he is known, would gladly have exchanged me for a quarter pound of wine gums and a gobstopper if mother had given him half a chance. Knowing mother, she would have traded me in for a year's supply of groceries and a free visit to the vet for father to be castrated.

My sister Elizabeth, 'Betty' for short, was eight years old and Dorothy was seven at the time. Both looked upon me more as a doll, and were given the pleasure of deciding my name. Mother, quite frankly, couldn't give a damn and had already decided to call me quits, as by now she was suffering from mother-in-law fatigue, a condition brought on by the constant deluge of abuse from my grandmother, morning, noon and night. "You're a harlot and a hussy, not to mention a whore, who led my son into the sins of the flesh." My father donned invisible ear muffs and turned a blind eye to it all.

In due course I was christened Valerie, the same name as a little German girl who played with my sisters. As far as names went, Hitler would have been sufficient. According to my mother and father I was as big an annoyance to them as he was to the world. The best way to get round this new obstacle was simply, 'If we ignore her she will disappear', hence I went through my early life feeling very shy, lonely and unloved. Never once did my parents tell me they loved me, and I can tell you it hurts, as anyone who has suffered the same fate can verify.

Those three words 'I love you' can cure a mountain of ailments. The way you are treated as a child has an influence upon the rest of your life. If you are reared with love it becomes second nature to be able to express love with ease. On the other hand, if you are reared with contempt, as my brothers and sisters and I were, you are inclined to be suspicious of other people's feelings. Furthermore, if you are used to love you can recognise the symptoms of being in love and can return love without feeling embarrassed. When I first fell in love in later years I was totally confused. Love to me meant sex and sex was dirty, according to my mother, so when a boy told me he loved me I froze with fear, and that would be the end of any relationship. Instead of feeling good about myself, I automatically felt I was being considered easy prey.

To be fair, I can't blame it *all* on my mother. She had her own sorrows to seek, as well as a mother-in-law who despised her and a husband who hadn't the guts to stand up for her. By rights if he had truly loved his wife, which I doubt very much, he would have told his mother where to go.

Not only was my father gutless, but he was vindictive towards my mother, especially as she was so hopeless at rearing a family. He considered her cooking and cleaning to be inferior to his mother's and reminded her of this frequently. He never hurt my mother physically, but mentally she must have been hurt just as much, especially by being continuously compared to her mother-in-law. Physical scars heal in time, but the mind is far more fragile, as I myself found out later in life. It's impossible to have come from a background filled with hate and animosity and emerge unscathed.

Even at an early age, the detrimental effects of my upbringing were revealed in often bizarre ways. If a relative showed affection in any way, be it ever so small, I would be immediately suspicious and run off like a scared rabbit to hide, usually in a cupboard or some dark recess. Or I would sometimes sit in the furthest corner that could be found, even behind the garage. In other ways it had the completely opposite effect, in that I would readily approach complete strangers outside the home. My parents never took the time to warn me about the dangers of this, being too wrapped up in their own pathetic world of bitterness. I shudder to think of what could have happened, for we lived facing a park and I would often sit talking to people I didn't know. Kind old men would say how pretty I looked even though I resembled a waif. I knew in my heart they meant well but I could see the pity in their eyes as they scanned my shabby shoes, socks that were pulled over my toes and tucked under my feet to hide the holes, an old hand-me-down dress, and my hair tied with a ribbon made from an old piece of torn-up vest. Maybe it was the sparkle in my large brown eyes – which, I am led to believe, always looked as if they were hiding some dark secret – that attracted people to talk to me.

It wasn't the fact that the family was poor, it was a more complex situation. My father was quite well off, as grandmother Linton let him keep a good part of his wages so that he could impress their wealthy friends. My mother was kept in the background in case she let my father down by revealing anything to them about her background. She did not have the money to clothe her offspring properly, having to beg for every penny.

My grandmother, by this time, was ill and mostly bedridden and now Betty, Dorothy and Chuck were feeling the pinch as well. Gone were the days when my mother could load her offspring in grandmother's direction. Mother by now must have been feeling suicidal, as she realised her dreams of grandeur were being shattered as the years flew past. The bank on wheels had taken on the appearance of meals on wheels. Bourgeois escapism is often claimed to be the opium of the common people; my mother's materialistic dreams had long since ceased to induce a feeling of wellbeing, and she became even more bitter. Her vitriolic manner only made people avoid her, which in turn made matters worse, especially when my father refused to let her accompany him on evenings out with friends. The atmosphere in the family home could best be described in one word – 'Hell'; and Hell hath no fury like a woman scorned.

Especially one who was addicted to the usage of Cardinal Red polish when in a temper. The fireplace tiles, and front and back doorsteps, were subjected to Charlotte's frenzied polishing attacks with the Cardinal Red until they shone like glass. By the time her temper had subsided, her face was as red as the tiles, while the sweat dripped from her brow, giving her eyes a glazed expression to match the polish. I often felt the heat of her wrath from the buckle end of my father's belt if I so much as looked at her sideways. In her temper she often beat me with this instrument of torture. Then, on seeing the marks that the buckle pin left on my legs she would panic at the thought of having to explain them to my father. He might have been mean with money and a mother's boy, but one thing he didn't do when we were young was beat us – though he was to turn to this when we were older. She warned me that if I as much as mentioned the beatings, I would receive another one as punishment for tittle-tattling. I really think the anger she took out on us children was as much to do with the anger she felt towards my father.

We always kept a female cat for catching mice, and it was forever having kittens. We always kept them for a few weeks to see if we could give them away, and also to allow the mother cat time to disperse her milk. I actually felt jealous of the love she had for those tiny creatures, a love my brother and sisters and I had been denied. It still disturbs me to think of the way I treated those little mites, although it was probably a reflection of how unloved I felt and how much I craved parental warmth and tenderness.

In order to see what love felt like I would try to smother one of these kittens almost to the point of death and then nurse it back to life. I would stroke and kiss it as if that little mite was my own flesh and blood. It was as if the kitten was me and I was acting out the part of my mother. I would tell it I loved it and it meant the world to me. I know most children can be very sadistic and cruel at times, but I can honestly say I did not possess any of these characteristics. In reality I was of a very gentle nature and even an argument in the home would send me scurrying for cover, as I knew I would usually be on the receiving end of Lottie's wrath, being the youngest and therefore most likely to be in the house at the time. The other three children were always out playing in order to escape the daily rantings and ravings of their mad mother. No doubt my attempt to smother the kittens was an outlet for my feelings, but it is not a happy memory to recall.

God help the wee mites – my dad would drown them the following week in a bucket. This made me feel really sad, it was so final. I can still recall that flaming bucket. It had a lid on it which kept them trapped; the feeble and distressing miaows as they fought for life would nearly break my heart. I would run behind the garage and stick my fingers in my ears so that I couldn't hear, and cry. I knew that all the kissing and hugging in the world could not bring them back, as I had seen my father perform this ritual on numerous occasions. Afterwards he would wrap them in newspaper and then throw them in the rubbish bin. As soon as he went back into the house I would remove the tiny lifeless creatures from where they had been so casually discarded and proceed to arrange a decent funeral. I used to collect boxes and pieces of material, and I cut up some of the cloth into suitable-sized pieces and carefully wrapped up each little kitten and placed it in a small box. I buried them in the back garden, erecting a small wooden cross and saying the only prayer I knew, which was the Lord's Prayer, taught to me by my Grandmother Linton, hoping this would gain them entrance into Heaven.

Every other week I became a gravedigger and exhumed the remains of those unfortunate felines and had a peek in the hope they would have come alive again. I was so naive I thought this act of morbid curiosity would miraculously bring them back to life. I had to give up this grisly practice after about a month, as by then they were as flat as pancakes. And so part of my early childhood was spent holding burial services for kittens, praying to God to deliver me from the evil of not letting the dead rest in peace, and avoiding arguments and beatings as best I could.

Religion was a subject my parents didn't bother to teach us about, it was something we had to find out for ourselves. In my case it came as rather a shock for I had been under the impression the Lord's Prayer was a religion on its own and entitled you to a ticket to Heaven if recited at the first hint of impending doom. Much of my childhood saw me spending a good part of the day in a praying position, for the feeling of doom oozed from every nook and cranny of the Linton home.

I started school at the age of five and I must have been one of the few children who actually looked forward to leaving their mother at the school gates. It was a very small school, having only three classrooms, a cloakroom and an outside toilet. The tiny playing area housed two air raid shelters. A ghostly reminder of the Second World War, lest we forget.

It was called 'Roseland Primary' and was situated in the Andersonstown area of the Falls Road. It was a Protestant school, even though it stood in a predominantly Catholic area, and I probably grew up with a respect for both religions because of it. Looking back, it was no bad thing and it was a sad day when they knocked it down. Two of the best friends I ever had – Anne and Jeanette –

went to this school and are remembered with fond memories. We stuck together like glue. The headmaster Mr Holmes nicknamed us 'The Three Graces' – Faith, Hope and Charity, with me being 'Hope' as I was always hoping something good would turn up, Anne being 'Faithe as she was such a faithful friend, while Jeanette was 'Charity' because she always shared her lunch. I enjoyed this, for her sandwiches contained meat while mine consisted of margarine and a dollop of jam, which was of the home-made variety and usually damson – a watery concoction which turned the bread mushy and pink by the time lunch-break arrived. This culinary delight was not enhanced by the odd damson stone mother couldn't be bothered removing before bottling the jam. I suffered many a toothache after biting down sharply on one of those blasted objects.

The pupils were all Protestants with one exception – a Catholic boy called Kevin. I felt sorry for Kevin as he was very shy like myself. He came from a very well-heeled family and why they sent him to Roseland Primary was a complete mystery as he could have had the best education money could buy. I'm not saying my wee school was behind in the education stakes; indeed in comparison to the larger schools it had a very high rate of '11 plus' passes and I know of at least one doctor, a few solicitors, and two well-known actresses who attended Roseland.

Kevin excelled himself in all subjects, but he was painfully self-conscious. I felt an empathy towards him because I felt the same way, even if for different reasons, and so we had a special friendship. Kevin and I were known as childhood sweethearts because we held hands in the playground in an attempt to comfort one another. A year is a long time to a child but inevitably we drifted apart. I made a mental note that if I ever had a family I would call my first male child after him. I kept this promise – my son also turned out to be very smart and ended up at university. It must have been an omen.

The most enjoyable part of the school day was milk-break, especially in winter when the small milk bottles were heated beside the classroom's blazing fire. This treat was made even more enjoyable if you were lucky enough to get your mitts on the bottle nearest the fire. Sometimes it was so hot the paper straw fell apart at the seams, giving you the welcome excuse to ask for another. If the teacher was in a good mood, she would often give you a couple extra and you had a spare for playing with at home time. My brother Chuck usually had the pleasure of using it for blowing barley at his sister's bare legs; either that or aiming for the back of the neck. His pleasures in life at the time were indeed simple, and included torturing me by inflicting 'Chinese burns' on my wrists.

It's a great pity that time flies so fast, people grow up, and childhood pleasures are no longer so easily satisfied. My mother found happiness very hard to come by, especially now that my grandmother's health was rapidly deteriorating. This was another cross for my mother to bear as she had to wait on her, hand and foot, a task she bitterly deplored, not having had any fond feelings for her mother-in-law in the first place. Now she was a bloody invalid as well as a 'damned moanie grey-haired old bat!' To make matters worse my mother was pregnant for the fifth time. However, she had one over on her crotchety mother-in-law – she could at least close the bedroom door on her feeble ramblings about how Bill lost his upper-class rearing because of a lower-class whore – or 'huwer', to be more precise, as this was the way she pronounced it with her Lancashire accent.

In due course, my mother gave birth to my brother Alan. From day one he was a sickly child and demanded her attention morning, noon and night, resulting in the rest of the family getting even less love, if that was at all possible. My father spent any spare time he could muster with his cronies, leaving my mother to sit in the house, nursing a not too healthy infant and a crabby old woman, as well as trying to rear four other children on a pittance. I'm sure that on more than one occasion she accepted that she had made the biggest mistake of her life, when she married for money instead of love. It turned out to be more pain than gain.

Many a time I had to go hunting for my father to get him to fetch a doctor to attend to Alan's convulsive fits, while my mother would go into hysterics at the sight of her delicate ailing child. Alan's looks resembled my father's in an uncanny way, which made matters worse, as it brought back unhappy memories to my grandmother of the thirteen boys she had lost in early pregnancy before my father was born. She kept harping on about it being a bad omen, and that he wasn't meant for this earth.

Oddly enough, while most of my mother's time was taken up with nursing Alan and trying to make the most out of a life of drudgery, I built up a friendship of sorts with my gran. Every day, after school, I sat on the edge of her bed and read the Bible to her as best I could. All the thees, thous and shalt nots were confusing, to say the least, especially with me being so young. The stories didn't mean much to me, as I couldn't understand them, but the attention I received for keeping her company more than compensated for my lack of knowledge. Even though she was an old woman it felt better than having no company at all. Alan was too young to talk to; Betty, Dorothy and Chuck, on the other hand, were too advanced and had outside friends to play with. I was piggy in the middle, so to speak, and a loner.

In February 1952 my grandmother died at the age of 82. I was nine years old. She had suffered from diabetes for a considerable time. As far as I know, she had an injury to the big toe on her left foot, which resulted in the onset of gangrene. Her toe gradually turned black and I must admit to feeling very curious on witnessing this strange phenomenon. When the doctor made his daily visit I would peak round the bedroom door and watch as he carefully unwrapped the bandage on her foot. I can remember the awful smell that filled the bedroom on these occasions. My parents had been very negligent with regard to her personal hygiene, especially when she had to use the toilet. While they argued as to who should take her to the bathroom the poor woman often wet herself as she feebly tried to make her own way, her weak bladder unable to take the strain and urine running down her legs into her carpet slippers. The odour of the pee-soaked slippers, combined with the smell of gangrenous tissue, became so overpowering the doctor himself was reluctant to breathe in the room and decided to admit her to hospital even if only for the sake of her dignity. Two days later she died, in a clean bed and in peace and quiet. A blessed relief, as the surgeons had decided to amputate her leg to try to stop the spread of the gangrene. This probably hastened her demise, as her heart gave in two hours after they informed her of their decision.

We had a parlour that we only used for Christmas gatherings and the weekly payout to the insurance man, and this was where she was reluctantly laid out for all to pay their last respects. I say reluctantly because my mother ranted and raved about the upheaval a funeral would cause to her routine. This was to be my first experience of looking at a corpse close up, and at nine years of age it was a very weird experience. All the relations had congregated in the living room. Everybody was being very polite to one another, which I thought very odd as usually they were at each other's throats.

My mother's two sisters, Maggie and Lilly, along with her brother Jack, were present. Her own mother and father were absent as they had gone to meet their maker a few years earlier. The 'bronkatus' had finally carried off Granda Russell, while Grandma Russell died from a blood disorder. The refusal to have her spleen removed did her no favours; had she given permission she would have lived a far longer life. The story that she refused because of a broken heart has been passed down through the family over the years – I suppose every family has its special tale to tell. There weren't many tears shed from my mother when her own parents passed away and even less on the demise of her mother-in-law. In fact, I could even detect a change in her attitude – she appeared unusually happy for someone who had just suffered a bereavement. The thought of having my father to herself and not having to compete with his mother must have given her a false sense of security – such elation was to be short-lived.

Anyway, while the relatives and friends of the family were busy chatting and drinking tea, my curiosity got the better of me and I bravely decided to venture into the parlour where my grandmother lay in peaceful repose. The first thing I noticed on entering the room was the distinctive odour of newly varnished wood. It was completely different to any furniture varnish. I knew this because my father was a carpenter and I was used to the smell of that particular substance. I wasn't scared as I approached the coffin, more curious than frightened. She was dressed in what looked like a white lace night gown and her face was covered with a veil. I was only about a foot higher than the coffin and, as I lifted the veil away from her, I was more or less face to face with what I can only describe as a marble caricature of what was once a human being.

The shock of witnessing this sight at my early age didn't help my nervous disposition. In fact I was petrified and, instead of dropping the veil back on to her face and running away, I did the exact opposite and stood rooted to the spot, staring in disbelief. What was this thing that lay in front of me – was it a horrible joke? It most certainly was not my gran. As if the sight wasn't enough to scare me outright, I had this compulsive urge to feel her face. I just let the back of my hand brush against her cheek. It was so cold it completely took my breath away. By now I was scared bloody witless, I can tell you. Turning on my heels I fled from the room like a bat out of hell. I ran to my Aunt Lilly and nearly hid up the leg of her knickers in fright. I didn't get any sympathy from my mother, no sir! Instead, I got a slap round the ear lugs for daring to go into the parlour without first asking, and for being so inquisitive in the first flaming place.

Now that my gran had died I missed my daily readings from the Bible, lying on my stomach beside her on the bed, my elbows supporting my weight while my hands cupped my chin to steady my head, my long gazelle-like legs bent at the knees and flaying from side to side like two metronomes, the pendulums of which were out of tempo with each other.

Seeing as children are fickle and flit from one person to another to command attention, I took to visiting my Aunt Ethel and Uncle Jack, who had taken over the Russell household on the Donegall Road. Had mother gotten wind of me walking the length of the Lisburn Road to Shaftesbury Square, and then up the Donegall Road on my own, she would have flayed me to within an inch of my life. Ironically, the same route would have been acceptable if she had needed groceries on credit but didn't want to make a personal appearance. No-one had the heart to refuse a forlorn-looking child clutching a begging note from its mother with the promise of payment at the end of the week (if they were lucky) hastily scribbled at the bottom. As for visiting relatives who were taboo in her address book – well, this was both unthinkable and despicable.

My aunt and uncle filled the void my gran had made by going and dying on me. I though it most inconsiderate of her dying without my permission. Didn't she realise I needed her company even though she was old and bedridden? At least I had been safe in the confines of her bedroom, especially as my mother hardly ever went in there to see how she was feeling.

My Aunt Ethel was the exact opposite to my gran – she enjoyed a drop of the hard stuff, in fact she devoured it as if it was about to go out of fashion. I used to wonder why she got merrier as the day progressed and the contents of the bottle on the sideboard gradually emptied. She gave me my own 'wee bottle of drinkies', as she would put it, and I poured my lemonade into a whisky glass and mimicked her as she emptied the cheap wine down her throat. After all the wine had been guzzled she craved for cider and scallops. She would send me scurrying to the chip shop in Sandy Row for two helpings of scallops and a bottle of cider in the off-licence. The owner of the latter would ask me who it was for, a suspicious look written on his face. "It's for my Aunt Ethel."

"Ethel Russell?" he asked as he took a juke out through the window to see if the coast was clear. Obviously he was well aware of Ethel Russell, for he knew the brand of cider she liked without having to be told. He wrapped it up well and told me to hide it in the bottom of my carrying bag as he would get into trouble with the law for selling alcohol to a minor. He also knew my aunt's penchant for fighting and the use of the aule fisticuffs; most likely he would rather have faced the magistrate than the wrath of my inebriated aunt furious at not getting her drink.

I did not care a jot as it meant the added thrill of receiving three pence spending money for my troubles. There was an old house-come-shop in my aunt's street; a half-door led into the front room that served as a shop. Trays of home-made treacle toffee, coconut-covered toffee, red-dyed toffee, mint-flavoured toffee, honeycomb and yellow man were lined along a makeshift table. Bottles of brandy balls, butter balls, mixed balls, cough rock, rhubarb rock and winter mixture, to name but a few, lined the shelves on the walls. My mouth watered at the sight, my eyes stung and my throat tingled with the aroma of the vinegar on the scallops and I wished life could stand still as I sucked on my brandy balls and skipped up the street for my tea of scallops and lemonade.

But life must go on, and the Linton household didn't change for the better. Lottie's elation was short-lived. Bill made sure she didn't have him all to herself. He still lived the high life outside the home and treated Lottie as his chattel. She still embarrassed him, so she stayed at home out of harm's way. But even at home she was still a force to be reckoned with. A very formidable woman, as half of the residents who lived in the area found out to their cost. Many a poor unsuspecting neighbour was left with their tail tucked between their legs after a tongue lashing from Lottie.

One of those poor individuals perchanced to be the local pastor. Lottie had an extreme hatred towards this particular species, and why he tried to change her outlook on the subject of religion was a mystery to all, as it was like flogging a dead horse. He must have been a glutton for punishment. Either that, or he imagined that converting my mother would entitle him to a ticket into Heaven. At every God-given opportunity the poor man would insist on trying to corner her.

On one of these occasions, he made the mistake of asking her if she thought she would go to Heaven when she died, for in his mind she didn't really deserve to go to Heaven, being so bad-tempered to her neighbours. Mother had a habit of putting on her posh voice when rankled, a most annoying habit as it did nothing other than make her sound more irritating than usual. Acting polite did not suit mother's bad-tempered demeanour. With arms tightly crossed under her ample bosom and head held high she haughtily retorted: "Will *you* be tharrr when you pass on, Pastor?"

"Indeed I will, Mrs Linton, indeed I will," he replied, his hands held in a praying manner while his eyes stared towards the sky as he searched for the highway to his Saviour; he certainly looked very pious. I tried to look invisible and covered my face with my hands to hide my blushes for I knew her reply would not be what he had in mind.

"In that case I would prefer to go to Hell, to avoid the likes of you!" she answered back, with an acid look on her face. "And another thing, Hell won't be full until you're in it," she added for good measure.

"May God forgive you, Mrs Linton!"

"Hell will freeze over before God forgives the likes of you, Pastor! Licking up to the sick on their dying beds until they put you in their will." He offered no answer and slumped up the Lane like a dog that had just been kicked up the backside, tail tucked between its legs.

I'm convinced that if the Lord himself had appeared to her in a flash of light she would have ate the gob off him for daring to come into the house without an invitation. The strangest part of it was that even though she tried to instil her agnosticism in her children, every time one of us got a hiding she would stop halfway to catch her breath and beseech God to give her the strength to carry out the remainder of the punishment. Very odd!

In 1953 she was once more pregnant, the same year Queen Elizabeth II came to the throne. Not that the two events had anything in common, other than one being crowned with pomp and ceremony, while my father was almost crowned with a cricket bat for being so bloody careless. I was ten years old at the time, and could sense the angry atmosphere in the home. Every time my father so much as looked in her direction, she would yell at the top of her voice, "I'm going to get rid of it!" I thought she was referring to the cat. Only in later years did I realize the significance of her taking three hot baths daily, plus a purgative every night.

This unusual display of hygiene served no purpose whatsoever, other than to make her feel weak and exhausted from the frequent trips to the lavatory. Added to this were her constant displays of hysterics, wondering how the hell it happened. As if she didn't know by now. As I grew older I realised I was perhaps responsible for my mother's condition – through a combination of frustration and the pin of a brooch. I had been frustrated at not being able to blow up what I presumed to be a balloon, and punctured it with the pin of a brooch that had been lying on the dressing table in my parent's bedroom. Sorry mother, at ten years of age I didn't know the difference between an everlasting condom and a balloon – please forgive me.

There were frequent visits by the family doctor to calm mother down during the first four months of her pregnancy, usually at night after my father came home from his day's work. The bedrooms in the bungalow led directly from the living room, and when the doctor arrived he and my father and mother would disappear into one of these bedrooms. I could hear my mother crying and pleading with the doctor. Being so young at the time, I couldn't quite understand what all the fuss was about. She didn't appear to be ill and I could hear the doctor tell her, in no uncertain terms: "You're a very strong healthy woman, Mrs Linton. Indeed, you should think yourself lucky to be in such good condition. Now pull yourself together, and stop trailing me out here every other night on matters I can't rectify."

Despite consuming all the pills, potions and laxatives she could lay her hands on, my brother Ian managed to make it into this world unharmed in November of that year. He was the spitting image of Winston Churchill. He was breast-fed up until the age of four (as were the rest of us – it was cheaper than dried milk), much to the amusement of my friends and to my embarrassment, as she never tried to conceal her enormous bosoms whenever Ian wanted sustenance. This maternal act was usually accompanied with the words: "shove that in your bake and stop snivelling." For some reason, he was the only child in the family to be shown any semblance of love.

This was to be the last child. My parents had finally come to their senses and called it a day as far as having children was concerned. They must have realised what was causing the problem!

Chapter 3

MEMORIES

Memories – everybody in the whole wide world has them. In my case the most memorable period of my life was the Fifties. Although the home atmosphere was oppressive, the early Fifties still bring back thoughts of quiet nights and gentle days. Halcyon days spent playing in sun-kissed hayfields; watching cricket players all dressed in white or fat ladies in tweed suits in action on the bowling green; the smell of melting tar on new-laid roads; ladybirds and crickets clicking in the grass or corncrakes in the fields; and, surprisingly, the smell of pig manure that clung to the warm summer breeze as it wafted over the Lane from the local farm. Or dressing up in my granny's crepe-de-Chine dresses, her feather boa draped round my neck, and scraping along in an old pair of her black button boots, one of her old hats plonked precariously on my head, with strings of jet beads dangling to my belly button and her precious Chinese hand-painted paper parasol flung nonchalantly over my shoulder. This last item came to a sticky end in a downpour of rain while I watched in horror – I was left with a handful of spokes and cane handle. I hid the evidence below a blackcurrant bush and every time the subject of a lost umbrella came up I sat with a look of angelic innocence and swore to God I knew nothing of its whereabouts, for fear of getting a hiding.

The Lane was a very pleasant area, a beautiful place, mostly countryside and full of fascinating characters. Belfast city, not to mention the rest of the world, might just as well have been on another planet as far as I was concerned. Apart from the Suez affair, which I knew very little about, world news seemed pretty mundane. My childhood, up until the age of eleven, or until I started secondary school, was spent in and around Stockman's Lane, except for the rare occasion when my father took the family for a jaunt to Rostrevor in our car. It was indeed a rare occurrence, as we witnessed more full moons than the sight of the sea. Not being the type to spoil his offspring with too many gifts or spontaneous outside activities, my father would struggle with his conscience for the better part of the morning until guilt, brought on by the anticipation shining from all our faces, would finally cause him to relent, while the moths in his wallet donned sunglasses at the prospect of seeing daylight when he bought petrol.

On these few and far between trips only three of the children were allowed to go, as any more would only cause wear and tear on the upholstery of his *real* pride and joy – his black Ford Popular. We would set out after dinner, about two o'clock in the afternoon, and drive straight to Rostrevor.

It was always bloody Rostrevor for some reason. It probably reminded him of the time his family had been evacuated there during the war, and brought back happy memories of his wartime separation from my mother. While the family was relatively safe from Hitler's bombs, he stayed behind to help make warplanes in the factory in Belfast. I have a suspicion he attached a photograph of mother onto the nose of each plane leaving the factory just to give Hitler an extra hint that Ireland was not a force to be taken lightly – we had Lottie on our side as an added deterrent. Our house was allocated to a British army officer and his family, while the lesser ranks had to be content with being billeted in tin huts in nearby Musgrave Park, alongside American forces. The latter were very handy for the odd pound of butter and bag of sugar as their way of saying 'thank-you' for a bit of Irish hospitality, these items being heavily rationed during the war. I was born two years before the war ended, most likely the product of father's weekend break from the aircraft factory. Rostrevor has a lot to answer for, as many a time I wished I had never been born at all.

Every time we drove around the little town my mother told the same story: "Your sister Dorothy actually saw fairies and leprechauns down in the fairy glen," the Glen being a small forest situated near the middle of the town. "I swear to God she did. Little people dressed in red and green."

My father always gave the same reply: "For Christ's sake, woman, will you shut up! That's nothing but a load of bollocks! There's no such bloody thing as hobgoblins and fairies." 'Bollocks' was his favourite word for something he didn't understand or agree with. He never cursed in front of us when we were young except for this one word. He used it on quite a few occasions, and when he was in a bad mood he had the ability to make it sound as if it was the worst swear word imaginable, letting it spew forth with a vengeance. It was either, "that's a bollocks", "he's a bollocks", or anything that didn't match up to his expectations was a "bollocks". In my opinion he was the biggest bollocks of them all the way he rambled on.

We then drove down to the harbour wall and sat looking out to sea for half an hour. Nobody got out of the car, we just sat and

35

stared at the waves breaking on the sea wall, afraid to utter a word in case we got a crack round the earhole for moaning. "Isn't that just lovely, Lottie? It sometimes makes me wish I had been a sailor." He was a man of few words and didn't say a lot but what he said was profound! My mother sat with a face that would have soured milk, her mouth puckered up like a purse on a draw string. She was probably thinking to herself, "I wish to hell you had been too, then maybe you would be on a slow boat to China this very minute, and I might not have been the mother of six bloody gurnin' youngsters."

The highlight of the day was an ice-cream cornet bought from the loose change my father found in his trouser pocket, counted out in pennies and halfpennies in the palm of his hand. We then headed home in his precious car, after he had inspected it for ice-cream stains, just in time for tea. The thought of having to eat out would have been too much of an extravagance, and his wallet had already been subjected to a hell of a shock when he had extracted the ten shilling note to pay for the petrol; indeed, this coupled with the ice-cream had completely buggered up his budget for at least three months. On rare occasions he brought his Brownie Box camera to capture the wonderful sight of the waves crashing on the sea wall and perhaps a snapshot of his car. Never a picture of us – oh no! In his eyes his car was a more precious memory to keep than the memory of his children growing up. As for my mother, it was enough that he had to live with her never mind having to look at her photograph.

Anyway, I was a home bird and preferred my own little domain, playing in Musgrave Park and the Bog Meadows at the back of the bungalow. Local farmers let their cattle roam freely in the Bog Meadows, the cow pats being evidence of this practice. We children made good use out of anything that could be turned into a game, and cow pats were no exception. One of my favourite pastimes was 'Jump the cow pat', a game I devised with my friend Margaret. A simple enough game for those with simple minds, as was undoubtedly the case with us. Anyone with their marbles in the right place wouldn't have thought up such a foolhardy activity. The easy part was running from one end of the field to the other. The hard part, the art of avoiding the droppings of our bovine friends, wasn't quite so simple. Points were lost if you miscued and landed in one of these sloppy mounds. I lost more points than a mongrel at Cruft's pedigree dog show, ending up plastered in cow dung right up to the ass of my navy knickers. There was only one remedy – go down to the local river. No, not to drown myself, even though the thought did cross my mind now and then as I knew the fate that awaited me when I returned home – but to wash off the offending mess. Shoes, socks, the hem of my dress, even my knickers – all had to be cleansed of the evidence of this foul-smelling substance. I ended up getting a hiding anyway for coming home wet. I never ever convinced my mother that I had accidentally fallen into the river, even on the days I actually did, trying to jump it and missing the other side by inches. I suppose I deserved this for crying wolf so often.

Stockman's Lane used to be a very narrow lane back in the Fifties, until the council took the headstaggers and turned it into a twentieth century nightmare. It's so busy now with traffic you could rear a family while waiting to cross the road. In the Fifties, one car overtaking the other would have been known as a traffic jam. Where the flyover is now situated, the Lane was no wider than fifteen feet, if it was that. A lovely little bridge, made from stone, straddled a river where the boys caught spricks in jam-jars. We also collected frogspawn and kept it in a bucket in the back garden, watching it change into tadpoles and then finally into tiny frogs.

Our pleasures were simple but then again educational. Not many people had televisions to turn the children into adults before their time. Observing nature at first hand is much more rewarding. There is nothing that can't be learnt from watching life at close quarters. We learnt all we needed to know about sex by spying on courting couples frolicking in haystacks. We tip-toed over slippery stones dotted in the shallow water that surrounded the islands in the park and played hide-and-seek among the bushes, or snitched apples and gooseberries out of Mr Breshaw's back garden. It was trying not to get caught which gave us a thrill, the apples and gooseberries usually ended up in the ditch, or else mother's tarts. She would have made a tart out of anything that held the crust up, usually cooking apples with the core thrown in to add to the bulk.

Most, if not all, of my spare time was spent outside the home, as it was thought a sin to sit inside and waste all that free fresh air. A spoonful of Virol or cod liver oil and malt was the order of the day if you complained of feeling tired or looked at all peaky. If you just mentioned the word 'bored' you would be given a job in the house or else thumped round the earlugs and thrown out the back door by the scruff of the neck. My mother's sentiments being: children should NEITHER be seen nor heard.

In a way she did me a favour. If I had sat in the house I would never have had the privilege of getting to know the characters who lived in and around the vicinity. A blind man, whose name now evades me, used to walk from the Lisburn Road end to the Falls Road end of the Lane and back every day come rain or shine. I often walked beside him while he warned me about bits of hedge that stuck out, so that I didn't scratch my legs or face on them as I passed by. He knew every inch of the Lane in his mind's eye. When I asked him how he managed this extraordinary feat he always replied: "You don't just need eyes to see. You can see with your hands, you can see with your feet, and best of all you can see by smelling and listening. And above all, never lose your imagination." These words meant very little to me as a child and yet I never forgot them and often now, when I lie in the dark, I can fully understand his words of wisdom. Imagination is, indeed, a powerful gift if used wisely.

Then there was May O'Doherty the fortune-teller, who lived in the red row at the Falls Road end. The houses along this stretch were small terraced homes made from red brick, hence the name 'red row'. The houses opposite were similar, only painted white, and the locals called this the 'white row' – it wouldn't take a university degree to work that one out. May's sister owned a hairdresser's shop on the Falls Road and only had to take one look at you and she could tell what was going to happen in your life. Nine times out of ten she was spot on. She never did tell me about mine. Just as well, I don't think I would have wanted to know. She scared me anyway, her dyed black hair held back in a bun, black clothes and black laced-up boots, plus a pair of gold-rimmed glasses perched on the end of her nose. She was about four feet ten inches tall; a broomstick wouldn't have looked out of place tucked between her legs. I was even more convinced of her supernatural powers when my mother sent me along to her shop to have my hair cut, much to my annoyance. I prayed for God to have mercy on a young lass such as myself, and allow me to wake up some morning with hair at least two foot long, rather than being continually lugged up to May's as soon as my locks touched the lobes of my ears. What with all the wires stretching from the perming machines to the curlers on the women's hair and the overpowering smell of ammonia – not to mention the aroma of singed hair – it was probably similar to Frankenstein's laboratory. I was convinced that not only did May resemble a witch, she was trying to turn half the population into little miniatures of herself. I thought these dreadful contraptions could make you shrink, such is a child's way of thinking.

Another memorable character lived at that end of the Lane. To most people he is well remembered as a famous actor, but to me Joseph Tomelty was just a kind white-haired gentleman who always bid you the time of day. Everybody knew Joseph and Joseph knew everyone. I can remember, as if it was only yesterday, the day he and I walked into the sweet shop at the top of the Lane. He bowed in an actor's fashion, ushering me into the shop before him, saying in that famous voice of his, "beauty before age." Even though I was only a child it made me feel very important. That was Joseph Tomelty – a true actor on and off stage.

It was one of his neighbour's children, a girl called Theresa, who first brought me into a Catholic church and scared the daylights out of me. Religion wasn't very high on the list of priorities in the Linton household. As my mother and father didn't attend church, the inside of a place of worship was a mystery and left entirely to my imagination. It was in St Agnes's Chapel in Andersonstown that I was given my first glimpse inside a Catholic church. Compared to attending the Salvation Army church hall in Bedford Street – which to me didn't look very holy inside, apart from the Bible which rested on the podium plus the inscription 'Blood and Fire' emblazoned on the wall alongside the picture of General Booth – this felt like entering through the doors of Heaven.

Theresa put the fear of God into me even before we entered the building. In those days it was considered an insult for a woman to enter a chapel bare-headed. As I didn't have anything to cover myself with, she gave me her handkerchief and slapped it on my head, almost knocking me into the following week in the process. "Now don't let that slip off your head, do you hear me," said Theresa. "If you do let it fall off, the priest will come round from behind the altar and beat the daylights out of you. And don't forget to genuflect and bless yourself with holy water from the font at the front door." I informed her that Protestants did not know how to bless themselves or genuflect. She got most annoyed. She grabbed my right hand and explained to me that blessing oneself was as simple as knowing the points of the compass, with my head being the north, my stomach the south and my shoulders east and west. At first I kept getting my easts and wests mixed up and received a tongue lashing for being so bloody stupid. She made me touch each point with the middle finger of my right hand, making sure everything was done to a 'T'. After a dozen or so attempts I finally mastered the art of blessing myself.

Genuflecting was quite another kettle of fish. She told me to imagine I had to curtsey in front of the Queen, informing me it should be no problem seeing I was a Protestant. She spat out this last remark, for she had been jealous the day I got off school for the Queen's Coronation in 1953, as the Catholic schools remained open and she had wanted the day off as well. Who, in the name of almighty, did she think I was? I might well have been a Protestant, but I didn't live in Buckingham Palace. I ended up flouncing about like a fairy who had just sat on a bunch of nettles. By now, Theresa was fit to be tied with frustration. She pushed me up the chapel steps so fast my feet went from under me and I fell flat on my face at the chapel doors. Things couldn't possibly get any worse. But that was to be the easy bit, as I soon found out when I entered this sacred house of God.

As I looked around, all I could see were statues and holy pictures. When I asked her what they were she ate the gob of me and told me to talk in whispers as God was inside a little cupboard at the altar and didn't like to be disturbed by people shouting, especially Protestants. By rights, she said, I shouldn't have been in there in the first place. As for the pictures, they were the Stations of the Cross and I was to genuflect and bless myself whilst saying a prayer at every one, otherwise I would go straight to Hell. By the time I got out I was a nervous wreck, fit for nothing apart from a lie down in one of the haystacks in the park. I ended up marrying a Catholic, so it gave me an insight into what was in store for me in the future. In a way, then, she did me a favour.

Whilst on the subject of religion, every eleventh of July we had a bonfire at the end of the houses on the 'white row'. Both Catholics and Protestants gathered together and a great time was had by all. There was no bitterness, just a few friendly jibes such as, "If it wasn't for us Catholics there would be no Twelfth of July to celebrate in the first place!" I suppose that makes sense. In fact, the only person who knew any Orange songs happened to be a Catholic. She was Mrs McGlonan, a woman who lived in one of the houses in the white row. She used to sing 'The Sash' to get the party going and would tell the Protestants they should be ashamed of themselves for not knowing any Orange tunes. The field where the Orangemen gathered after the march up the Lisburn Road was situated behind her back garden and she let them have use of her outside toilet. After they used it she always said, "B'God, I can't sae nay differ'nce in Orange pee an' Green pee, it's all the same colour tae me." For a laugh she used to hang a picture of the Pope, draped with a pair of rosary beads, on the toilet wall.

No-one ever took offence at what Mrs McGlonan said, not in those days anyway – it should still be the same today. She was just a jolly, down-to-earth, rosy-cheeked wee woman. A typical mother-earth individual who smelt of bleach and sunlight soap and waddled rather than walked. This had most likely resulted from years of child-bearing and the fact that she almost always had a child in her arms, its legs astride her hip bone. She always wore a wrap-around pinny and a pair of mutton dummies on her feet. When it was cold she wrapped a shawl around her shoulders, covering both herself and whatever child she happened to be carrying that day, not necessarily one of her own. The fact that she would have looked more at home leaning over a half door of a thatched cottage in the boglands of Donegal than in Stockman's Lane didn't bother her in the least. She was almost first at the scene on bonfire night to get the party in swing, regardless of religion.

The occasion was mainly an excuse for the boys and girls in the Lane to get together, never mind it being the Twelfth of July celebrations. We danced around the bonfire, holding hands in a circle and sang "Round goes the bun, the jolly old bun; round goes the bun once more, I'll pick the prettiest girl in the ring and kiss her on the floor." The thought of being picked for a kiss usually got the girls all excited. All this debauchery and not a drop of alcohol in sight. Oh, if only time could have stood still. We might have been easily pleased then but we were happy, not to mention a lot healthier.

One thing we did not do was spend most of our time in front of the television screen. Although some people did have television, as yet it wasn't looked upon as the one-eyed master of the home – the killer of conversation. In 1953 my father rented a television for the princely sum of seven shillings and sixpence a month, so that we could witness the Coronation. There wasn't really all that much to watch at the time. I looked forward to 'Watch with Mother', 'Bill and Ben, the Flowerpot Men', or 'Andy Pandy'. Tuesdays and Thursdays it was 'Rag, Tag and Bobtail' – all a far cry from the violence the children of today are subjected to.

In fact, the radio was far more interesting. Valentine Diall's 'The Man in Black' horror stories, although tame by today's standards, were enough to send you scurrying under the bedclothes at night. Comic relief was provided by the 'Goon Show' with Spike Milligan and Harry Secombe, 'Meet the Huggets', and 'The Glums' with Ma and Pa Glum. 'The Archers: an everyday story of country folk' pleased the housewives, along with 'Mrs Dale's Diary'. Then there was Wilfred Pickles with his catch-phrases 'have a go,' 'are you courting', or 'have you had any embarrassing moments lately'. No smut here apart from a few double entendres for those with dirty minds.

My brother and I went to the cinema every Saturday morning – usually the Majestic Picture House on the Lisburn Road, which held a session called A.B.C. Minors especially for children. It cost fourpence admission, and to make up this amount we went round the neighbours collecting jam-jars, as a local shop gave twopence for each one, there being a shortage of glass because of the war. We always managed to raise the money, and Chuck, who was very canny, could usually even manage to gather extra for sweets. We clanked our way up the Lisburn Road as the jars rattled together in my mother's shopping bag.

Although Chuck was five years older than myself, he wore short trousers up until the age of fourteen, as did all the boys at that time. You got your first long trousers when you started work and not before. The boys looked forward to this auspicious occasion as it was a sign of reaching manhood. The day boys received their long trousers was indeed a day to celebrate. Chuck was no exception. The day he eventually received his he thought he ruled the world.

We resembled the Bisto Kids, with Chuck still in his short trousers, very badly knitted pullover (mother had used two different sized needles, as she never managed to find two the same) which had holes in the elbows, socks at half-mast and hair that hadn't seen a comb in days. He also smelt to high heaven with the aroma of pig manure – his favourite pastime was mucking out the pigs for the local farmer. A sharp contrast to the way he turned out in his later teenage years, when he kept himself preened to perfection.

I always walked three steps behind Chuck as I couldn't keep up with him. He always did things in a hurry, a trait that has stayed with him to this day. On many of those trips to the cinema he hadn't the patience to wait for me to go to the toilet after the films, and he was the fault of many a pair of wet knickers. He used to be disgusted at my inability to control my bladder, as it usually occurred in front of his mates. He let on he wasn't with me, telling me to 'bugger off' out of the side of his mouth. If I didn't obey his command at the double I got a wallop round the back of the head, plus a warning that if I ever peed in my knickers again he'd personally take them off and rub then round my ugly bake. He would then proceed to pick me up by the scruff of the neck, kick me up the backside and shout "piss off, git". One of his favourite sayings used to be "If I don't get you, you git, some other git will get you, so get you, git!' Try to make sense of that. If he had been heard to use such language at home he would have been annihilated by my father. The two didn't agree for more than two minutes and each rubbed the other up the wrong way. After a few of those visits to the cinema I didn't give a damn whether the Lone Ranger and Tonto had saved the Wild West, or Superman had saved the world, I just wanted someone to save me from my supercilious brother.

Hallowe'en was another nightmare outing with Chuck. I was Stan Laurel to his Oliver Hardy in 'The Stooge'. While Chuck pocketed the money after a night's pickings and let off the fireworks, I had to be content to stand and observe while my pockets bulged to bursting point with nuts, fruit and home-made toffee. He relieved me of the toffee; for badness he left me the nuts and fruit, two items of food I detested with a vengeance. If I objected he remarked, "That's too bad, camel gob, go shove them up your hump."

The Lone Ranger brings to mind another character who resided in the Lane, known as 'Big Jim'. Jim had been adopted in America by a couple who lived in Stockman's Lane. Before he arrived in Ireland, rumour had it he was in his twenties and very handsome. Being American was an added bonus, and we visualised this tall good-looking cowboy. To us any American male must be like John Wayne: tall, handsome, talking with a drawl and walking with a swagger, as if his ass was chewing a caramel. We were to be disappointed by the reality. Jim was, to say the least, a little short of the grey matter between the ears.

He was in his thirties but had the mentality of a twelve-year-old. I don't mean to be disrespectful to individuals with this handicap, as to me they are God's children and he probably made them this way so they would go through life without worry. But people can be cruel, none more so than children, and Jim was known as the village idiot. He was quite handsome in a rugged sort of way. He was also tall and did talk with an American drawl but this was where the similarity to John Wayne ended. Jim had red hair and he didn't swagger. In fact he gave the impression his arse was on fire and he raced up and down the Lane like a thoroughbred racehorse. His adopted parents owned a grocery shop and used the house for storing any surplus stock – items such as cigarettes, sweets and tinned foods. Children, being children, abused Jim's lack of responsibility and persuaded him to hand over sweets left, right and centre, along with the more than occasional packet of cigarettes. All the kids had a ball. I am ashamed to say I was as guilty as the rest. We ate sweets until they were coming out of our ears. Most of the boys started smoking just for the hell of it. As long as Jim was handing out the goods he was the greatest thing since sliced bread. But all good things come to an end and Jim was found out. The house was emptied of all these goodies overnight and he had to find other ways of finding friends.

As children can be mercenary little brats, Jim was ostracised. He was of no further use to us obstreperous whippersnappers. Looking back on it, it was not a nice thing to do. I myself should have known better, coming from a background filled with hate and animosity. Just because my mother and father never showed me any love, it was no excuse to turn my back on a person who, by a stroke of nature, could only express love. God had not inflicted him with the burden of knowing the feeling of hate. Big Jim did not hold it against us, he just took all cuts as compliments and in the end he was accepted by most of the residents of the area. A few snobs took umbrage, feeling he lowered the tone of the Lane. They thought he would have been better off in a home for the mentally retarded, but they were overruled by the majority. Even when he took to sleeping rough every full moon and the local farmer began losing chickens and eggs, everyone turned a blind eye. Evidence of this unusual activity were the burnt-out fires in the surrounding fields and the bones of the chickens he had consumed in order to keep body and soul together. At the end of his solar activities Big Jim emerged bearded, but otherwise unharmed. He would then make his way over to the farm from where he had stolen the chickens and proceed to muck out the pigs as a way of 'thank-you' to the farmer, who hadn't the heart to chastise him for his pilfering. He knew in his heart that Jim did not think of it as stealing. In his mind he thought mucking out the pigs was fair exchange for a few measly poultry.

The star of the television series 'The Lone Ranger' visited Musgrave Park Hospital in the Fifties. I think it was because the hospital treated polio victims, mostly children, that the visit had been arranged. On hearing of this event, Jim haretailed it over to the park like a ferret up a trouser leg, and managed to divest the Lone

Ranger of one of his silver bullets. I don't think the man knew what hit him. I doubt very much if the bullet was real silver but Big Jim was convinced it was and that was all that mattered. Mother, who hadn't time for her own children, must have had a soft spot for our friend for she fed him her home-baked apple tart, dinosaur stew (we nicknamed it this because it contained more bone than meat) and platefuls of porridge. He was the only person in the Lane who didn't get the gob eaten off him for knocking the back door, so she must have had a gentle side hidden somewhere within her hostile exterior. Either that, or the fact that he told her "Your food's really tasty, mam," was what endeared him to her heart, as everyone else thought it revolting.

I have only mentioned a few of the characters who lived in the Lane, but it was such people who helped ensure that my early childhood wasn't all doom and gloom. In fact, Stockman's Lane was a lovely area to grow up in, compared to some places. We had the countryside and good clean air. Not that everything we indulged in was necessarily good for our health – I still have vivid memories of sugar-coated marshmallow biscuits, liquorice flavoured bubble gum, threepenny Cinderella rock and the taste of my first ice lolly, a change from the butterscotch gums and 'My Lady' caramels we had to be content with for quite a while after the war. In hindsight, if my parents had been more tolerable it would have been more than perfect. But then again, not many people can claim to have had the perfect parents. I'm sure I will not be looked upon as being perfect by my offspring, even though I do try.

By the age of eleven I was preparing for secondary school, a far cry from Roseland Primary. In September of 1954 I donned the grey and red uniform of Graymount Secondary School for Girls and headed off into the big wide world. A slight exaggeration as, after all, it was only situated in Newtownabbey, two bus trips away. However, to someone who had never ventured beyond a two mile radius, it was indeed an adventure. It meant as much to me as a trip up the Amazon would to David Attenborough.

The reason I enrolled in a school so far away from home was because of my friend Margaret. Her mum picked this school as it was the only respectable all-girls secondary school at the time and her Margaret would just have to have the best, being spoilt rotten. Margaret and I were inseparable therefore I had to go to the same school as her even though the cost of four bus trips a day would be a heavy burden on my mother's already slim purse. She could have saved her money – Margaret left after only three months when her mother decided to pay for her beloved daughter to attend grammar school nearer home. We lost touch after this, and Margaret's memory became that of someone smug and spoilt whose dressing-table drawers had bulged with brilliant white underwear and knee socks. No more would I have to listen to her make fun of my tattered knickers and socks riddled with holes.

There were so many classrooms I frequently got lost in between lessons. The school also had a laboratory, something I thought only existed in Frankenstein movies, and a gymnasium. It was in this building – or, more accurately, in its showers – that I first learned the facts of life. Girls are often far cruder than boys; males tend to be concerned about the size of their manhood and that's it, while girls talk about everything under the sun – boobs, bums, and bodily functions, the three 'B's. I also found out about 'the curse', or the menstrual cycle, and how to use this as an excuse for getting out of netball and hockey. In the Fifties we still lived somewhat in the dark ages, with old wives' tales in abundance, such as the notion that washing one's hair or feet when menstruating could lead to fainting fits or, even worse, an untimely death. As we were made to shower after games we used to tell the teacher we were 'unwell', to get out of doing P.E. This backfired after a few months, for she got suspicious when she realised most of the girls were having their period every other week and demanded a note from our mothers on such occasions. This really put me in a fix, as I didn't even have a period to begin with.

A shower was a novelty I hadn't known existed, for even taking a bath in our house was a rare event. My father was so mean he wouldn't allow anyone to pull the damper out in the fire to heat the water as it meant burning up too much coal, and coal cost money. If we complained he always snapped back, "Bollox you and your bath, I haven't money to burn, you know." So we washed ourselves from the sink, filled with a kettle of hot water – as far up as we could go and as far down as we could go. A whole bar of soap was a novelty; we usually had the remains of about four bars stuck together. After it had done the rounds of the family it resembled a large piece of snot. The face cloth felt as if it had been dipped in wallpaper paste, while the towels were beyond description.

On top of this the house was freezing in the winter, though my father never noticed as he always wore a blanket-type dressing gown in the home. He purchased this article of clothing in a second-hand clothing shop for a few shillings. The sight of him wandering about with this wretched garment (which reeked of mothballs) over his long-johns, the crotch of which hung to the knees – not to mention a long-sleeved simmit and socks pulled over the long-johns, with a scarf wrapped round his neck for good measure – was enough to put a girl off men for life. My mother never told us girls in the family the facts of life. She probably thought the sight of our father in this get-up would be a sufficient deterrent in itself.

I did have a childhood sweetheart. We would walk through

Musgrave Park, holding hands and shyly looking into each other's eyes. Now and then we would steal a childish kiss, our lips tightly pursed. Someone must have told him about French kissing, for he opened his lips on one occasion and gave me a big wet slobbering smackeroon. I slapped him round the face and told him never to do such a thing ever again, as it was a disgusting habit and he should have been ashamed of himself. He blushed to the roots of his hair with embarrassment and gave me a red spider brooch the following day by way of apology. I was going on eleven and he was fourteen. As I was too scared of telling my mother, I threw it away when I got home. Eventually I outgrew him, for by the age of eleven I was fully grown in height while he remained static, as boys are inclined to do.

I often wondered why my mother warned me not to go anywhere alone with a boy, but never gave it much thought. I knew certain things were wrong, such as letting a boy see your knickers (not that mine were much to look at) but that was the height of it. Naive wasn't the word, just uneducated on such matters. My mother and father never demonstrated much affection for one another. Most likely the dressing gown was the fault. They certainly never kissed or hugged each other. Love was a dirty word. I knew a pregnant mother when I saw one but didn't know how the baby got in there or how it got out. I also heard my sisters telling each other they had their period and saw them hide packets of 'thingies' (sanitary towels) in the bottom drawer of their dressing table. They were always arguing with each other about who stole each other's thingies. I just wondered what the hell they used them for – I thought they were to wrap around a sore throat. My two sisters were seven and eight years older than me respectively, and had also matured earlier than I had. They probably thought my friends would enlighten me on the subject, the way their own friends had done with them years earlier.

It was in the showers in school that I learned the truth. My new friend Anne, who had now replaced Margaret, explained the facts of life to me as we dried ourselves with towels that measured no more than two feet by one. The shock of it all was almost too much to bear. 'Christ', I thought, how the hell will I tell my mother what's wrong with me when that happens, I was scared stiff of her as it was. What was her reaction going to be?

I soon found out. One Saturday morning, about three months later, when I was eleven and a half, nature took its course. I very nearly fainted with fright. Making a beeline for the bedroom, I hurriedly opened the bottom drawer of the dressing table, for I knew by now what my sisters' 'thingies' were for. Horror upon horrors, they were all gone! I ran into the bathroom to look in the hot press. No luck. There was no point looking for toilet tissue to make a makeshift sanitary towel, for it would have been of little use, as on the very rare occasion we did have this luxury it was the slippery, non-absorbent type. We usually used the *Belfast Telegraph* cut up in squares and hung on a hook beside the toilet, a habit my mother had not lost from her 'street rearing', as my father often remarked. He would be especially irritated when she would cut up a newspaper he had not finished reading. Anyway, by now my stomach was cramping as well and I was terrified. I thought I was going to die and felt my head go light. My mother happened to be passing the bathroom door when I staggered into the hallway.

"What the hell's wrong with you!" she yelled. "Are you constipated?" She most likely thought this as I usually was, and looked quite ill on such occasions. I had no other choice but to tell her.

"I've took my period," I replied, swaying back and forth, the cold sweat lashing from me in buckets. I didn't know what attitude she would adopt, and when I found out I wished I hadn't told her. She put her hands to her head and screamed: "Bloody hell, what in the name of Christ am I going to do now! You're nothing but a bitch, do you hear me, a bitch in heat!" At this point I wasn't quite sure who needed the help, her or me, for by now she was beating her breast in despair.

"But mum, what will I do?" By now I was crying.

"There's one thing you won't do and that's go near boys, do you hear me? No boys! If I ever see you with one I'll break your bloody back!" She then proceeded to go into the cupboard under the stairs where she kept all the dirty rags, tore a piece of old sheet up and threw it in my direction. "Put that on and get out of my sight! And remember – no boys!"

Two years were to pass before I would again let a boy kiss me on the cheek, she had me so afraid. I had even begun to believe that a kiss made you pregnant. It was at this age that my own tall, good-looking American guy made an impact on my life. Not in the flesh but over the airwaves. Betty, Dorothy, Chuck and I were listening to the Top Twelve records of the week on Radio Luxembourg. There was nothing really out of the ordinary or different from the usual assortment of the time. There was Bill Haley's 'Rock Around the Clock', and Doris Day, Pat Boone and Johnie Ray were the heart throbs. Michael Holliday's 'Hot Diggity' had us tapping our feet and swaying like Germans at a beer festival while Ruby Murray's 'Softly Softly' had us waltzing with the yard brush as a substitute for the man of our dreams. My sister Dorothy liked smoochy love songs. She was courting at the time and was inclined to daydream to Nat King Cole's 'When I fall in love'. She passed through the house like a will-o-the-wisp in dreamland, which made my father question her state of mental health. "She's on this world but not in it, the gormless gop. In the name of heaven stick a bit of pepper up her bum to put a bit of life in it, for Christ's sake." But Dorothy ignored his remarks and turned up her nose in defiance.

Chuck was more concerned with the Plasticine he was moulding into funny faces. He was browned off, it being Sunday night with nowhere to go. The disc jockey announced a new singer who had gone directly to number 2 that week. I wasn't really taking all that much interest when the sound of 'Heartbreak Hotel' filled the room. It was completely different to anything I had heard before and I sprang to life as if hit by lightning. "Who's that singing?" I yelled excitedly, at the same time turning up the volume knob on the wireless.

"Some eejit called Elvis something," Chuck snapped back, as I had startled him, making him accidentally drop his work of art. He gave me a look that would have melted stone and cursed under his breath, "flamin' sisters, they would give you the pip."

"Elvis who?" I shouted at the top of my voice; by now I was jumping up and down like a chicken on a hot griddle.

"I don't know," Chuck replied, his face stuck up against mine. "Now piss off or shut up." He then thumped me on the head with a large piece of Plasticine. "Maybe that will knock the air out of your head and give your brains a chance." Anyway, the disc jockey answered my question when the record finished. "That was Elvis Presley, folks. He's sure to be a big hit."

It was the understatement of the year. A big hit? More like an atom bomb. From that day to this I have been an ardent fan. He was to help me through life without me ever meeting him. A ray of light that shone when I would become so depressed I could see no reason for living. He had a song for every mood I found myself in, whether happy or sad. Little did I realize on that Sunday in May of 1956 that a man who never even knew I existed was to become a friend for life through his music. From then on, no other singer was to so inspire me or have anything near the effect Elvis Presley would have on me.

In later years Elvis impersonators would try to duplicate the look Elvis had, with little or no success. Some may resemble him in a certain way, other singers may make an attempt to sing like him, helped by special sound-effects. Others have made pathetic attempts at trying to emulate his body movements. But Elvis Aron Presley was a 'one off' – no-one could ever recapture his charisma. All the plastic surgery and dressing in jump suits won't create another Elvis; the aura that surrounded him cannot be manufactured by human hands. As Bruce Springsteen was to say: "There have been pretenders. There have been contenders. But there is only one King." He was and still is a very special person in my life.

Elvis came into my early teens when I was feeling low. He was to make a dramatic comeback in my later years (not that he was ever forgotten in between) and help pull me back from the brink of suicide. At that time I was to feel a strong empathy with him. I had a feeling that he too felt trapped behind walls of glass, as this was how I felt, having to listen to people talking behind my back. They couldn't understand I did not contemplate suicide for the love of it, there was a reason. I too was to find myself a victim of prescribed drug addiction, although not to the extent Elvis was.

He was on uppers and downers, the uppers to get going, the downers to put him to sleep. The army had started him on this habit as it used uppers to keep soldiers awake on night manoeuvres. He got to the point where he needed a pill for almost every bodily function in order to survive. He had colon problems and was prescribed cortisone, giving him a bloated look which most people put down to obesity. Others made an issue out of the fact that he was barely capable of keeping his eyes open on stage because of drugs. The guy had glaucoma, he had to have injections in his eyes before performances. Those people who have stood in the full glare of stage lighting will be aware of this problem. If the sweat is capable of blinding a performer, what would the added problem of having glaucoma be like? Personally I don't think Elvis could have performed on stage if he had been as drugged as people tried to make out. Anyway, why make a big thing out of Elvis's drug use when most of today's pop groups are on the same road and are put on a pedestal for admitting it. Maybe he was sick to the eyeteeth with the Memphis Mafia stuck up his backside from morning to night and wanted to go into a state of oblivion to rid them from his mind. I found myself addicted to one prescribed drug in later life; I most certainly could not have performed two shows a night in Las Vegas – even if I could sing! It is a sad state when one finds oneself in the position of not being able to live with a drug and yet not being able to live without it. A living hell.

Chapter 4

ONE SIDED LOVE AFFAIR

1957 – a year had passed since I first heard Elvis on the radio. He had by now almost taken over my brain – nothing or no-one else mattered. As far as I was concerned my whole family could have emigrated and left me behind, just as long as they left me the wireless and a few shillings to go to the cinema, for Elvis was now appearing in films.

Actually, for a couple of years my mother had been unsuccessfully trying to talk my father into emigrating to Australia with the family. His expertise in woodworking would have entitled him to the £10 emigration fare. Perhaps if she had let him go on his own he would have jumped at the chance. However, he was not of pioneering stock, whereas my mother could have taken on the world single-handed. She nagged at him so much, he once almost broke his rule of thriftiness and contemplated buying a bottle of Sandymans Port to get drunk, but reneged at the last moment – he thought it easier on the wallet to sit in the garage for half an hour and pull on a Woodbine cigarette.

I continued to get high in Elvis, now that I could see him in the flesh, albeit on celluloid. Having previously had to be content with his singing, supplemented by the odd magazine photograph, his appearance on screen revealed to me just how handsome the guy was. His first movie 'Love me Tender' had me weak at the knees even before it made the cinema in Ireland. I had my own image of Elvis – Elvis was mine as far as I was concerned, he had come into my life at a time when I had been feeling very low in spirit. I didn't have many friends, apart from my new school-friend Anne. I was introverted and shy, and spent most of my spare time listening to Elvis records or staring at his photographs. I told him all my secret thoughts, looking upon him as a father confessor. I could detect a shyness in him even though people had been calling him obscene because of his body movements on stage. But, as many other Elvis fans can verify, when his body was exuding sexuality his face retained a look of disbelief, as if to say, 'My body is doing something my brain has no control over'. His cheeky lop-sided smile coupled with his sleekly combed-back light-brown hair gave out a childish innocence, almost amusement, but which nevertheless seemed to mask some inner fear. That was exactly how I felt – perhaps that was why I became so attached to him.

I did not feel embarrassed telling his photograph my innermost secrets, I had a gut feeling he would have understood. Anyway, a photograph was safe, it didn't tell you to bugger off and give its head peace. Although Elvis was very handsome, his looks were not intimidating, unlike some of the so-called heart-throbs of today.

The only drawback for me was that I was labelled the family nut. Chuck, then nineteen years of age, found it very bemusing. Whenever he discovered me in a state of ecstasy listening to my heart-throb, he always told whoever was in the vicinity, "she's gone with Elvis". When someone knocked at the door he would yell for all to hear: "That's Elvis at the door, Val, he's come to take you out for the night." This backfired when my younger brother Alan actually thought I *was* going out with him and told his friends I was dating Elvis Presley. For ages afterwards, whenever I went out some snotty nosed little brat would ask the same bloody question – "Your brother said you were going out with Elvis – what's he like?" – then turn on their heels and run up the Lane snorting in mockery like a pig. I found it easier to answer "Yes, I was", rather than argue with the brats. I gave Alan a wallop on the head with the palm of my hand, telling him I would put a stop to his growth if he didn't shut his clap-trap. "But Chuck told me you were seeing Elvis." At which point he'd start gurnin' and rub the top of his blonde bonce. "Shut up, ye wee shite, or I'll shove my boot up your arse." I had a wicked streak and a foul mouth when it came to defending Elvis.

Looking back on it, it really wasn't Alan's fault, after all he was only eight years old, and he believed all he heard. I should have shoved my boot up Chuck's arse, but one thing prevented me – he was bigger (and uglier) than me! To tell the truth I really loved Chuck when I was a teenager; only for him I would have been penniless, unable to buy any records or go see Elvis films. He always threw me a couple of shillings from his pay packet every Friday night.

I also had him robbed stupid behind his back. My father had renovated the loft, turning it into a bedroom for our ever-increasing family. Chuck had a secret hiding place where he saved the odd sixpenny bit and occasional shilling, as he intended emigrating to America in the future. This place did not stay a secret very long – yours truly discovered it. As fast as Chuck was depositing his hard-earned money I was withdrawing it. Of course mother got the blame, seeing as the family knew she was hard-up. No-one suspected the quiet, introverted picture of innocence sitting in the corner, with a Mona Lisa smile on her gob, being sent into another dimension by the dulcet tones of the man from Memphis. May God forgive me, for I sat and watched my mother squirm as my brother accused her of robbing him. I found it easier to feign innocence than admit to my guilt and submit myself to a good hiding, not only from Chuck but my mother, who I knew would use the buckle end of the belt on my skinny posterior.

The guilty always get caught sooner or later, in my case sooner than expected. Chuck set a trap – he lay in wait under the bed, curled up like a snake awaiting its prey. His patience paid off. Just as I was about to divest his bank balance of yet another sixpence, he leapt from under the bed in a swirl of dust and feathers, grabbed me by the wrist and yelled, "Drop it! drop it, or by Christ I'll cut the hand aff ye, ye thievin' bitch. That's it, no more Elvis money, you've had it! I'm going to beat the thoughts of that hip swingin', lip-curlin' eejit right out of that pea-sized brain of yours!"

I almost wet myself with fright at being caught. "I'm only borrowing it, Chuck, honest to God I am!" I was nearly on my knees pleading for clemency.

"You're effin' stealin' it, ye gabshit!" Chuck hissed in my face.

"I'm not!" I cried.

"Call it what ye like – purloined, filched, pilfered, swiped – it still adds up to stealin'! You sneaked up the stairs and robbed my safety deposit box of half its bloody contents, ye bitch!"

My face burnt with embarrassment at hearing my beloved Chuck calling me a thief. That word hurt more than a knife between the shoulder blades. I was not a thief – a 'borrower' perhaps. He looked as hurt as I felt, almost as if he was trying to say 'You only had to ask.'

Chuck had a hard shell wrapped around his soft centre by which he protected himself against the spiteful remarks my father directed at him regarding his so-called misspent youth – all a pack of lies, for Chuck was a hard worker. It had more to do with my father's jealousy that Chuck's expertise in handling wood now matched his own.

"Don't tell me Da, and for Christ's sake don't tell me Ma, she'll beat the crap out of me. Com'n Chuck, gimme a chance, I'll clean your shoes for a month, I'll even press your trousers. I tell you what – I'll pay you back by the week." By now I was on my knees pleading for mercy.

"If you effen' licked my ass, I still wouldn't let you off with it. That was my American money, git! You're goin' to wish you'd never been born before this bloody day's out!"

However, his bark was worse than his bite, and he didn't feel the need to tell my parents, knowing the threat alone was sufficient.

Furthermore, he knew rightly that had he told them my mother would have thrown him out of the house for originally blaming her. Yet he did get his own back – he banned me from listening to Elvis on the radio or playing his records. He sat at the living room table and watched every move I made with those dark eyes of his, his chin cupped in his hands. If I so much as made a move towards the radio he would menacingly mouth the word 'Ma' – he knew this would do the trick. He also kept me to my word – I polished his shoes and pressed his trousers for a month. As for paying him back – well, you can't get blood from a stone.

For a month I was as depressed as hell – no Elvis to cheer me up, no money to even listen to him on the jukebox in the cafe at the top of the Lane, no Chuck to complain to, for he had sent me to Coventry as an extra punishment. The simplest of tasks became a drag, going to school depressed me almost to the brink of suicide and I slopped around with a face the length of a yard stick.

Almost as bad as the face of the conductor of the school bus. He wore the look of someone who had been asked to fight World War III on his own and had lost the will to live, while his uniform looked as though it had already been through World Wars I and II. Mind you, he did have an army to tackle – a bunch of unruly schoolgirls, all dressed in the grey and red uniform of Graymount Secondary School for Girls, some of whom were armed with hockey sticks, some with tennis racquets, but all wearing the armour of youth, a commodity the bus conductor was sadly lacking.

It wasn't the fact that he was old in years. The state of his uniform just seemed to accentuate his look of misery. The ass of his trousers was trying to escape down the back of his legs, while the knees stuck out in opposite directions. We often felt sorry for annoying him and sometimes apologised at the end of the journey, hoping it would make up for his feelings of desolation.

On a few occasions I didn't even get on this bus. I played truant so that I could dander around Smithfield Market in Belfast. I passed the time fingering through old records in second-hand shops in the hope of finding a rock-'n'-roll record for the price of the bus fare I had saved mitching school. Although my idol was Elvis Presley I still listened to other singers. Bill Haley and his Comets had quite a few hits in the Fifties, as did Buddy Holly. You could say I was there for the birth of rock-'n'-roll. Indeed, I felt as elated as a new mother, for it was a very exhilarating period. Teenagers had now got music they could call their own. Before then we had had to be content with the crooners, swingers or romantics such as Nat King Cole, Jimmy Young, Johnnie Ray, Doris Day and Alma Cogan. Great as they were, they did not have the charisma Elvis radiated. Sexuality oozed from every pore, his voice literally begged to be listened to, and he had the ability to make you believe he was singing only for you. It's no wonder he was banned from being shown from the waist down on television. Most teenagers had been accustomed to reasonably sheltered lives up until then – and now here was someone throwing messages to their bodies and minds in a manner most adults felt worthy of an X-certificate. My father thought he was the biggest load of bollocks that ever graced the world of music.

"No way will that man ever overtake Bing Crosby or Al Jolson. By the time the year's out he will be history." Was he ever to be proved so wrong. "Give me a good dose of George Formby any day, thon headcase needs a good clearin' out with a strong laxative; you'd think he'd worms up his ass and couldn't get rid of the itch. As for his voice, if he stood behind a bus ticket you wouldn't be able to hear it." Any comment he made about Elvis invariably included one about myself, with me being referred to as 'that' or 'it'. He'd look in my direction and mutter, "Christ, that's living proof of life after death; it looks like a bloody zombie sat there beside that set. Light a fire under its backside to see if it will bring it back to the land of the livin'."

Mind you, he was hardly one to pass remarks about anyone else resembling a zombie – he could well have passed for an Egyptian mummy, the way he went around the house dressed in his white long-johns and long-sleeved simmit. As for the dressing gown, it made him resemble Scrooge out of Charles Dickens' 'Christmas Carol'. Talk about the ass of the pot calling the kettle black!

My love for Elvis was the nucleus of my life, everything else in my life became secondary. No amount of beatings or verbal abuse could stand in the way of my listening to or watching him. I constantly mitched school to save on bus fare, sold my dinner tickets for half price, asked for sweets on my mother's credit in the local shop then sold them at reduced prices to the other kids – all to get the money together to see him in 'Love me Tender'. A true case of begging, stealing and borrowing.

Anne, my friend from secondary school, and I prepared for our night of ecstasy at the Troxy picture house. Anne lived on Belfast's Shore Road and the Troxy was situated just in front of her house. It was better me going to her house rather than have her traipse to my house and then back again. Anyway, the boys on the Shore Road were better looking than the boys in the Lane.

It was arranged with precision, right down to the minutiae. We embroidered Elvis's name on our knickers – what for, God only knows, as no-one but ourselves would ever know. Not that they would have tickled the fancy of any male admirer should they have been seen, for my patient needlework had been wasted on a pair of navy blue elasticated-legged school passion-killers. We managed to scrape up the money to buy two Park Drive cigarettes at the confectionery shop beside the cinema to help calm our mounting excitement at our first and long-awaited glimpse of the one and only Elvis Presley in his film debut. Like myself, Anne loved Elvis, although we often argued as to whether my love for him was deeper than hers. "Anyway, Elvis doesn't like girls with dark hair," I reminded Anne, unaware that he actually preferred brunettes.

His name beckoned us in red lights above the entrance to the cinema, blinking on and off and teasing us in the process. The letters beat the same rhythm of my heart – El-vis, El-vis, El-vis. The faster I walked, the further away the cinema seemed to be, and by the time I reached the door my chest was heaving with excitement. I felt like crying – which I guess was a strange reaction on what should have been such a joyous occasion. Yet here I was, the moment I had been longing for all year – and I felt intensely sad. I thought I had all rights to Elvis, he was *mine* – but now my dreams were shattered as I surveyed the queue of females, all of whom looked exactly the way I felt. I realised then, with much regret, that I had to share him. A crowd of boys had gathered, mockingly gyrating to a tuneless rendition of 'Heartbreak Hotel', each one curling their upper lip in a pathetic effort to emulate Elvis's good looks. A lot of the girls laughed, telling the boys to get stuffed and catch themselves on. This only added fuel to the tension that already existed and almost ended in tears, until finally the cinema attendant made an appearance and threatened, "If you don't behave, the film will be replaced by another – so settle down, or else you can all bugger off!"

The girls obeyed, the boys sheepishly joined the queue, while I breathed a sigh of relief. To tell the truth, I was a little disappointed when the film began, for I had expected Elvis to make an appearance right from the start. The story was of no importance; I scanned the screen in anticipation of my first glimpse of the man who had now occupied my mind for the guts of two years. Finally, he appeared in the distance, pushing, of all things, a plough. The building echoed with the screams of maniacal females mixed with the obscene remarks of jealous males. Not a word of dialogue of that film was heard above the furore. The only quiet part was when Elvis was shot – no-one had envisaged this ending. For a moment there was a stunned silence, then mayhem broke loose. The girls cried hysterically, whereas it gave the boys more ammunition.

Someone from the back row shouted, "The bastard's bit the dust, for Christ's sake give him one in the head, finish him off before he decides to get up again!" "Shut your faces, assholes!" the girls yelled back through floods of tears. For a while we forgot to keep our dignity in our shock at Elvis's untimely demise. "He won't be needin' his Blue Suede Shoes again, girls; now Don't be Cruel on us guys, we will always Love You Tender." They were really bleeding the situation dry.

A girl from the front row stood up and yelled back "Eff off, fish face! Your Ma must have gave birth to a trout and put it in nappies instead of eatin' it!" The cinema attendant began racing up and down the aisles in a rage, his torch trying to search out the troublemakers with its small round ray of light. All to no avail, as by now every irate Elvis lover, or hater, was standing on their seat hurling insults at one another.

In the middle of it all Elvis's ghost appeared on the screen singing 'Love me Tender'. This only made matters worse. "The buckijit effin' lived!" exploded another boy, pointing at the screen from the balcony. "For frig sake someone shove a stick of dynamite up his arse!" I was cringing at the cursing that was going on, for I didn't curse at the time – well, not in public anyway! Although my brother cursed, it was unknown to my mother and father, for he would have been thrown out of the house on his ear had it been brought to their attention.

"He IS dead," the females all chanted together. "Well, he doesn't friggin' know it, for he's still standin'!" shouted some comedian, who was just emerging from the toilets. At this point the film came to an abrupt halt and the lights were turned on full power, blinding the lot of us in the process. There wasn't a dry eye among the females, while the males were doubled up with laughter, and the cinema attendant was shouting commands like General Custer at the Battle of Little Bighorn, using his torch as a pointer. "Boys to the right, girls to the left. Now file out the side doors in an orderly manner." The sweat sat on the top of his lip, his eyes were wide open and his temple pulsated with rage. Hitler would have been proud of him – all he would have needed to do to complete the scene was break into a goose step.

What had started out as a night to remember turned out to be a night best forgotten. The tirade of abuse continued outside until some people who lived opposite the cinema threatened to call the police if we didn't piss off pronto. Anne and I smoked our Park Drives to calm our frayed nerves, a bad habit to start at such an early age. I have smoked ever since.

Being so incensed at the whole shindig and the embarrassment of it all, we stomped up Anne's stairs in a huff and threw ourselves on her bed with such force the springs nearly touched the bedroom floor and the headboard blattered against the wall. Her dad bellowed from downstairs: "What in the name of blazes have youse two up there? A couple of donkeys per chance, or a carthorse with iron hooves?"

"It's not fair, Da, they all made fun of Elvis!" Anne cried into her pillow. She hit the headboard repeatedly with her fist and her dad came running up the stairs two at a time to see for himself what all the fuss was about.

"Hear this, the two of ye! Elvis Presley isn't goin' to mend that bloody bed after you two have finished dismantlin' it in yer temper fit! I've to work to earn the money to pay for that furniture. Wrigglin' my backside and shakin' a leg at the boss doesn't pay my wages, unlike that head the ball with the curly lip. If ye can't control yer bloody selves, take yerselves by the hand an' clear aff." We were affronted – how could anyone run down our hero. The record player was turned up full blast, and as Anne's Da bellowed down the Shore Road – after he had thrown us out by the scruff of the neck – the sound of Elvis's 'Blue Suede Shoes' could be heard fading in the distance.

Looking back on the whole thing, I suppose the boys were just jealous, as they too liked to rock-'n'-roll to Elvis's music. They were just none too happy with his looks. But my world of make-believe had been shattered. I cried myself to sleep that night – not only had I to share my love for Elvis, I had to defend it. I have always been on the defensive side. I can't tolerate people who criticize what they don't understand, or people who run down others they have never even met.

I have said certain things about my parents that do not sound very flattering, but I lived with them, I witnessed their quirks and foibles. I don't mean to be cruel by recounting certain events – I forgive them their human failings. I hope some day my children will forgive me mine. I accept too that my father did reveal a comic streak on occasion. For example, he had us in fits of laughter at his Egyptian sand dance, performed in his winter underwear and grey socks, the heels of his socks usually around the soles of his feet while the crotch of his long-johns almost hit his knees. His bony knees and elbows made the legs and arms of this ensemble sit out at curious angles. He topped this masquerade by putting a hanky, with the four corners tied in knots, on his head. In retrospect, I firmly believe my father could have been a totally different person had he married the right woman. My mother unwittingly alienated herself by trying to monopolize him into giving her 100 per cent of his attention. He enjoyed company, be it with his upper-class acquaintances or the ordinary person in the street. Like many other men, he enjoyed being titillated when in the company of women, without being labelled a dirty brute by his lawful, or perhaps I should say 'awful', wedded wife. Unlike my mother, he was apparently not spiteful or malicious towards others before he married. That seed was sown, germinated and nurtured like a lily until it matched its fellow fleur-de-lys, and its petals were poisoned with malice and intolerance.

It's no wonder I grew up stoical, and found it extremely difficult to express my feelings verbally. You are indeed influenced by your parents' attitude towards each other. This probably explains my so-called one-sided love affair with Elvis, which resulted in intensely jealous feelings towards other Elvis fans during my teens. I retreated into a world of my own, talking to his picture as if it were flesh and blood and listening to the words of his songs as if he were singing only for me. In my naivety I thought it was only a matter of time before he came to rescue me, like a knight in shining armour, from the tower in which I was being held captive. With hindsight, it was.

My sister Betty married her sweetheart Sam in September of 1957. I can't remember a lot about their actual wedding, but can recall her wedding gown down to the last detail. The ivory silk brocade seemed to have been made by the fairies, woven with threads of silver and gold by the light of the moon. In my opinion it was the most beautiful creation since Cinderella's ball gown. I caught my breath at the sight of it spread over the bed in the room we three sisters shared. Betty was very meticulous, and had been inspecting it for imperfections. The only imperfection I could detect was the well-worn eiderdown it rested upon.

"Can I touch it, Betty? I promise I'll be careful." I felt as if I was in the presence of royalty.

"Are your hands clean?" she asked.

"I'll wash them first, okay?" I went into the bathroom and gave them a quick rub with the slimy face cloth.

As I bent down to touch the precious garment I sneezed. Betty was horrified. "Christ, she's snattered all over it!" She proceeded to inspect every inch of it, while I took refuge behind the dressing table at the window. After scrutinizing her matrimonial finery for what seemed an eternity she declared it snot-free. I was told to have a quick feel of the thing and then clear off. I half-heartedly touched the dress, as the novelty had now worn off, and then ambled out of the bedroom muttering obscenities under my breath.

She must have put a curse on me after the incident, for my eyes broke out in styes. I spent weeks with my eyes covered in bread poultices, and on the day of the wedding I looked as if I had gone ten rounds with Rocky Marciano.

At least Betty was able to walk out of the family home without any undue alarm, unlike my other sister. The following year Dorothy planned a quiet wedding; so quiet, in fact, that none of the family even knew about it. That is, until I unwittingly put my big foot in it, which led to one unholy row the night before the event. Somewhere along the line Dorothy must have revealed her plans to someone she thought she could trust. Not trusting people should have been the eleventh commandment – 'Thou shall not trust anything other than thine own shadow, lest you want the world to know.' Anyway, I had been walking along the Lane minding my own business, when the local gossip pulled alongside in a car, and smiling like a Cheshire cat, asked me what time of day Dorothy was going to tie the knot with Jack, her fiancé.

"Dorothy isn't getting married," I answered, feeling a little puzzled. Could I have missed out on something as important as a family wedding? I wondered whether I had gone so completely bananas over Elvis that my brain had ceased to function properly.

"She's getting married tomorrow. She told a friend of mine the other day."

Some friend – she had blown the gaff on poor Dorothy, who had just wanted to slip away without any fuss. My mother and father had moaned on and on about the expense of Betty's wedding the previous year. (This was a complete lie as they were not out a penny, not even the price of the carnation my father wore in his lapel, for Betty and Sam had paid for the lot. My father did give one tip, and this was to the taxi driver – he told him never to get married!) In all honesty Dorothy just couldn't bear the thought of having to listen to such moaning for years to come.

Of course, what did I do? I flew like a bat out of hell down the remainder of the Lane, ran straight into the house and asked my mother what dress she had ironed for me to wear at Dorothy's wedding. My mother was washing clothes in the kitchen sink and was up to her oxters in suds from the Sunlight soap that was being transmogrified in an attempt to remove the odour from Chuck's socks.

She turned in surprise, at the same time rubbing her hand against her sweating brow and then across her upper lip, leaving a blob of suds on her hair and another stuck to the end of her nose. Her large bosom was heaving with exhaustion and her breathing was deep and slow. "What in hell's gates are ye on about? Did I hear ye right – did ye say our Dorothy's weddin'?"

"Well, Mrs Mulholland said Dorothy was getting married tomorrow. You might have let me know. Or am I not goin'?"

"Nobody's bloody goin'! For she isn't gettin' married, she's only goin' to Portrush for the weekend with a few girls from work. Aule Mulholland's not right in the flamin' head." I pondered on Mrs Mulholland's words for a while, but she had definitely said Dorothy.

My mother must have been pondering on it too. "By Christ, you could be right," she said, wiping her hands dry on the old piece of pyjama leg she had been using as a dishcloth-come-floorcloth – she was not the most hygienic person in the world. "She's been seein' a lot of thon Jack this while back, and she's as deep as a drawn well. The quiet ones are the worst, you don't know what's goin' on in their minds." She left the kitchen and went into Dorothy's bedroom, where she searched the wardrobe and dressing-table drawers. All Dorothy's clothes were gone, except enough for one change!

By now mother's face was beetroot red; she kept going on about people getting up the skite, then about losing Dorothy's pay on a Friday night. "Wait till she gets in tonight; by God she's some explainin' to do! Do you see if this is true, she'll hand me a fortnight's money, mark my words – no-one leaves this house without first giving notice." She ended up screeching, "Do ye hear me! do ye hear me!" in a voice befitting one of the three witches in Macbeth. Her hechin' and pechin' could be heard a mile away as she continued washing at the sink, her face crimson with rage. I was dumbstruck, as I thought she was going to disappear up the leg of her knickers in her distraction.

Dorothy took it all in her stride. She confirmed to my parents that she *was* getting married the next day, and as she was over twenty-one there wasn't a damn thing they could do about it. She looked my father straight in the eyes and said, "I don't know what's worrying you – that's two children you've got rid of without having to put your hand in your wallet. No doubt a man of your thrifty nature will find this a great comfort." He was gobsmacked.

I left school in 1958 and started work in July of the same year. My mother, not being one to lose out on the money stakes, had not rested on her laurels. I left school on Friday and started work on Monday. My first job was as a shop assistant in 'The Spinning Mill' in Royal Avenue. This only lasted a month as the boss was a slave driver. He had me lugging bales of curtain material up and down the shop, a job more befitting a man and not a slip of a fifteen-year-old girl.

It was here I made my first friend since leaving school. Carol had long blonde hair tied up in a pony tail and was extremely pretty, whereas I had short blonde hair and was extremely gawky. I was envious of Carol's petite figure – it came out and went in, in all the right places. I was shaped like a Co-op milk bottle – I just went in at the neck, while the rest of my anatomy was straight.

She too left within a month, after her father gave the boss a belt round the chops for treating his daughter like a carthorse. I got a belt round the chops from my mother for being so bloody weak. "If you had flamin' well ate fruit when you were young you'd have been a bit healthier." Her memory was short-lived; she knew I had a revulsion against fruit of any kind, and still have, especially oranges and bananas. Yet every Christmas as a child I was given an orange and an apple from Father Christmas in my stocking. As I cried with anger at Santa for giving me these two items, my mother told me "Father Christmas doesn't know you don't like fruit." How cruel can a mother be to her own child, I ask you. To the present day I will not handle an orange or banana which has been peeled – it would make me vomit.

Carol went into hair-dressing; I went into a box-making factory, a vast difference. Hair-dressing was feminine and smelt nice; box-making was dirty and smelt of rotting horse-flesh, for the glue was made from horses' bones. Which meant I smelt like a dead horse at the end of the day. Looking back, it was not a bit of wonder Carol got all the good-looking boys, while I got stuck with the ugly ones. It's a curious fact, but when boys go around in pairs, one is normally good-looking while the other could usually land a part in a horror film. It's the same with girls too – one usually looks beautiful while the other looks like a dog – my mother should have called me Lassie!

Carol and I had some good times all the same. She owned a record player, an old Dansette that could hold eight records at a time. Little Richard was her favourite singer, and we often argued the piece out as to who was the greatest. She was out-voted by her own mother who took my side – she liked Elvis and even bought his records. I thought she was really with it, and envied Carol having a mother so young at heart. In fact she was only in her early thirties, but that seemed ancient to us.

She never, ever, accused Carol of resembling a whore for wearing make-up, nor did she reprimand her for talking to boys. She had a look of sweet innocence, a look Carol must have inherited. Carol certainly did not inherit her father's looks as he always wore a scowl, his temper having a very short fuse. Carol lit this fuse on quite a number of occasions. The time she dyed my hair as an experiment almost led to one of the biggest explosions since the dropping of the atomic bomb. That particular night, when by accident Carol turned my hair bright red, instead of strawberry blonde, will go down in the history of my family as one of the greatest cock-ups ever made. We were all blonde in our family when young, varying from light to dark. I was a natural platinum blonde, the envy of all blondes, the colour a lot of women would have died for – or dyed for, depending on how you want to look at it. Although my mother did not have a loving streak for me as a person, my hair, however, was her pride and joy. I might not have had a lot of it, but what I had was beautiful.

Carol thought she knew it all, after working in a hairdresser's for all of four months. She had the idea that strawberry blonde meant going ever so slightly pink, and my hair being the perfect colour – in actual fact no colour – would be the canvas on which she would create her masterpiece. After a lot of adding and subtracting different dyes, we decided to apply a red dye, but only keep it on for the minimum of time, so that we would obtain the perfect results.

Talk about a bollocks – to use one of father's expressions. Not realising blonde hair is extremely porous, it turned out as red as a fluorescent tomato. Following the initial shock when we realised it was permanent, repeated shampooing notwithstanding, Carol set about sculpturing it into a beautiful new style. We decided it looked rather sophisticated and put it to the test. Carol put her brain into gear and came up with the perfect judge of beauty – the man who owned the corner shop.

Now this example of the male species was a randy old git, and anything that wore knickers was in mortal danger of being sexually harassed. The man was speechless, and in my naivety I thought it was at the sight of my beauty and not from shock. He looked at Carol and enquired if it had been all her own doing, or had I been mistaken for a pillar box due its annual paint job. We went back to her house to review the situation. I was considering hari-kari as a way of avoiding the inevitable scene at home, when Carol's father came in. Normally he never took us under his notice, except for now and then muttering some profound anecdotes about juvenile delinquents. But not that night!

"What the friggin' hell have you done!" His eyes stared in disbelief at my unusual coiffure. "You did that, ye head bin, didn't ye?" he yelled at Carol, the spit flying out of his mouth. "Her Da will kill her when she gets home, and see if he does, I'll stand as witness for his defence. I'll plead insanity on your behalf. Only someone insane would do a thing like that!"

"You'll better get home, maybe by some miracle your Ma won't notice," pleaded Carol. "If she does notice, don't for Christ's sake say it was me who did it." Who the hell was I going to say did it – the fairies? On the way home I met Big Jim. At least he liked it, for he asked me for a date. Coming from someone who went ga-ga at the sight of a full moon didn't settle the rumblings in my stomach and the diarrhoea that would follow when I was confronted by my parents. My father was out, but mother was in when I reached home. I sheepishly put my head round the door, at the same time praying for God to have mercy. But neither God nor mother had mercy on me that night.

After mother's temper had subsided to just below boiling point, and my ears had started to adjust to the explosion of verbal abuse, I was subjected to yet more shampooing with scouring powder, Sunlight soap and toilet cleaner. All to no avail – my mother just had to accept a redhead for a daughter. She made me wear a headscarf in my father's presence, and just hoped it would grow out quickly or fade with more vigorous attempts at removing the offending colour with household cleaning agents. This did not improve the condition or the colour of my hair, and only resulted in it standing on end like the bristles of a yard brush. I was nicknamed Wee Willy Harris after a singer of the same name, who had a shock of red hair as his trademark. My hair never regained its natural colour, much to my mother's chagrin. It did grow out blonde, a dirty blonde, not the beautiful platinum my mother had been so proud of.

Elvis joined the Army in March of 1958; he was now known as Private Presley, U.S. 53310761. I watched him on the television news and cried as they cut his hair. I felt as if he was leaving me for ever. God almighty, there were thousands of teenagers crying as far as I could make out, but I was different – I was Irish and Americans loved Irish girls. I would send him a photograph along with a letter pledging my undying love; he would then send me a letter back and our love would blossom. Oh, how I miss the innocence of youth.

Chuck left for America that same year. I would miss him dearly, for I looked upon him not only as my brother but as my friend and confidant. Although he laughed at my love for Elvis, I knew in my heart he understood. He knew it was a form of escape from reality and that some day I would have the chance of making a life of my own, just the way he was going to make a new life in America.

I cried an ocean when Chuck departed the house for the airport on that cold winter's night. I threw myself onto my bed and sobbed into the pillow. I thought I was dreaming when a couple of hours later Chuck entered the bedroom.

"Are you not going?" My heart soared, for I thought he had changed his mind about leaving.

"No, the airport was fog-bound, the plane couldn't take off. I leave in the morning instead." My heart fell to my belly like a brick from a roof. God, this meant another 'goodbye' – how much could I take in two days! "Ah, com'n there, Val, it's not that bad." He could sense my sadness, especially as the pair of us had always been so close. "You know I will write home."

He sat on the edge of the bed and put his right arm around my shoulders, pulling my head into his chest with his left hand. The tears flowed more freely and soaked his new shirt. "Are you goin' to wash this camel gob? For if you don't I'll make you sniff my feet for the rest of the night." He laughed at this but the joke had lost its sting; my chin was almost touching my knees with depression. Who was going to tell us silly jokes, jokes that no-one but the family understood? We were not worldly-wise, we lived in a private world where we lingered on Chuck's every word as if it were gospel. I even went so far as to carry his photograph around to show to my friends. I thought he was the funniest person on earth (good looking as well, even if it chokes me to admit it, Chuck!)

He joked about telling Elvis to write to me when he got there, as if Pennsylvania was just a stone's throw from Memphis and he and Elvis were going to be buddies. For a long time I believed him. I looked forward to his letters in the hope a photograph of him and Elvis together would fall out. Failing this, a few dollars to buy a few records. My record collection was my pride and joy; I had most of the early '78s' which I cherished with tender loving care. The record player (a cabinet for which my father had made out of wood, and took pride of place in the living room) shook with the echo of Elvis's voice, as needle after needle was pilfered from the small tin box and screwed into the arm. The needles wore down very quickly and had to be replaced quite often. Being a glutton for punishment, I received more than the occasional hiding for using up more than my quota. It did not deter me from playing Elvis at every possible moment, that is until the blasted record player gave up the ghost, refusing to work at all. In my desperation to receive my regular fix of Elvis, I made the mistake of lending my collection to a boy I imagined I fancied, who owned a record player. Looking back it was really the record player that attracted me to him, it couldn't possibly have been his looks for he had a face that resembled the backside of a goat. He talked me into parting with my collection with the promise of letting me sit in his house to listen. He omitted to inform me of his family's intention to move house, and absconded with my treasured collection never to cross my path again.

My heart and spirit were broken, and life became a monotonous drag without the sound of Elvis to brighten my dull existence. Chuck's dollars were used instead to buy tickets to the cinema to see Elvis, who, before entering the army, had made a few more movies which were now doing the rounds, even though I never quite got the jist of them as I cried and screamed the whole way through. His movies did not cheer me up the same way as his records. With the records I could pretend, but with the films I suppose it was jealousy watching him get the girl, and with that girl not being me it was too much to bear. I did however get a photograph taken to send to him in the hope of getting a reply. I chickened out at the last minute; I didn't have the guts to send it because the shock of receiving a reply would have killed me. Anyway, the more I looked at it the more I thought I did indeed resemble a camel – I take back all the nice things I said about you, Chuck!

Chapter 5

ALMOST IN LOVE

It was the spring of 1959 and as Elvis was well ensconced in the American Army, hopes were fading fast of a romantic encounter with the man of my dreams. My love for Elvis knew no geographical bounds, but Germany, where he had been stationed, wasn't exactly down the road. A little closer than Memphis perhaps but still not close enough. As I hadn't two halfpennies to rub together, a ticket to Germany was quite out of the question. Even if I had managed to achieve this journey of love I doubt very much if he would have been swept of his feet with unbridled passion by the sight of a gangling fifteen-year-old. Little did I know he was dating a girl a year younger than myself. Perhaps if I had sent him my photograph, I might well have beaten Priscilla to the post – wishful thinking. Ah well, one can dream, there's no law against it.

At fifteen years of age your hormones are falling out with one another constantly. The slightest trauma can send you into a decline so great as to almost make you feel suicidal, so in hindsight ignorance was bliss. Had I known about Priscilla, that green-eyed monster called jealousy would have driven me to distraction. Mind you, it would not have taken a lot to distract a gormless eejit such as myself. I still held the silly notion Elvis was singing for me alone – aye, me and millions of others!

I had again changed my job, as the dreadful smell of the glue in the box factory was starting to ooze from my pores. I found it hard enough to get a boy, without first having to explain why I smelt like a dead horse. I was now working as a shop assistant in a home bakery. Half of my time was spent moping about like a love-sick cow, continuously lamenting on my undying love for someone way out of reach. "If only Elvis hadn't joined the army I could have had my brother Chuck bring me over on holiday. At least I could have seen him on stage, and perhaps, just perhaps, by some miracle, had the good fortune to be sitting in the front row. Then our eyes might have met and... " WHAM! I had been thinking out loud again.

"For Christ's sake, give it a break, ye never give up rabbitin', do ye! It's Elvis this, Elvis that; as sure as hell there's air gettin' in somewhere. Do you honestly think for one minute Elvis would give YOU a second glance? One look at ye sittin' in the front row with an expression on yer gob that resembled a lunatic whose brain has gone on vacation, an' he'd be aff that stage like a rocket to get the men in white coats to lug ye away to the nearest asylum. You'd put him aff singin' fer life with a gob like that!"

Violet, who worked in the same shop, had come to the end of her tether – she was firmly convinced that I was a raving nutter in urgent need of medical attention. Her eyes rolled as she gazed towards the ceiling in search of heavenly consolation, and she inhaled deeply. "Lord Jaysus, help me keep my sanity, for any minute now I'm goin' to strangle this half wit!" She had just about had her fill of my constant rabbiting on about Elvis Presley, who in her opinion was well and truly unavailable. My time, according to her, would be better spent trying to meet someone a little more obtainable; that is, someone who lived within a few miles radius of myself and could afford a night out at the cinema plus the price of the bus fare home. Not a lot to hope for, you might think, but in 1959 half the guys who did take you home on a bus usually did so in the hope of a quick court up an alleyway as payment. If you didn't oblige they promptly asked for the fare back. On the other hand, if you did comply, they were happy to walk home. I always had to give the money back. I wasn't so much frigid as dead from the neck down, as well as dumb from the neck up.

I promptly brought to Violet's attention that I wasn't the ugliest girl in the world and did have the privilege of having a few boyfriends in the short while I had been on this earth. I also reminded her of the one who had run off with my Elvis collection, not realising I had mentioned the dreaded 'E' word again. Violet, who didn't mince her words or suffer fools gladly, told me in no uncertain terms where I could shove Elvis if I ever let his name pass my lips in or around her presence, starting from that very moment. This was not an easy task as Elvis was uppermost in my mind every minute of my day. Even in my dreams he made the more than occasional visit.

"Why don't ye go out with me to the Plaza Ballroom for a night an' meet someone more yer own age, not to mention more available." By this time Violet was strutting up and down behind the shop counter in her bright orange overall, chucking soda farls and barmbracks onto the glass shelves with such ferocity half of them bounced back onto the floor. She promptly retrieved them, dusted them down with the cuff of her sleeve and proceeded to place them back on the shelves – and us professing to be the most hygienic bakery in the town.

"The Plaza!" I asked in amazement. "Did you say the Plaza?"

"No, the institute fer the mentally deranged," she replied

sarcastically. "Of course I said the flamin' Plaza. Why, what's wrong with it anyway?"

"But Violet," I cried in despair, "I'm only fifteen and three quarters." The emphasis was on the 'three quarters'. "You have to be eighteen to get into the Plaza." I must admit to feeling a little nervous at the thought of undertaking such a drastic step, as the nearest I had been to a dance was the annual hoe-down at the Salvation Army where the most daring act of indecency was to remove your bonnet.

"Well, let on you're eighteen, have ye no grey matter between yer ears at all, or has the thought of Elvis been too much fer that pea-sized brain of yours?" she gasped, as she jabbed her forehead with her middle finger in exasperation.

"And how in hell am I going to manage that with my shape – at least you've got a bust?" Which was the understatement of the year – you could have set your plate on one of her boobs, your cup and saucer on the other, and then eaten your tea. Anyway, she was a few years older than me and had a head start. At this point her patience was beginning to fray even more and her chest was heaving to such an extent she resembled a Rhode Island Red in her bright orange overall. Violet also had a habit of strutting with her backside stuck out and flaying her feet as she walked – she did indeed resemble a hen in more ways than one. To ease her temper she lifted the bread knife and proceeded to cut wheaten bannocks in half to put aside for customers.

This was the very same knife I had used the day before to fend off a flasher who had been trying to show off his manhood at the shop window. There was something about Great Victoria Street that gave a lot of men an obsession about their wedding tackle. They were known as the dirty raincoat brigade. By the look on Violet's face and the dangerous way she was wielding the knife, I had a gut feeling she was using the bannocks as a substitute for my head.

She grabbed me by the hair on the back of my head and, twirling me round, hissed into my face. "Fer Christ's sake, have ye never heard of cotton wool? Get some an' stuff your effin' bra with it, an' plaster yer ugly bake with make-up!" By now she was spitting bullets and hand grenades.

"But Violet..." I was trying to tell her my Ma would go doo-lally at the thought of me going to the Plaza, when she interrupted.

"Don't Violet me! If ye want to get a boy, God knows even if it's only to get Elvis out of yer mind... Christ! now you have ME mentionin' his name! Take a tip, do as I damn well tell ye, or belt up!" She stuck the knife in the bread board; I could almost feel the pain in my back.

I thought to myself – how the hell did this flaming argument start. I didn't say I wanted a boy in the first place, I was content living in a world of my own. I had merely mentioned Elvis, now I was being forced to go somewhere my parents would beat the living daylights out of me for daring to even think of going to in my dreams. I half-heartedly relented just to keep the peace, for Violet was beginning to turn purple round the gills and it was definitely not a pleasant sight.

I went through the motions of trying to at least look like a shop assistant for the rest of the day, at the end of which Violet reminded me of the coming Saturday night dance. "Now don't forget, get the cotton wool, pad the bra, borrow a little make-up and be outside the Plaza at eight o'clock sharp or forever haule yer tongue." The full length mirror that hung in the shop teasingly reflected my youthful image. I took a long lingering look and thought to myself 'Mission impossible', but as I worked alongside Violet I would have to go, or never again would I be able to air my grievances in her presence. Little did I know what lay ahead, and, more to the point, little did Violet know what lay ahead.

Apart from my regular chat with his photo, Elvis took a back seat for the rest of the week as I planned for Saturday night. My mind was otherwise occupied with thoughts of subterfuge. I slinked round the home like the 'Pink Panther', trying to salvage any odd bits of lipstick, eye shadow and face powder my sisters had long since lost. My father became a trifle suspicious at my antics and asked my mother, "Lottie, why's that flamin' headcase runnin' around like a fart in a trance. Is she all right, or is she sickenin' for somethin'?"

"Ach, her bowels have most likely seized up again, give her a couple of laxatives and she'll be as right as rain in the mornin'," my mother mumbled angrily, tut-tutting because he had interrupted her evening doze. She had a habit of falling asleep bolt upright in front of the television.

I panicked a little at the thought of being caught betraying my parents. I envisaged the rows and mother's tantrum fits that would follow if I was found guilty of daring to disobey their rules. However, I decided to take the chance, as I thought 'nothing ventured, nothing gained', even if it meant a hiding for my troubles. Getting my friend Carol to cover for me would be simple. If my parents asked where I was off to my answer would be, "I'm baby-sitting with Carol." Not being on the phone in those days there would be no way of checking up other than go to her house. Perfect – as long as I was back in the house for eleven o'clock at night no-one should be any the wiser.

As for the make-up and the filling out of the upper regions, this could also be left to Carol. I would call at her house an hour earlier and perform this metamorphosis – to change from child to adult in the space of sixty minutes. I could worry about turning the clock back two and a half years again when the time came. My mind was also focused on what to wear. My wardrobe contained one blue straight skirted dress with a navy checked collar that resembled a workhouse uniform, a couple of bedraggled dirndl skirts ready for the bin, a black straight skirt, the arse of which was shiny with wear, and a blouse that had seen better days. It was just as well I wore an overall at work; my mother didn't believe in spoiling you for choice – she couldn't afford to in the first place. I opted for the blue dress and prayed that any beauty I possessed, with the help of some make-up, would compensate for the motley raiment that would adorn my body.

All this planning was quite exciting but I must admit to feeling very guilty, as somewhere in the back of my mind a tiny voice was arguing with my conscience. I had often heard my father call my brother a gigolo just because Chuck took dancing lessons when he was seventeen years old. If he was called a gigolo for this innocent pastime what on earth would my father's reaction be to his fifteen-year-old daughter going rock-'n'-rolling in a dance hall that attracted sailors and married men on the hunt for women. He most likely would flay me to within an inch of my life, while my mother would stand back and watch, beating her breast, asking God why he had delivered her such a wayward child, and on the other hand trying to convince herself there was no God or she wouldn't have been afflicted with such trying children.

Despite all my fears I resolved to go, and ignored the possible consequences. To me the Plaza was just another dance hall. The fact that it was situated in Chichester Street close to the docks didn't mean one iota, as I had been born and reared in what was then considered countryside. I might have worked in Belfast but this did not necessarily mean I knew the city.

Saturday came and I prepared myself for a night that would change my life dramatically. As I stood outside the Plaza waiting for Violet I felt like a fish out of water and tried to make myself look invisible. I was conscious of my padded boobs which resembled two ice-cream cones in my sister's whirlpool bra, borrowed without her knowledge. This was already two sizes too big, and had to be stitched at the sides so that the straps met at the back, and I'm sure I had overdone the make-up – panstick – again borrowed from my sister Betty.

All of which would add up to a bloody good hiding if I was caught out. I almost forgot about the high heels and stockings. Now not only would I be due a good slap around the head, I would have to wash dishes for a month. It's known as the Cinderella effect, the only difference being I would not turn into a pumpkin at midnight – my body would more than likely be turned to pulp! The only items that belonged to me were my dress and knickers plus my four false teeth. Mind you, even this might have been debatable as I don't think my mother had paid the dentist, so I might not have been the legitimate owner.

The wait for Violet seemed endless. I pretended to look at the forthcoming events advertised on the walls of the building. It's amazing how uninteresting things suddenly take on new meaning when you're trying to pass the time. Now and then I sneaked a quick look at some of the people going into the dance-hall. A group of teddy boys, or square heads, passed, and eyed me up and down. I blushed and they laughed, informing me the church meeting was in the Ulster Hall further up the road. A cluster of teddy girls dressed in sparkling sweaters, full dirndl skirts, waists drawn in with tight belts, bobby socks, flat B-bopper shoes and hair tied up in pony tails, also passed by, and they too eyed me up and down in my Sunday go-to-meeting attire. They had a good laugh at my expense and I felt my legs turn to water at the thought of what lay ahead. This didn't help my ego one little bit and I was on the verge of going home when Violet finally showed up, shoulders back, chest and backside stuck out like a hen preparing to lay an egg and in a flap as usual.

After running her eye over my persona to see if I met with her approval, she grabbed my arm and came out with her famous one-liner: "You'll do, me aule Pan Yan Pickle." I had passed the test, for this was a sign of endearment from Violet. Not everyone was called "Me aule Pan Yan Pickle"; one had to know her well to receive such a compliment. Actually it meant something very rude – males or females were greeted with "How's yer aule Pan Yan Pickle today?" I need say no more...

At the ticket kiosk she reminded me not to let Elvis's name pass my lips or she would thump me so hard I'd land in the middle of the following week. I meekly agreed as I followed her into the powder room just off the foyer, where all the girls were reapplying their make-up, fixing their hair and straightening the seams of their stockings. Now and then the cry of, "Has someone got a sixpenny piece to hold my stocking up – I've just broken the button on my suspender belt?" could be heard over the din of chattering females, who were preening themselves in the hope of clicking for the night, or, even better, meeting a man for life. Some of these females were well past their sell-by date and were quite desperate. As long as 'it' wore trousers and shaved, any male was in mortal danger of finding himself up the aisle of a church within a very short period of time, and then informed he was to be the proud parent of a baby he couldn't recall ever having had the pleasure of fathering, being most likely drunk on the night in question. Quite often he wasn't the father, but what the hell.

After the preening ritual, Violet and I headed off towards the

70

staircase which led to the ballroom. As the music wafted down the stairs towards us my heart momentarily stopped and I froze on the spot. I couldn't believe it – my God, it was Elvis himself singing 'All shook up'! As it wasn't time for the band to play, records were being played to fill the gap. I looked at Violet out of the corner of my eye to see her reaction.

She was in the first throes of a nervous breakdown. "Jaysus, I don't believe it!" She was leaning against the flocked wallpapered wall at the side of the stairs. "You can't get away from the bloody man! As sure as hell if you joined the Orange Lodge they would most likely change the words of 'The Sash my Father wore' to 'The Blue Suede Shoes my Father wore'!" At this point they changed the record to 'Won't you wear my ring around your neck', one of my favourites and my face lit up as if I'd lost sixpence and found a two-shilling piece. Violet's face dropped as if the opposite had happened. "One word, one flamin' word, that's all, and you will be all shook up and wearing my hands round your throat! As far as you're concerned, I didn't hear it and neither did you!"

My God, for one terrible moment I thought I could hear undertones of mother as I was pushed up the stairs of the dance hall. I shuddered at the thought. I was starting to feel disillusioned as, quite frankly, I didn't really want to forget Elvis, in fact I would have been happy to have listened to him all night. Anyway, Violet was wasting her breath as he was played at least a half a dozen times that evening. We made our way to the top of the stairs to find the place buzzing with activity. The hall was in semi-darkness except for the bandstand which was circular and brightly lit with spotlights. It was circular because it was turned around halfway through the evening for the main attraction, usually one of the more popular bands. The only other room lighting was provided by large rotating glass globes which hung from the ceiling, throwing out small silver beams around the dance hall. To a greenhorn like myself it had a magical feel to it, a fairyland saturated with the aroma of cheap perfume, Brylcreem and cigarette smoke.

Most of the females stood to one side of the hall, the males to the other. The bottom end facing the bandstand was pretty well mixed, while the wallflowers attached themselves to the outer limits of the dance hall, pretending they didn't care whether they were asked to dance or not, yet praying fervently that some member of the male species would perchance to stray in their direction and pluck them early in the night to prevent them from wilting with frustration. I had a feeling I would be keeping them company. Violet warned me to stay away from the bandstand area as this was where all the 'good things' stood. "Ye can tell from their mottled legs an' pimply faces they've got V.D. – the chain round their ankle proves it," said Violet with a disapproving look on her face. Like an idiot I believed her, not realising the mottled legs were a result of sitting too close to the open fire at home, not having the luxury of central heating. I never had this problem as my parents never let you sit too long at the fire – household chores such as polishing the lino with Mansion Polish or doing the ironing were more important. More to the point, we never had big enough fires to acquire mottled legs. My father was more worried about the price of coal than being able to boast of having daughters with perfect legs.

The dance hall had the feel of a cattle market: the better-looking the cow, the better the chance she had of being asked to dance on the dancing area that was set lower than the rest of the hall. If you made it down that step you were halfway assured your passport of approval, as all eyes were trained here to see what was on offer. I don't want to paint a bad picture of the Plaza, although it did attract a handful of undesirables, and bouncers were employed to keep them to a minimum. Once in, you had to behave or you were thrown out on your posterior. Actually it looked very posh inside – the foyer was like a first class hotel and not all the punters were bad'uns. A watchful eye was also kept on the entrance at the top of the stairs by both male and female on the lookout for fresh meat. Being new to this game I felt very vulnerable, on view to all and sundry. I didn't know what to do with my hands. I fiddled with my hair, toyed with my pearlised flower-shaped earrings, or rummaged through my handbag. In other words I just acted myself, a half-witted country bumpkin let loose for the night.

"Let's get up on the floor together an' dance. We stand a better chance that way, at least we'll be on the floor instead of standin' here like two long weekends waiting on Easter," said Violet, digging me in the ribs. "With a bit of luck maybe two fellas will ask us to dance."

"For Christ's sake, mind the chest! You nearly knocked my boobs off, they're loose as it is!" I exclaimed, looking down at the offending lumps that had been stuffed with old nylon stockings, for I had been unable to get my hands on cotton wool.

"Come'n grumpy, where did ye leave the rest of the dwarfs?" Violet grabbed me by the arm and I was on the floor before I knew it. After rock-'n'-rolling for about ten minutes Violet was tapped on the shoulder by a fella. Not a word was spoken as she gave me the thumbs up and winked as if to say, 'That's me lifted, you can do whatever the hell you like, mate,' and danced off, leaving me high and dry. Trust Violet to be lifted first. I felt as if the eyes of the world were on me as I walked off the dance floor. I stood like a ha'peth of dates waiting on paper for what felt like an eternity, while I was eyed up and down by every other male as if he were an Arabian Prince on the lookout for a concubine for his harem. As sure as God I felt so bad that night I thought to myself: if there was only one man, a goat and myself in the dance hall, with my luck the fella would have asked the goat to dance.

Just as I was beginning to lose hope of ever being lifted I was tapped on the shoulder from behind, and my heart skipped a beat. I turned around in the hope of finding my own Elvis look-a-like, only to be confronted by a short fat balding man who was at least fifty years of age. He was sweating profusely and the smell of body odour was overpowering. He had barely six teeth, all of which he must have been extremely proud of, for he had no hesitation in flashing them with the broadest smile imaginable. His wife must have taken pity on him and let him out for the night. To my young eyes he was ready for the knacker's yard. "Are ye gettin' up?" – an Ulsterman's way of asking you if you wanted to dance. 'Why me, Lord?' I thought to myself, but hadn't the heart to say 'no'. He must have thought his luck had taken a turn for the better.

To make matters worse it was a slow waltz, which gave him the opportunity to hold me close. His smile got even broader and he panted in my ear like a dog in heat. Horror upon horrors, the worst was yet to come, as the old hand-slipping act went into action, down my back onto my bum. I just stopped in my tracks, stared him in the ugly gob, told him my friend was calling me from the side of the dance floor and raced off, leaving him standing scratching his head and with a look of bewilderment etched on his none too handsome fid. As I passed Violet I gave her a look of disgust and pulled her away from the bloke she had been dancing with.

"Excuse me, I want to have a word in your ear – did you see what lifted me?" She just laughed, much to my irritation. "Go on, have a good laugh, only the next time he asks me to dance the laugh will be on you – I'll tell him you fancy him and you're dying for him to ask you to dance," I said sarcastically.

"He's the nearest you'll get to Elvis tonight," she joked, doubling up with laughter.

"Want to bet? You've got my hump up tonight making fun of my Elvis, you're not doin' so well yourself. That thing you were dancing with looked a bit decrepit, he wasn't far off his own old age pension."

"Now don't be obnoxious," Violet tittered, "The nearest you'll get to Elvis in the Plaza is a sailor from an American ship, and maybe with a bit of luck he will wiggle his pelvis in yer direction."

"Sarky cat," I answered, walking off the floor in a huff. I spent the next hour trying to avoid the toothless wonder I'd been dancing with earlier. Every time I looked over my shoulder he was there, ready to pounce at the first opportunity. I was scanning the hall in desperation in case he caught up with me, when out of the corner of my eye I spied this tall dark male nodding his head in my direction and indicating he wanted a dance. I didn't bother to look around me to make sure he wasn't indicating to someone else in my vicinity, but ran across the dance floor and grabbed him by the hand. Whether he meant me or not he had no choice in the matter – he was going to dance with ME, full stop. I blushed with embarrassment at being so brazen, buried my head in my chest and held him at arms' length.

I was indeed my mother's daughter – if one thinks back to a certain night in St Aiden's Church Hall when my mother nabbed my father!

Chapter 6

BABY I DON'T CARE

We didn't say much to each other. My vocabulary was limited to "yes", "no", and "I don't care". "Yes" in response to "are you enjoying yourself?"; "no" to "do you come here often?"; and "I don't care" to "do you want to dance the next three dances?" (the band always played three dances in a row). I wonder if this is where Elvis got the title for his hit song 'Baby I don't Care'. After every third dance I held on to him like a limpet, as if defying him to walk away and leave me to the mercy of the ugly one. To tell the truth I didn't take much notice of his looks, apart from noticing that he wasn't over forty, had all his hair and teeth and was taller than me. To hell with the fact that he might not have wanted *my* company – he was the best offer I'd had all night and he wasn't going to get away. He told me his name was John, I told him mine. He informed me he was an electrician by trade – very impressive – and that he lived in St James's Road at the top of the Donegall Road. I had a feeling of déjà vu at this last remark. When I told him I lived in Stockman's Lane there seemed to be a slight hesitation on his part, but I thought nothing more of it.

The sweat was dripping from me and I was relieved when he asked me if I would like a Coca-Cola. On the way to the cafe behind the bandstand we passed Violet. She gave me a smug look as if to say, 'I see you managed to click after all – I told you you'd get a boy at the Plaza.'

She grabbed me by the arm and whispered in my ear. "You'll be alright now, me aule Pan Yan Pickle, I'll leave you alone to get on

74

with business." She gave a sly wink and ambled off. I never saw her again that night.

John and I drank our soft drinks, as alcohol was prohibited in the Plaza. It only led to drunken brawls, even though most of the guys were already half cut before they came in. My heart was pounding as I sipped my drink. Not with passion, or the thought of finding the man of my dreams. No, it most definitely wasn't due to the effects of love at first sight, but was more to do with guilt at sitting here with a stranger, who I knew to be in his early twenties, and me only fifteen (and three quarters). I had a quick peek at my bust to make sure my bra hadn't caved in. The whirlpool bra, as it was called, had a habit of doing this. Although it was pointed and stiff as a poker, it often dented like two small volcanoes when dancing too close to your partner, especially if you didn't possess the ingredients to fill it in the first place. However, all was in order so I relaxed a little. That is, until John came up with the four words I was dreading.

"What age are you?"

"Er... I've just turned eighteen." The words were catching in my throat, and like Pinnochio I'm sure my nose grew a fraction. But I must have sounded convincing for he didn't pursue the topic. I glanced at the clock on the wall and nearly died of fright – it was half-past ten and I had to be home by eleven o'clock sharp! "I'll have to go now," I informed John, at the same time standing up with a jolt and almost knocking the glasses from the table in my haste.

"Can I leave you home?" John asked very politely. I later learned he had spent most of his teenage years in England, and this had smoothed the rough edges from his Belfast accent. It was indeed déjà vu, as it reminded me in a way of my father and mother, the only difference being I didn't come from the Donegall Road – he did, or so I thought. I didn't know, and he didn't know, that our conversation had been riddled with lies from the start. Realising that I had to be home by eleven o'clock with my make-up removed, my mind jumped from one thing to another – should I risk the chance of landing a date (for he was quite presentable, and he had a good job – according to him anyway) or risk a hiding for staying out late? I opted for the latter and answered.

"Yes, you can leave me home – if you have the bus fare!"

We arranged to meet up in the foyer after I collected my coat. I thought to myself, 'he'll most likely change his mind and do a runner while I'm in the cloakroom.' But no, he kept his word, and when I entered the foyer there he stood in his black crombie coat – the spittin' image of Humphrey Bogart in a scene from 'Casablanca'. We caught the Balmoral bus outside the C&A department store in Donegall Place. It was five minutes past eleven according to the clock on the King's Hall when we alighted. I prayed to God John wouldn't be one of those fly men who wanted a quick court up an alleyway as payment for my bus fare home. I didn't have the time to argue. John, being unaware of my predicament, started to walk at a slow pace towards Stockman's Lane. I, on the other hand, proceeded to walk fast and almost broke into a trot. I made a mental note to wring Violet's neck on Monday morning for getting me into this bloody predicament. As luck would have it John was the perfect gentleman and didn't get up to any hanky-panky, but just made polite conversation and walked a little faster in order to keep up with me. As we turned the corner at the little shop in the Lane, I could see my mother standing at the gate, arms akimbo, yelling 'Valerie' at the top of her voice. It sounded more like 'Vaaaal-reeee!'

John wanted to know who the yodeller was. "Christ, that's me Ma! She'll kill me for not being in for eleven." I panicked when I made this remark, as it might have made him very suspicious of my age, but luckily he didn't cotton on. "She's very strict is my Ma," I told John. "You may stay here until I get in, then slip past the house without her knowing."

"Can I see you on Monday night?" I answered 'yes' just to get home and told him to meet me outside the shop at half past seven, then scurried up the remaining part of the Lane, at the same time removing my make-up with a hanky as best as I could. As luck would have it my mother was too busy trying to get me into the house before my father came home and told me to go straight to bed. It must have been divine intervention that had kept my father out half an hour longer than usual. Fate must also have played the top hand in its deck of cards – for I had met my future husband. It was to be a very rocky road ahead, a very traumatic as well as rocky road. I found it very hard to get to sleep that night as I thought I had committed a blunder by making a date with John, especially telling him to meet me so near my own house. Also, for the first time in years, I had gone to bed without saying goodnight to Elvis's picture on my wall. Somewhere in the back of my mind, lurking in the recesses, a voice must have been trying to tell me I had finally met someone who could compete with Elvis.

At work on Monday I relived the whole evening's events with Violet. I had mixed feelings about John, the age difference especially was nagging at my brain. When you are fifteen, a five-year difference can seem an awful lot greater. I regretted having made the date as I now would have to meet him without my make-up, not to mention my padded bra. What a cock-up! It brought to mind the saying: 'What a web of lies we weave, when we practice to deceive.' But at least it had achieved the impossible – I actually got through a day without mentioning Elvis, much to the delight and relief of Violet.

"Go, fer God's sake, I saw him an' he's stikkenout; a bit of alright, min' ye – nice long legs an' smartly dressed."

She had taken in more than I had. For all the notice I had taken of John, he could have had short hairy legs and been wearing a kilt under his crombie coat. Getting rid of the old sugar daddy who had been pestering me all night had been uppermost in my mind – anything would have looked better than him.

"What about the age difference, Violet – he thinks I'm eighteen? If you were in my shoes what would you do?"

"Look at it this way. If it was Elvis asking you out, you would be off like a pedigree greyhound and he's eight years older. Just imagine it is Elvis and I'll guarantee you'll have him beggin' for mercy before the night's over."

"If only," I answered wistfully.

"Jumpin' Jehovah! Well, I'll be jiggered! I take ye out fer the night, I get ye a man an' still ye aren't satisfied."

"What do you mean, get me a man? May I remind you I got this one on my own bat, and just to show you I'm capable of keeping him for more than a week – unlike some people I know who are all ass and tits – I'll go out with him for badness."

"Suit yourself, Linton, but I'll tell ye this much – he's in fer a hell of a shock if he slips the haun and finds out yer chest's nothin' other than two currents on a bakin' board."

"Piss off, ducks' disease, jealousy will get you nowhere. Anyway, more than a handful is wastage!" A scone hit me on the side of the head, bounced off and hit the floor just as a customer walked through the doorway. We burst out laughing and I could just about serve her in between giggles.

Carol called at the house on Monday night just as I got home from work, wanting me to go out with her. I nudged her into the parlour and whispered, "I have a boy to meet."

"Ach, you don't want to go out with a boy tonight. I've nowhere to go and my Da is in a bad mood. I don't want to stay in. Ah, go on, go out with me," she pleaded.

"What's all this, did I hear you say you had a boy to meet?" It was mother – she had heard every word, nothing escaped her attention. And so I had to admit to it, although I did add he was very nice and he had a trade. This was a very important factor in our house, for my parents weighed a man's character by the job of work he held down. As I told her he came from St James's Road she thought it a good chance he was a Protestant, for that area was well mixed in its religious composition. "Well, as long as your father doesn't find out, I suppose it will be all right – and as long as you're in by eleven."

I couldn't believe my ears, my mother was actually letting me go out with a boy! What had got into her? Carol was fuming and tried every trick in the book to get me to change my mind. She even offered to cut and set my hair if I stayed in the house and kept her company. Seven thirty arrived and exactly on time John passed by the front garden on his way to the shop for our meeting. If nothing else, he was punctual. "That's him!" I squealed. My heart was pounding in my chest so hard I thought it was going to come up my throat. It was the first date my mother had ever agreed to and I looked at her, hoping for her approval.

"Well, he seems presentable," she remarked as she stood on her tip-toes, craning her neck to the hilt in order to get the best possible view of John as he disappeared up the Lane.

"He's got a big nose; look at the size of his conk, it's huge!" Carol was resorting to personal insults in order to get me to stand up my date. "And he dresses like a teddy boy."

"Catch yourself on," my mother retorted, "he does not, he looks very well turned out in his nice blue suit, red tie and white shirt – in fact he looks very patriotic."

By God, mother didn't miss much, she must have had eyes like a hawk to take all this in within the blink of an eyelid. Little did she realise the truth – things aren't always as they appear. The fact that he came from the Falls Road end of the Lane should have been a clue.

"He does look like a teddy boy, he's got a Tony Curtis hairstyle – only teddy boys have those," quipped Carol with a smug expression on her face.

"Don't be so daft. If that's the case, why isn't Tony Curtis a teddy boy?" To my amazement I found myself defending John, probably out of spite, as on many an occasion Carol hadn't given a damn if she left *me* high and dry to go out on a date.

"He's as thin as a poker; if his nose was smaller he could hide behind a lamp post." Carol's sarcasm was starting to irritate me as her own choice of boyfriends left much to be desired. What gave her the right to lambast my choice of male companion?

"That's it, I'm going – no more arguing. God almighty, you'd think I was going to run off with him – after all, it's only a date!" If I could have looked into the future I would have seen the beatings and bad names I would soon have to endure for falling in love – for indeed this turned out to be far more than just a date.

"Well, take yourself off now and don't keep him standing like a stewed prune waiting on custard, with his arms the one length. Now go on and meet him, at least he doesn't have ducks' disease and his arse doesn't hit the kerb when he steps off," my mother remarked as she guided me towards the front door. "And mind he doesn't make any untoward advances or he will have me to answer to." This last remark turned my legs to jelly. I could just picture the scene if I did come home and told her he'd slipped the hand. She would most likely haretail it up the Lane after him, grab him by the scruff of the neck with one hand and beat the living daylights out of him with the other. I shuddered at the thought.

I had mixed feelings about my first date with John. It most definitely wasn't love at first sight, more an ordeal, as I was very shy and introverted. Odd as it may appear, I think it stemmed from the fact that I was allowed to go on this date at all, the shock of which had unsettled me completely. I was more used to sneaking out to meet a boy and usually the excitement carried me through on such occasions. My emotions were fraught with guilt. I felt guilty about lying over my age, and the fact that my bust had disappeared over the weekend while my face was now bereft of make-up made me very self-conscious. I tried to hide the evidence of this by walking two steps behind John with my head bowed and my shoulders bent forwards. I must have resembled a depressed camel.

"He has a big nose!" Carol's remark rattled around in my head. Elvis had no imperfection – his nose was not big, it was in proportion to his face. I lifted my head ever so slightly and had a quick shufty at John's neb. Well, it did have a bump on it, but otherwise it wasn't all that long. I felt consoled by this. But Carol's voice just wouldn't go away. "He's so skinny he could hide behind a lamp-post." It was as if she had planted seeds of doubt in my subconscious. I took another hasty juke at John. Admittedly, he was no Charles Atlas, and if it wasn't for his two-inch crepe-soled shoes the wind might have carried him off like Dorothy in 'The Wizard of Oz'.

John noticed my furtive glances. "Why are you staring at me with a funny expression on your dial all the time?" he enquired.

"I'm not staring at you!"

"You are indeed. You keep lifting your head and squinting at me as if I had just landed from outer space."

"I'm not, honestly!" I lied.

"That's all right, then," he answered, a bit too abruptly for my liking.

'He has a Tony Curtis hairstyle.' Ohh... shut up, Carol! I quickly put my hand over my mouth, for I had spoken out loud without realising it. John grabbed me by the elbow and swung me round to face him.

"Are you talking to yourself?"

I bent my head and in a timid voice answered, "No, I just sneezed." Further up the Lisburn Road I had another peek. 'Well,' I thought to myself, 'his hair is similar to Elvis's. I guess one point out of three is better than none at all.'

"Where do you want to go? The pictures or a walk?" asked John. He didn't believe in spoiling you for choice.

I answered with my usual one-liner, "I don't care." He could have asked me to step behind a hedge so he could have his wicked way with me and most likely I would have given him the same answer, I was so nervous. I chose the cinema – at least I wouldn't have to talk much there. As well as that it would be dark and I wouldn't have to keep my head bowed the rest of the evening to hide my youthful appearance.

"I hope that thing Presley isn't on. The last time I took a girl to the cinema he was the main picture and she screamed her head off all night. Nearly done *my* head in – my ears rung for a week. Needless to say, it was the last time I took her out. I hope you're not one of those eejits?"

Maybe I should have gone out with Carol! I felt like a turncoat as I lied, "No, I'm not that fussy on Elvis." I made a mental note to apologise to his picture when I got home. Luckily it wasn't an Elvis film – otherwise it would have been the shortest courtship in history. I'm afraid I couldn't have controlled my emotions and John could not have withstood the assault of my screaming and gurning upon his lugholes.

As we walked up the steps of the Regal cinema I imagined all sorts of hurdles. For a start, what if he asked for tickets to the back stalls? This always signified an interest in snogging rather than in the film. After all, being older he would be more worldly-wise and therefore more sexually experienced than myself. What would I do if he made advances more fitting to a girl of eighteen? I decided to play it by ear and just hope the problem wouldn't arise... if you excuse the pun.

"Two tickets for the back stalls please, preferably the back row." 'Jesus, this is it!' I thought, 'I'll soon find out – there's no backing out now.'

I had been worrying over nothing. Apart from putting his arm around my shoulders and holding my hand, nothing else happened. In fact, I was a little disappointed he hadn't kissed me – I even began to doubt my own femininity. I thought he had gone off me on our very first date and I actually felt dejected. There's no pleasing a female. However, the night was still young and I had the walk home in front of me – he might try for a kiss then. Stockman's Lane in the late Fifties was full of nooks and crannies for courting couples, especially a certain alleyway just a few houses up from the little shop.

John had his arm around my shoulder as we walked home. On approaching a particularly dark and secluded part of the Lane, he automatically steered me in its direction. My legs turned to jelly as I thought to myself 'Oh no, now I have to worry all over again'. I silently prayed that he would keep his hands to himself. Why did I get myself into this situation; my experience of the male species up until then had been mostly limited to kissing, imagination and childish pranks – I had a feeling my childhood days would soon be history. He had just about time to give me one kiss when the dulcet tones of 'Vaaaal-reeee!' could be heard resounding from the direction of my house. Hells bells, or should I say saved by the bell! It was mother calling for her offspring. Eleven o'clock had arrived in the nick of time. Thank God I didn't have to fend off wandering hands, I could rest in my bed with a clear conscience. Mind you, John was not so pleased – my female intuition had picked up certain vibes. He wasn't breathing heavily because of ill health!

"Does your mother call you in like a dog every night at eleven o'clock precisely? You would think you were about fourteen years of age."

Not too far out, I thought to myself. I turned my head to the side so he wouldn't see the expression on my face, turned my eyes towards Heaven and prayed to God for guidance. Phew – that was a bit too close for comfort; get me out of this one, Lord, and I owe you one.

"Ach, she's an awful worrier is my Ma. Don't take any notice and she'll go back into the house. It's my Dad that has her like that. He's an old skinflint – unless the lights are out by ten past eleven he starts sweating buckets in case the electric bill goes sky high." Well, it was partly the truth.

"In that case you'd better go on in." I didn't know whether he was being sarcastic or understanding, for he looked quite disgusted and frustrated. I had a quick peak round the corner to see if the coast was clear. It was. "Come on, make a run for it before she comes out of the house again." Talk about trying to hide from the Gestapo! Even though she had given me permission to go out with John she wouldn't have been too happy at the thought of us canoodling up some alleyway. I remembered her warning about him making any untoward advances, as she was the sort who would have grabbed him by the throat and interrogated him until he knew nobody.

"Can I see you again? Say Friday night, and we'll go dancing?" This one wasn't going to give up without a fight; at least my mother hadn't put him off.

"All right then, but hurry up, for God's sake!"

"What time, and where will I meet you?"

"Same time, same place as tonight. Now come on quick." He pulled me towards him for another kiss. I automatically pushed him away. "We have no time for that now, just run like hell's gates!" I could tell he was embarrassed by this rejection but I didn't give a damn. I just wanted into the house as quickly as possible to avoid any arguments.

My father met me at the back door with his usual greeting – a good strong kick up the backside. "Get in there, bitch, do you know what time it is?" Nothing unusual here, this was almost a sign of endearment compared to some of the welcomes I received on arriving home late. "Lottie, something will have to be done about her coming in at this time of night. You don't know what the hell she's up to. From now on she'll have to be in by half past ten at the latest, do you hear?"

"Yes Bill." My mother always agreed with my father. Half past ten! This had definitely thrown a spanner in the works – how do I work this one out? I just hoped that Violet would have the answer.

"How did the date go?"

As soon as I walked through the shop door on Tuesday, Violet started bombarding me with questions.

"Did ye go on the date at all, where did he take ye, was he a fly man? Hurry up an' tell me, for God's sake, before Alec comes in with the mornin's delivery!"

"Yes, I did go on the date, we went to the Regal, and no, he wasn't a fly man," I lied. "Any more stupid bloody questions?"

"What's wrong with ye then, get out of the wrong side of the bed this mornin'? Didn't ye like him then, or was it because he doesn't look like Elvis?"

"You can wipe that smug smile of your gob, I do like him."

"You've a face the length of York Street. Had ye to pay yer own way into the Regal then?"

"It's my Da. Just because I was five minutes late getting in I have to be home by half past ten in future. The aule git."

"Don't take any notice of that. If my Da told me to be in at that time I'd tell him to take a runnin' jump. Ye don't always do as yer parents say."

"In my case you do, or the hide will be flayed off you, make no mistake."

"Well, suit yerself," answered Violet, "but fer heaven's sake don't start rabbitin' about it all bloody day. Did he ask ye out again?"

"He wants to go dancing. If I tell him I have to be in at that time he's sure to smell a rat. He'd think I was away in the head leaving a dance at ten o'clock, and sure the bloody dance would only be starting at that time. Frig my aule lad anyway, it's only his dirty mind. He's under the impression sex begins after ten at night."

"Don't worry yer wee head about it at the moment, you've got three days to think about it."

My mind couldn't concentrate on my work all that day. John wasn't too bad-looking, mind you, a bit on the skinny side and a bit flashy in the way he dressed. But more importantly he was mature, not like the spotty-faced Herberts who usually asked me out. Indeed, he made me feel quite grown up.

While Violet was all for me seeing John, Carol tried to talk me out of seeing him again. "I don't know for the life of me how your mother didn't see he was a lot older than you, and odds on he's a Catholic, coming from the Falls Road. Sure he's got a Fenian look about him."

"What do you mean 'a Fenian look'? What the hell kind of look is that! Of course *you* would know seeing as you go with one yourself. I don't tell you not to go out with *him*, do I?"

"He's dark haired, swarthy and his eyes are close-set."

I told her to catch herself on. "Get a grip of your knickers, your own Da's dark-haired and swarthy and he's in the Orange Order." This argument went on for the rest of the evening and I *was* beginning to have doubts although I wouldn't admit to it. This made me all the more determined to see John on Friday even if it was only to prove Carol wrong.

At work I questioned Violet on the chances of John being a Catholic until she was almost blue in the face.

"What the hell does it matter what religion he is. Maybe he's a Hindu an' that will confuse the whole bloody issue. Then I suppose you'll worry whether or not he's a Protestant Hindu or a Catholic Hindu. Now clear aff an' give my head peace. In fact why don't ye do a bit of work – stack those shelves with bread or wash the flamin' floor!" Violet believed in speaking her mind. If you were offended by it that was too bad.

In the home I threw a few hints at my mother to see what her reaction would be concerning another date with John. "I wasn't late home intentionally on Monday night, you know. We went to the Regal and the picture wasn't over until later than usual!"

"Listen here, my girl, the point is that you were late. Your Da didn't know you were meeting a boy or you wouldn't have got out at all."

She was busy beating some butter and sugar in a bowl to form the basis for one of her tasteless cakes. The bowl was tucked under her left arm like a pair of bagpipes, while her right arm holding the spoon rotated at the speed of light. The more she whipped, the redder her face became. Red for danger – she was working herself into a frenzy, cursing the mixture for not turning white and cursing me for getting her into a sticky situation.

"If he finds out I gave you permission he's going to hit the roof. Don't you dare tell him, do you hear? My life's hard enough rearing a pack of brats without having to lie for their enjoyment. No-one ever stood up for me, so I'm most certainly not standing up for the likes of you."

I was almost too afraid to ask about seeing John again after listening to these loving words from my beloved mother's lips, but eventually picked up the courage to ask. "Does that mean I can't see him again?"

"Let me tell you something. You're only fifteen, and if my eyes aren't deceiving me I would say that lad is in his twenties. Am I right?" She grabbed my arm and stared me straight in the face. I looked down at the floor hoping that if I didn't show my face she wouldn't see the lie I was going to come out with.

"He's eighteen and a half."

"If he's eighteen, I'm Hitler's mother. Thon lad's gone twenty-one if his looks are anything to go by. If he's only eighteen he must have had a hard life. Did he tell you he was eighteen?"

"You saw him go by the window – why did you tell me to go out with him if you thought he was too old?"

"I don't know what the hell I was thinking about! Maybe I didn't want him hangin' about the Lane. If the wee man in the shop had seen him mossyin' around he might have called the police – he's a bit shifty lookin' an all. Where did you say he came from?"

"St James's Road." I had a sneaky feeling Carol was maybe right.

"Did he give any indication what his religion was? What's his second name – it doesn't start with an 'O' by any chance?" He had told me his second name was Maher. I thought it sounded a bit Catholic so I added a 'T' and told her it was 'Mather'.

"Hmmm." She looked at me with her eyes squinted and mouth pursed, her hand resting on the kitchen table while her fingers tapped out a most annoying rhythm. "And another thing – where did you perchance to meet this over-ripe teenager? I'm sure it wasn't in a milk bar."

"He calls into the shop now and then. We just got talking and he asked me out."

"Oh, I suppose it was a case of two soda farls and what are you doin' tomorrow night?"

"Can I go out with him again," I pleaded. I knew she was suspicious, but there was no harm in asking.

"No, with a capital 'N'. Your father wouldn't like it." She always referred to my Da as 'father' when her dander was up. There was no use wasting my energy arguing. But I wasn't going to give in, not without a fight. When you're told not to do something it often makes you all the more determined to do it.

After work on Friday I locked myself in the bathroom, had a bit of a wash down, changed my clothes, applied a little make-up, put on the high-heeled shoes I had found in the cupboard under the stairs, even though the soles were full of holes – but what the hell, no-one would see those anyway – and sneaked out through the back door while my mother was having a doze in front of the television. Alan and Ian were playing in the kitchen and as I crept past I put my finger to my lip and warned them to keep hush.

"I'm telling on you," Alan and Ian rhymed together.

"Do and I'll wring your bloody necks, obstreperous gits. Not only that, I'll tell Ma you were the ones who stole her eggs for an egg fight!" There was a sudden silence as they pondered the possible consequences. I ran up the driveway and headed towards the shop, at the same time praying John would be there on time. True to form he was – punctual as usual.

"What's all the rush in aid of? You ran up the Lane as if the Hound of the Baskervilles was after you," laughed John. I wasn't joking when I told him he could be right. Nor was I lying when I told him we didn't have time to go dancing.

"Why not?"

"Just don't ask. I have to be in by half past ten so we'll just go for a walk."

"A walk on a Friday night! Come off it, at least go for a drink – I know a nice bar in Belfast."

Oh shit, I thought to myself, the cat will be out of the bag now – no bar will take me for eighteen. Just because John believed me when I told him I was eighteen didn't mean the whole of Ireland was as gullible. Ah, to hell with it – in for a penny in for a pound!

"All right then, let's go!" I might as well have put my neck in a noose. We ended up in Kelly's Cellars in the city centre, but I felt guilty and uneasy the whole time. When John asked me what I wanted to drink my brain seized up, I didn't know what to ask for – this was the first time I had tasted alcohol.

"Would you like a Pims?" What the hell was that? Out of the corner of my eye I spied an advertisement for Babycham.

"I'll have one of those, please," pointing to the advertisement. Not being used to drink I ended up quite tipsy after my third, my nose felt numb and I hadn't a care in the world. The world took on a rosy hue, my mother and father weren't really such ogres, just caring. After the fourth drink I felt very brave, the world was my oyster, and my mother and father could take a running jump. "Come on, let's go to the Plaza! To hell with being in by half past ten."

John asked if I was sure. He looked more worried than I felt.

"Of coursh I'm shure!" By now my words were slurred. As we walked along Chichester Street I put my arm through John's as if we had known each other for years. I was walking on cloud nine. In fact, when we danced I wrapped my arms round his neck. I felt comfortable in his arms. He held me close and I felt loved for the first time in my life. Nothing else mattered in this world. Even though I was drunk I sensed that John felt the same. We were lost in a time warp – until I sobered up. I got home at half past eleven. My father was in a blinding rage and slapped me from one end of the house to the other.

"Only whores stay out to this time – whores and pimps!" I had an idea what a whore was, but enquired what exactly a pimp was.

"That thing that left you home, I saw him from the window.

That's a pimp, he looks like a spiv as well as a pimp. Lottie, did you know she was out with a man! Jesus, and her only fifteen! See if you bring trouble to this house you'll go out that door in a wooden box for I'll kill you stone dead, you slut!" My father had the ability to hurt you to your very soul – making you feel worthless was something he had perfected to a fine art. In his eyes all females were bitches or whores.

I have often wondered why he held this attitude. I've come up with two possible explanations. One, his disdain for my mother who had trapped him into marriage. Two, my grandmother's attitude towards my mother, which had rubbed off on him. I wasn't the only female in the house to be at the receiving end of the stick when he flew into one of his tempers. My two sisters were also hurt by his frequent outbursts about how low the female species could sink. I can only say that his choice of female friends outside the home must have left much to be desired if he held such an attitude towards women – maybe he had a guilty conscience.

I felt so humiliated a lump gathered in my throat and tears welled in my eyes, but I tried my hardest to hold back the flood. No-one, least of all my father, was going to rob me of the affection I had experienced that night. If my mother and father never showed me love, no way were they going to deny me the chance of finding it outside the home. I looked at my mother in the hope of some support. Even if she reprimanded my father for calling me a whore it would have been of some comfort. Why didn't she stand up for me, just a little bit. After all, she was as much to blame for pushing me out to meet John in the first place.

I could see she was flustered. She wouldn't look me in the eye and her cheeks were scarlet with guilt. Why, I thought, do you do this to yourself? Stand up to the man, don't you see what he is doing to his own children. He's already forced three to leave home because of his filthy imagination. It's only a matter of time before you will be left on your own with him, and you will be two very lonely people, for not one of us will be able to show any love towards you, only contempt. Rear your children with contempt and that's what you will receive in return.

I went to bed with the words whore, slut, pimp and bitch ringing in my ears. In the privacy of my own room I cried. Elvis's picture smiled down at me from my bedroom wall and I wiped the tears from my eyes. 'What should I do, Elvis?' I got out of bed, walked over to his picture and rubbed his cheek, then let my fingers gently touch his lips as if willing them to speak. But no matter how fervently one wishes, a picture cannot talk back. So I put words in his mouth. I spoke for him, saying the things I wanted to hear. His slow Memphis drawl echoed in my head.

"Jus' you do what you wanna do, girl. You ain't a chil' no more,

jes you tell your ol' maw an' paw it's all raight by me. Tell 'em old
El here said that guy you're seein' is jes raight on. He'll do till I can
come raight over tharr an' take you back to Memphis to be ma
wife." I giggled to myself. At least it brought a smile to my face as
I imagined him say, "Ya'll come back now tomorrow naight, do ya
hear me, gal?" Well, who's to say he might not have fallen for my
photograph had he clapped eyes on it? He might have written those
words 'to be ma wife' in one of his letters to me.

My father's cruel remarks did not deter me from seeing John. I
had tasted the high that only love can bring even though I had only
known him for a week. It might not have been love at first sight but
the feeling was growing.

Once again Violet had to listen to my woes. "Do ye mean to say I
have to listen to ye preaching about the virtues of the book according
to Saint John. First it was Elvis, God's gift to women, now it's Saint
John, God's gift to Valerie the moan. There's a woman waiting to
be served, take yourself aff by the hand an' see what she wants, an'
give over gripin'. I'm taking a tea break to get my head showered.
An' stop worryin' about yer Ma an' Da, sure they were like that
before ye met John. If yer Da thinks you're droppin' yer knickers
that's his worry, you know you're not an' that's what counts. Now
no more moanin' or I'll wrap yer knickers round yer neck an'
strangle ye with them."

Violet's bark was worse than her bite. I never took umbrage at
her remarks, for she meant well. Like myself, she kept her emotions
under wraps, for she had a lot of heartache in her own life. Her
attitude to life was to try and see the funny side and not to dwell on
the sad side – laughter heals quicker than tears. Indeed, by the end
of the day we often found ourselves staggering about at the back of
the shop in fits of laughter, holding our stomachs lest they should
explode.

These fits were often brought on by the customers themselves –
unknown to them, of course. We had some real characters in Great
Victoria Street. Such as the prostitute with the wooden leg who
hated men. She spent her day walking up and down the street
clouting any man she didn't like the look of with a swing of her
handbag, followed by a torrent of foul language. How she made a
living was a mystery to us all. She also had a hatred of young girls
and often came into the shop to annoy Violet and myself just for the
sheer hell of it. Her right arm got some exercise trying to get her
handbag to connect with our heads as we huddled together behind
the counter waiting for her temper to subside. She usually succumbed
to exhaustion and limped out of the shop uttering every conceivable
swear word.

Another oddity was the old woman who called every morning

for stale bread because it was cheaper. She resembled a badly stuffed teddy bear, with the lower half having had more share of the sawdust. She was found dead in an old flat in Great Victoria Street with enough paper money tucked down the legs of her knickers to stuff a pillow.

Or the old man who legged it up the middle of the road without a stitch of clothing, apart from a pair of army boots and a pith helmet. We had our happy moments to compensate for the sad. They would have been happier if my mother and father had been a bit more understanding towards their offspring.

Despite my parents' threats, I continued to see John on a regular basis, even if it did mean sneaking out at night and lying to my eyeteeth. I still had to keep up the pretence of being eighteen years old, as we occasionally went to the Plaza and usually spent an hour in Kelly's Cellars for a drink before going. Anyway, the drink gave me the courage to face the night ahead.

As the weeks went by John was beginning to get more amorous. I don't mean to imply we were having a passionate love affair, but John's instincts were those of a mature man, while mine were still those of a child. Although my knowledge of sex was limited, I had an idea of what was acceptable and what was unacceptable behaviour. The practice of no hands above the knee or below the neck still applied, much to his amusement and most likely his frustration. Every time he stopped for a goodnight kiss I immediately went on the defensive. Instinct told me when to call a halt to the night's courting and I always had an excuse at the ready to get me out of any embarrassing situation without being hurtful or giving away my age. I would suddenly break into conversation, just as John was about to break out in a sweat.

It was during one of these untimely conversations that I learned the truth about John. For a start he was not an electrician, he was unemployed, or, to use his own words, 'in between jobs'. In my book that meant he was on the dole. He didn't live in St James's Road, he only told me this because foolishly he thought it sounded better than the Whiterock Road where he really came from. Because I lived in Stockman's Lane he thought I was upper class and wouldn't want to associate with anyone from his area. And yes, he was a Catholic – was I in deep trouble!

He had all the faults my father hated – not one, but all three. He hadn't a trade, he came from the Falls Road and he was a Catholic. Even if he had a trade, had been a Protestant and came from the Shankill Road the chances of me being allowed to go out with him at my age were almost nil. My chances were now non-existent.

I made the mistake of relaying this news to Carol, but much to my dismay she revelled in the news. "I knew it! You can't trust them." She couldn't contain her delight at being right. "Now you will have to give him up."

"Why should I?" I answered indignantly.

"Because you will get murdered if you don't – do you think your Ma won't find out? Your Ma's as cunning as Sherlock Holmes, that's why."

"Well, I'm not going to stop seeing him. Would you find it so easy to give up your boyfriend at the drop of a hat? I don't think so."

My mind dwelt on little else but the thought of having to stop seeing John. I concluded that I couldn't; he was beginning to mean too much to me. My life at home, the verbal abuse, the hidings, had become easier to bear knowing I could escape for a few hours at night with John. He had an understanding nature, though how he stuck my moaning God only knows. He must have felt some love for me, and I detected a feeling deep down in the pit of my stomach, a feeling I had never experienced before. I couldn't put my finger on it but I just had to keep seeing him.

My heart was breaking at the thought of not seeing John again and I concluded that for a heart to break it must have love in it. I felt scared, I had so much on my mind for one so young. Continuously living a lie day in and day out was beginning to take its toll. My sisters were married and had lives of their own to live, so I couldn't burden them with my secret. As for my mother and father – there was no way they could be persuaded to yield.

I prayed to God my parents wouldn't find out the truth about John. I also prayed John wouldn't find out about me. I was living a double lie. John knew I was a Protestant but he didn't appear unduly disturbed over this; he probably thought the romance wouldn't last anyway. Elvis's songs took on new meaning. When I listened to 'Love Me Tender' or 'Loving You' not only did I now have an imaginary love but a real love as well, and I cried for both. When I cried for Elvis my imagination ran wild. What if one day, by some miracle, I should happen to meet him and knocked him off his feet? I knew in my wildest dreams, however, that it could never happen – and what if I gave up my real love for an imaginary love? I had a feeling my romance with John was going to be more than a seven-day wonder (even if John didn't think so), and to give this up for a dream – for that's what it was, no more than a dream – I would not have been right in the head. Young love is so painful.

I also cried at work much to Violet's annoyance. By now she was sorry she had ever mentioned going to the Plaza Ballroom. The strange thing about John was the fact he never asked me out on a Saturday night, which gave Violet an idea.

"Let's go to the Fiesta Ballroom this Saturday. With a bit of luck you will meet someone younger and a Protestant to boot, then all your problems will be solved. No more tears, no more fears." To keep the peace I half-heartedly agreed.

"That's it then, me aule Pan Yan Pickle, the Fiesta it is." I went through the same procedure to go to the Fiesta I had gone through to make it to the Plaza, only this time I didn't call at Carol's to put on my make-up. No way was I going to let her make fun of me again; as far as I was concerned she could take a long walk on a short pier – she was history.

I hid behind Violet as she paid for the tickets, hoping the doorman would be too busy to take full stock of my youthful looks. I put on my make-up in the ladies' room, feeling less excited than when I had gone to the Plaza, and my mind kept wandering to thoughts of John. The dance floor was alive with activity, a lot friendlier than the Plaza, and a younger crowd as well.

"For heaven's sake cheer up, the end of the world isn't nigh or anything as drastic fer that matter. Let yerself go, make a few eyes there at the boys." Violet was digging me in the ribs and winking her eye as if she had just told a dirty joke. This time I was the first to be asked to dance, and I sniffed in her direction, closing my eyes as if in defiance. She just laughed and made a rude gesture with two fingers.

I just couldn't cheer up. The fact that the fella who had lifted me was four inches shorter than me didn't dispel my misery one little bit – I could see right over his head with the greatest of ease. The slow music must have got to him for he became quite amorous. He buried his head in my chest and was getting a bit carried away when I spotted a tall slim dark-haired male dancing nearby with a girl. It couldn't be! Yes, it was – it was John!

The sneaked git, I thought to myself – so this is where he gets to on a Saturday night! He wants the best of both worlds – a girl for weekends as well as a girl for during the week! No way was he going to get away with this without a good explanation. I forgot about the boy I was dancing with – he just became an obstacle between me and John.

In the late Fifties and early Sixties dancing always involved the male taking the lead in guiding the female round the floor – it was commonly known as moodying. Couples got so close you could have held a postage stamp between them without it dropping. Apart from rock-'n'-rolling this was the most popular dance. Of course one could go ballroom dancing but this was for squares or has-beens. On this occasion, however, I took the lead and guided my partner in John's direction. He looked up at me with a startled look.

"What the hell's going on here, I'm supposed to be leading you; don't you know how to dance?"

"Don't argue, just go where I lead you, there's someone over at the other side of the hall I have to see!" He looked at me as if I'd lost my marbles.

John was dancing away oblivious to the fact that he was being hunted like a lion's prey. How dare he hold someone else so close after going out with me for over a month. I was green with jealousy. The two-timing slimy toad! Carol was right, you can't trust a Fenian after all.

I tapped John on the shoulder and he turned round. "Remember me?" I asked sarcastically. "So this is where you go on a Saturday night?" It was really very ignorant of me to do such a thing in the middle of a crowded dance floor but my dander was up, plus the fact that I felt quite hurt, having believed he felt the same about me as I did for him. For one awful moment I thought he was going to tell me to piss off, for he looked quite alarmed at being interrupted in the middle of a dance. The four of us stared at one another in bewilderment. The guy who had been dancing with me pulled me to him as if to say, 'she's mine', while the girl dancing with John grabbed him towards her as if to say 'he's mine'.

"Hang on a minute!" I said, pushing my partner away. All of a sudden I felt very brave. "You don't own me, *he* does," I said, pointing at John. "Now clear off!" As luck would have it the music stopped just at this point in time. I grabbed John by the hand, trailed him off the floor and headed towards Violet.

"This is John, Violet. You told me you wanted to meet him." Violet stared at me in amazement, for she had said no such thing, then looked at John in disbelief. "Er, hello John – pleased to meet ye."

John was so taken aback he could hardly answer. At that moment I realised what I had done. I blushed to the roots and Violet pulled me to the side.

"I don't believe this!" She covered her face with her hands in despair, then pulled her fingers down slowly as if she were trying to scrab her face with frustration. "What are ye tryin' to do to me, drive me bloody mad? I brought ye here in the hope of forgetting that flamin' man an' what happens – he's only bloody here isn't he! It could only happen to a string of misery like yourself!" She sighed and shook her head from side to side, her spirit broken. "Go on, clear aff, just don't come moanin' to me when things go wrong, tell someone else yer woes!" I knew she didn't mean it – or did she?

That was the last of John's secret Saturday night rendezvous. His excuse was that he did not see a girl on Saturday nights until he had been going out with her for more than a month. From that night on he took me out at weekends. We continued seeing each other on a regular basis. I told him of my parents' suspicions that he was a Catholic, and explained that it would be safer if we met somewhere else other than outside the shop in the Lane. I also told him my father was very bad tempered, that being one of the reasons I had to be in early at night. I refrained from telling him about the nightly hidings and verbal abuse I had to endure in case he decided it would be better for me if we just stopped seeing each other. I felt safe with John, even though he wasn't a saint. He had the sexual urges of any healthy young man, but nothing that couldn't be handled with a firm 'No, you can't.' He took it quite well apart from the strange look he used to give me on the odd occasion. It was the same look he had given me in the Plaza when I had said I came from Stockman's Lane.

My curiosity finally got the better of me. "Why do you give me that strange look whenever I don't give in to your advances?"

"Oh, it's nothing." Which meant it *was* something.

"Come on, out with it. There's something on your mind. You might as well spit it out." I was quaking in my shoes as I thought he was going to tell me he didn't want to see me anymore.

"It's just something my mate said, it probably doesn't mean a thing."

"What did he say?"

"Do you know a Joe McManus?"

"The name rings a bell, why?" I answered uneasily, as indeed I did know him. He was a fly piece of work at that.

"He told me he left you home one night. He said you were easy pickings. Mind you, he did say nothing happened but you made a date to meet him the following night with a friend. He said you told him to bring a mate along for a double date."

"The lousy git!" I answered, "I only told him that to get rid of him – he was coming on a bit strong and I was frightened. I had no intentions of turning up the next night."

"I know you didn't turn up."

"How do *you* know?"

"Because I was the mate he brought with him for the blind date!" he laughed. "I had an idea it was you by the way he described you. He said you had a funny name, it sounded like Linseed."

We both broke into fits of laughter – at last the mystery was solved. "You were every bit as bad for going with him," I said. "Hell, slap it into you for believing him. From now on no funny looks and no fly moves – you're only wasting your time anyway."

"No harm in trying," he said holding his arms out and shrugging his shoulders. We often had a laugh about this. Every time I told him off for getting fresh he always hit back with the same words: "Remember Joe McManus. He might have been telling the truth, maybe you're not as innocent as you look." Of course he was only joking – I think.

Those first couple of months were idyllic. I felt wanted, I felt I had an identity, I was a person in my own right, not merely some object who brought in a wage to complement the measly pittance my father begrudgingly handed to my mother. Most important of all, I felt loved for the very first time in my life, for John did not find it an effort to express his love in words.

I also felt confused. As I was never shown love as a child I didn't know how to express it in return. John grew up with love, and even though his father had to give up work at an early age and money was in short supply, material things didn't play an important part in his family life. His parents had seven children. Each one grew up knowing they were wanted and loved, so loving in return came easy. I usually felt grateful for any love shown to me, not just flattered like anyone else might feel. I always had the feeling love had to be bought. I often felt guilty in saying 'no' to John's sexual advances. More than once it passed my mind to give in, just a little, as payment for affection, only to be brought to my senses with not only the moral side but the legal issue as well. Being under age it would not have been fair to John, especially as he was unaware of the truth. My young mind must have been in turmoil to have even thought of such a thing. I stuck to my morals with the thought that good girls don't do those sort of things, no matter what their father believed.

And so I continued seeing John behind my parents' backs. I knew that if this deception was discovered I risked the threat of even more emotional and physical abuse from my parents. The situation came to a climax when my mother accidentally found out I was still seeing John from someone she worked with. This so-called 'friend' must have gained sadistic pleasure in telling her, because she was not all that fond of my mother in the first place. My mother's acrimonious manner led to her having many enemies, who were only too glad to bring her down a peg or two with the slightest bit of tittle-tattle regarding our family. To make matters even worse she informed her of John's religion, where he came from – everything. When I came home from work that fateful day, I was greeted with a slap on the face.

"What was that in aid of?" I asked.

"That's only a taste of things to come, my girl, if you don't give that Fenian his marching orders!"

"I don't know what you're talking about," I lied.

"Do I have to spell it out? It's that so-called over-ripe teenager you're cavorting about with all over the place behind my back. Apparently our warnings have gone unheeded. If your father had known he was one of the other sort on top of everything else, he would not only have beat the daylights out of you, I'd have got a rollicking as well for letting you go out in the first place."

"Who told you?" I meekly enquired, hoping it was someone I knew so that I could ring their scrawny neck in retaliation. Why couldn't people mind their own business; why did they have to go poking their nose in my affairs. I had felt happy for the first time in my life and now this was going to be ruined by some spiteful person out to get one back on my mother.

"That's neither here nor there, my girl. The fact is, firstly he's a Catholic, secondly he has no job, and thirdly he's far too long in the tooth to be going out with you. Plus he's no right to take advantage of your good Protestant upbringing into the bargain."

"What are you talking about?" I was taking my life in my hands answering my mother in this tone, but I was flabbergasted by this last remark. "Protestant upbringing! What upbringing are you talking about? I wasn't even reared up – I was dragged up! All my life I've had to beg for love, and now someone is showing me what love is you are going to deny me this pleasure? Anyway, what would you know about love? There isn't much love shown in this house! You should know plenty about that side – what love did my father show you apart from siring six children?"

I had gone too far. "Don't you talk to me like that, you filthy-mouthed mongrel! We don't flaunt our feelings like animals! Catholics behave like animals – they commit sin through the week, then go to confession on a Friday and think all is forgiven. I know, I work with them. They wear the knees out of their trousers praying in chapel then wear the ass out of them sitting in pubs. You wouldn't find your father in a pub, he wears himself out working for other people to keep all the brats in this house fed."

"He's not out working, he's deliberately staying out of your way, you're an embarrassment to him. That's why he doesn't bring you with him." That did it!

She pushed me out of the kitchen where the argument had started, up the hall into the living room and started to hit me all over again with a strength equal to that of three men. My head was hurting, but I wasn't going to give in, not now. It didn't matter any more. What the hell – I was being hit for nothing, I might as well be hung for a sheep as a lamb. As her temper subdued she fell back onto the settee with exhaustion. Her eyes filled with tears and I almost felt sorry I had said such hurtful words, that is until she called me a whoring bitch and that I should have been drowned at birth. I reminded her that I had not asked to be born into this world in the first place.

"No, and I didn't ask to be burdened with you or your brothers and sisters. Damn the lot of you for ruining my life; not one of you would be here if I had got my own way in the beginning!"

I thought this a very cruel remark. Not only had she stabbed me in the back, she had twisted the knife in the process. Any pity I had felt for her vanished out the window. I knew then she would never stand up to my father when he called me those names, not while she echoed his filthy insinuations. Words cannot express the sorrow I felt at that moment. I had no-one in the home to lean on for comfort. My sisters were not there, and Chuck, who I had relied on so much, was far away in America. I retreated into my bedroom and cried.

I cried for the days when Chuck would give me a few shillings, pat me on the head and tell me to go buy an Elvis record to get sent into ecstasy. He knew what it felt like to be on the receiving end of false accusations. But when you're young your hurt soon heals, words run off you like water off a duck's back, even though your brain stores them up like a computer. We don't have to press a few buttons to recall these unhappy memories of life, they have a habit of popping up by themselves in later years when the people who caused them grow old and forget, and then expect love in return.

I don't think my mother actually told my father the truth about John after that particular argument. Maybe she was afraid of what his reaction would have been; he may well have taken it out on her as a release for his own emotions, not being too enamoured by his own choice of matrimonial partner. He did find out in time though, when he was returning from his evening soiree and spied John walking up the Lane after leaving me home. He enquired why "that pimp was still stalking" Stockman's Lane. By this time I had found out what a pimp was, and I often thought to myself: how did he know what a pimp looked like, maybe he knew a few? I prayed to God to forgive me for such thoughts and prayed also that I hadn't been cursed with my parents' tarnished intellect concerning matters of the opposite sex. This time he didn't just call John a pimp, he was a praying mantis as well, the stick insect which resembled someone saying their prayers with their hands clasped. This was his sarcastic way of calling John a Catholic. From then on it was, "Here's that blasted praying mantis on the prowl, creepin' Jesus, Papish bastard," to name but a few of my father's terms of endearment.

He knew he couldn't stop me seeing John, other than locking me in my bedroom and putting bars on the windows, so I suffered regular verbal and physical abuse on my return from each date. John didn't know anything about these incidents for a long time, as I was afraid of telling him in case he gave me up out of pity. Although I had only turned sixteen, my quest for love had turned me into an adult before my time.

I confided in Violet a lot, no-one else being available. She advised me to tell John of my predicament. In her opinion if he loved me he would stick by me.

"It's just like this, Val," she said, as she handed me a hanky to wipe away my tears. "He has to know, he has to share yer fears as well, or ye will never know his true feelings. Ye must love him or ye would not be puttin' yerself through hell and high water to go out with him. This way ye will know if he loves ye, and yer worries will

95

be halved. Christ, you're too young to have such heartache. Take it from one who knows. I too have a lot of heartache but at least I'm five years older. I might shout at ye now an' then, but my bark's worse than my bite. Take the bull by the horns, tell him tonight."

John and I went to the cinema that night. I toyed with the idea of telling him my real age, then made up my mind to tell him I was seventeen not eighteen. This wouldn't be so big a shock to his system. On the way home I hardly spoke two words.

"What's wrong with you tonight?" John asked. "Don't you want to see me again?"

"It's not that. I'm worried, that's all."

"Well, you can't be pregnant, that's for sure. You can't put the blame on me – you could always blame Joe McManus," he joked.

"Don't make fun of me." I burst out crying and John turned me around by the shoulders to face him.

"Look at me, lift your face and look me in the eyes. What in the name of God is it? Christ, you're shaking. Have you been told bad news or something?"

I told him everything – how my father hit me every night I came home from our dates, and the verbal abuse I had to suffer from both of my parents. I even told him he was known as a praying mantis and maybe it would be better for him if he didn't see me again.

"Catch yourself on! Are you right in the head – don't you know I love you? If it will make things easier I'll have a talk with your Da. That's if you want me to, or maybe *you* want to give me up?"

"No, I don't want to give you up!" I wanted to tell him I loved him in return, but I couldn't, I found those three words 'I love you' so very hard to say. I never had cause to say them to anyone before then, they were alien to me. They only belonged to films and books, not the real world.

"Do you love me, then?" John asked.

I could only answer 'Yes', I couldn't say the actual words.

"That's it, then, I will speak to your aule man," he replied.

"There's one other thing – I'm not eighteen, I'm seventeen," I confessed, my eyes avoiding his as I tried to hide my guilt.

"Bloody Nora, are you sure that's *all* your secrets?"

"Yes." I lied.

"Well, cheer up for God's sake and smile. If you died with a face like that no-one would bury you." He put his finger under my chin, lifted up my face so he could look me in the eyes. "Now pull yourself together, it's not the end of the world!"

I thought to myself 'not quite', but the worst was yet to come!

Chapter 7

TAKE GOOD CARE OF HER

John and I had to give up the foolhardy practice of meeting in the Lane, as my parents were in a permanent state of cranium unsteadiness, more commonly known as the headstaggers, at the sight of John passing the house to meet me for a night out. I usually got hit going out and a good walloping for good measure when I came home. The neighbours' dogs got better treatment for crapping on the lawns.

My sanity was now in a serious state of deterioration. No tradeless Fenian bastard (to use my father's very words) was going to get their feet under the Linton table. The thought was enough to send my father into a blue fit. Ironically, it was somehow perfectly in order for my father to earn a living working in Catholic chapels, making altars and pulpits from which the priest delivered Mass, or even to make the pews and praying sills for the congregations to wear their knees out while praying for forgiveness! It was also an honour to be asked to do private work for the local priest.

As far as I was concerned my parents were simply hypocrites. They did not attend church, yet called upon the services of the clergy when it suited them – weddings, funerals, christenings. I'm afraid I can't make excuses for them. I have long since tried and failed to understand their mentality. Their bigoted attitude was not something they inherited from their own parents. My paternal grandparents who came from England couldn't give a tinker's ass, while my maternal grandparents insisted their table cloth was their flag. It was all a case of too much religion and not enough Christianity. I am glad to say my parents' views on religion did not tarnish my own mind – I went out with John regardless of his religion.

In the late Fifties we usually obtained our information through the 'grapevine'. Unlike today, the telephone was a privilege and a luxury only wealthy or business people could afford. As neither John's nor my own family fell into this category, the next best thing for communicating with each other, apart from hearing through a third party, was if your place of work was situated within shouting distance of one of these marvels of modern technology.

The furniture store situated next door to my workplace had the misfortune of possessing a telephone. I say misfortune, because the girl in the office of Whitten's Furniture Store was run off her feet, not to mention scundered to the eyeteeth, by having to sprint from one shop to the other with the message that my beloved was on the other end of the phone. John had a very deep voice, and to those who didn't know him he could have been mistaken for someone far older than his twenty-two years. Marie from Whitten's was no exception and was under the impression I was dating a very mature man.

"There's an aule lad on the phone for you, blondie. Dare I ask what the nature of the call may be, or are you by any chance takin' up datin' sugar daddies?" Marie was decidedly red in the face, having dashed from the furniture store before John's few pence would run out. Her curiosity was also getting the better of her. She told me to get my skates on and to remove the look of a cow peering over a wall from my face. It got to the stage where John was on the phone every other day.

Violet was also going steady by now and the first ten minutes of each day was spent comparing the goings-on of the previous night's courting habits. Boys overexaggerate their sexual exploits so as to sound macho, while girls tend to tell the truth and have a bit of a giggle. Many a time we found laughing hysterically as we exchanged stories about our escapades. We talked a lot about sex but practised very little of it. We came to the conclusion that men weren't ruled by their brains but by another part of their anatomy. It would be wrong to imply we were angels, for we dabbled on the fringes, but we always called a halt where the fringe joined the hem for fear of getting up the skite.

Another important concern was the fear of never getting another boy, as men in those days would have been very dilatory about walking up the aisle with a girl who was not virgo intacta. If she was not in this state, it was to have been by his doing and no-one else. Our attitudes to sex were very much a product of prevailing social attitudes. I even thought it quite daring for Violet to make remarks on the smallness of my bust.

"A bit of haun rearin' wouldn't go amiss in that department, if ye ask me."

I told her, "Your aule lad must have been goin' like a dinger in his efforts to get yours in that condition; it certainly wasn't the heat of the sun."

"God," she answered back, "you're a dirty blirt coming out with a remark like that!"

"Listen to the pot calling the arse of the kettle black – sure you started it!"

Needless to say we just laughed it off and put it down to experience, or the lack of it. My mother got even more suspicious at not seeing John pass the house, plus the fact that I was always out at night when my friends came looking for me. She was nobody's fool, and suspecting I might be seeing him she put every obstacle in my path. She divested me of all my weekly earnings apart from my bus fare to and from work. She never bought me any clothes, which led me to borrow from my sister, who was now staying in the house with her husband and young son David while they awaited word of a new home from the Housing Trust. This led to even more arguments as Betty was very fussy about her clothes. She washed, ironed to perfection and hung everything neatly in her wardrobe, while her underwear was placed tidily in her dressing table drawers. As quick as Betty was putting her clothes away I was taking them out again. I was not so fussy and left them back in a complete mess. Nothing was sacred – even her knickers, bras, stockings and suspender belt. I even took her baby son's nappies to dry myself with after washing as there usually wasn't a clean towel in the house. I couldn't win – if I wasn't getting hit by my parents, I was getting clobbered by Betty.

I managed to dispossess my father of a few shillings – unknown to him, I should add. He always left his loose change beside the clock on the mantelpiece before retiring to bed. Now I was not so stupid as to take the money there and then. I shoved the odd half-crown under the clock and waited to see if he noticed next morning when he put it back in his pocket. For all my father's meanness he must have been a trifle gormless – he never ever made a check, and so the plan worked.

Once he was out of the house the half-crown was soon deposited in my pocket. I didn't know at the time that my brother Alan was at the same lark. If I had known I would have blamed him if my father had cottoned on, but he never did. My mother was not so easily taken in with the slyness of her offspring. She became really suspicious of my movements when she called into the shop one day and I was absent. Violet had let me out for a couple of hours on a slack day to meet John in the Botanic Gardens. My mother's eyes scanned every corner of the shop and she started flapping about like a whirling dervish.

"Where is she!" she screeched at Violet, who was by now having kittens at the sight of my frenzied mother, as she circled the shop in her search for her wayward daughter. "I said, where is sheeee!" She was beating her breast like an ape while Violet continued stacking bread, desperately trying to think up some excuse.

"She's... emm, she's emm...." Violet's bowels were on the point of working involuntarily as she felt fear take a grip on her innards.

Mother was behind the counter by now and staring directly into Violet's face.

"She's not here, is she? She's out with that long-legged over-the-hill teenager. Just wait till she comes home. No way will she go out unbeknownst to me with that one! I'll bate her with a wet dish-cloth 'till she knows nobody!"

"She's up in the Newtownards Road branch today." This sudden brainwave of Violet's was brought on by fright rather than cleverness. "They were short-staffed," she added as an afterthought. This seemed to appease my mother somewhat, but she informed Violet she would check up in case she was being lied to.

My mother had just left the shop ten minutes when I returned. "Fer Christ sake, don't ye ever do that on me again! That aule barge of a Ma of yours was here an' you're in for a quare gunk when ye get home. Look after the shop fer five minutes while I go up to the bog, the insides are leaving me. I'll give ye the jist of it when I come down. Prepare yerself to do some cover-up work."

Violet relayed the whole story word for word. Our brains worked overtime trying to think of a way out of the situation.

"Listen", said Violet, "go next door, ring up the Newtownards Road branch an' tell them to cover fer ye before yer Ma makes it there. If she finds out yer kaileyin' about during working hours with John-boy, I dread to think of the consequences."

I didn't argue, just obeyed and prayed the ploy would work. My mother half-believed it, but described in detail what she would do to me if I was caught lying. I cringed at the thought and made a mental note to be more careful in future.

I knew things were getting serious between John and I when he took me home to meet his family. The entire brood had stayed in to see what John's latest flame looked like. I could hear his sisters giggling behind my back and sensed they were making fun of my posh accent. Being reared in an upper-class district had rubbed off to the extent that we did know how to conduct ourselves as far as speech was concerned, even though my parents' general attitude towards life left much to be desired.

John's family on the other hand were rough and ready but the love shone through the unrefined exterior. His parents were the complete opposite to mine, they were very quiet and spoke softly, maybe not with the poshest of accents – in fact it was a very broad Ulster tongue – but they did made you feel at ease.

His father Tommy was very Jewish-looking, bald, swarthy, with a hooked nose, and always had a smile even though he never wore his false teeth. Out of the corner of my eye I saw a photograph of him in his younger days dressed in the uniform of The Highland Light Infantry. His military training was still reflected in his bearing

– he was wearing a spotless white shirt, newly pressed trousers and shoes shined to perfection. He did not work due to ill health, for he had asthma, a bad heart and other complaints too numerable to mention.

John's mother Ellen reminded me of Pope John XXIII in looks. She was the typical wee down-to-earth mother figure, forever preparing meals, frying in a huge cast iron pan or boiling clothes in a bucket on the cooker. She also reminded me of Mrs McGlonan from the Lane – I later learned they were friends and had grown up together in the same street. Like her she never wore her false teeth except for weddings and funerals.

I looked around their living room; it had a homely feel to it. A glass cabinet filled with china tea sets, figurines and various pieces of oriental design, most probably mementos from Mr Maher's army days. A holy statue resting on the fireplace reminded me of John's religion, and for a short moment I felt like an intruder, but the family's warmth, not to mention the warmth from the large blazing fire, enveloped me like loving arms. I felt as if I had come home for the first time in my life, and I had to quell the urge to embrace Tommy and Ellen as if they were long-lost parents.

They sensed my uneasiness as I glanced at the holy picture of the Sacred Heart hanging beside the window, but they did not make apologies for their religion, nor did they try to make apologies for mine. Their kindly smiles answered my silent thoughts, 'Don't be afraid, child dear, you are not here to be judged, only God has the power to judge.'

A shiver ran through my body as a picture of my mother and father flashed before my eyes – I could feel it come alive. They were damning me for feeling happy in a house filled with Papish bastards who scraped and bowed to statues – their words, not mine. I tried to blot out their image with pleasant thoughts of a better life in the future; after all, I was seventeen, not too far off marrying age, when I could make a life of my own.

John's father had one failing, however. Now it was not one that would send him into hellfire and damnation, but nevertheless it was an embarrassment to his family – he was unable to hold his wind, and farted at the most inopportune times. He had been warned by John not to pass wind in my company – if he had the urge he was to go to the toilet. But mother nature does not take heed of mortals at all times, and John's breath was wasted. All was quiet and we were having a cup of tea on our knee (another sight I was unaccustomed to, for in our house we had to drink our tea at the table, and the sight of such an act would have offended my father) when this short but loud fart echoed round the room.

All eyes turned to John's father who was trying to suppress a giggling fit, and in doing so his body looked as if it was in the first stage of an epileptic fit. As he had asthma he started to cough. A fart accompanied every cough, which only made matters worse, because the more he coughed the more he farted. John gave his father a look of disgust, and he in turn tried to blame it on the legs of his chair being loose.

"Ellen, somethin' will have to be done wi' these chairs. They make an awful noise when ye move."

By this time John's sisters had made a beeline for sanctuary in the scullery, and his mother grimaced at John as if to apologise, while John looked at me, his face and neck crimson with embarrassment. I glanced over at his father who smiled at me and said, "Ye can't haule what's nat in yer haun, love."

God love him; in his own way he had broken the ice, and from that day nothing or no-one in the Maher household could embarrass me. Ellen, John's mother, proceeded to tell me all about my beloved's birth, a fault of which all mothers are guilty.

She always pronounced her words wrong. I realised this when she informed me that John's legs were blue with 'stagnation' when he was born. The penny dropped when she proceeded to tell me how she had to sit up all night and rub them vigorously to get the 'circling' back into them, obviously referring to his bad circulation. "Nat only were his legs stagnant, they were that long they hung aff the end of me knee like two blue ribbons wi' knots aun the end o'thim. Nat only that, the midwife thought he haud no head, fer there wis nay sign of it when I started pushin'."

John had a look on his face no artist could paint as he tried under his breath to tell his mother to shut up. But now that she'd started she was going to finish. "Mindye, it cuda been wurse, the woman daun the street hadta go in to be seduced she wus that overdue. An' that's awful embarrassin' havin' a maun hokin' at ye whin all ye want isa bita pase to git an wi the jab yoursel'. Minye it's a quare detergent agin gettin' thon way again ina hurry."

Now it was my turn to turn red round the gills with embarrassment, as I didn't know what on earth she was talking about. What was all this talk of pushing and 'seducing', not to mention babies having no heads? She must have thought I knew all about such things. Then we went directly onto the subject of death, and she informed me that she was the local 'handy woman', who helped out at births and the washing of the dead.

"Me an' Mrs Fitzpatrick made a great jab a thon wee maun roun' the corner, John. Ye know the maun I'm talkin' about – wee Wullie who lived at number ten? He luked awful well he did, niver seen him luk so well in me life. By the time we'd laid 'im out he hud a smile aun 'is face. As long as he keeps his bum to the wall he'll be all right, his shroud couldne meet at the back he wus so fat."

The mind boggles – why the smile? By now I was highly

amused, for I had never in my life heard such stories. I was completely engrossed by what I heard and could have listened all night, while John sat mortified. Then the photographs came out of hibernation, albums frayed at the edges with age and shoe boxes overflowing with pictures of people long since departed. "John's the spittin' image aff his Da when he wus his age, he's the same nose an all."

His father burst out laughing at this point. "That's somethin' to look forward to, John. You're goin' to end aff bald an' toothless by the time ye reach forty."

"Indeed, I won't," John argued back, his voice an octave higher than usual. "Look, my hair's thick and wavy!" He was pulling at his hair to prove his point.

"So wus mine till it waved goodbye," his father answered back in a fit of giggles, which only made him start farting all over again.

As John walked me home that night he tried to apologise for his family's foibles. I told him it was the best night I had ever spent, and if he wanted to witness quirks and foibles, a weekend in my house would not go amiss.

I spent my days off work in John's house – at least I got fed. Whenever I came home from a hard day's work at home I was usually the last in the queue for dinner. This meant making a boiled egg and toast or going without, as my mother never ever made enough to go round. My father had his piece of steak served on his own table beside the fire, while we lesser mortals sat in the scullery and contented ourselves with sausages and sniffed the frying pan in order to savour the aroma of the steak. If we closed our eyes we could always pretend we were eating meat. We knew when father had finished his dinner, for he tapped the sides of his plate with his knife and fork as if he was playing the snare drum. This indicated satisfaction with his meal, and we always knew he was displeased when he smashed the plate against the kitchen wall and yelled, "Do you call that a bolloxing dinner – the vet feeds better to his dogs." The nights he got dinosaur stew were the worst. He picked the bones out one at a time and threw them at the wall just before the plate made contact. "There's more bolloxing bones in that bloody meal than in a graveyard."

John's mother, on the other hand, had the art of making the simplest of meals taste like manna from heaven. Her fry-ups had you drooling at the mouth before she even lit the gas under the heavy cast-iron frying pan. It had been used so often it was seasoned to the point were a slice of bread tasted like roast beef when dipped in the juices. Her soup was perfection – poetry to a ravenous stomach, salve to a rumbling belly.

The Maher house became my place of refuge. The only argument I ever heard was over whether or not it was a sin to eat meat on a

Friday or who was entitled to the crispiest Kennedy's bap of a morning for breakfast. The ritual of the bap never failed to amuse me. Kennedy's bakery delivered at five o'clock in the morning. Peter the delivery man had the key to almost all the homes in the Whiterock area and let himself in while the residents were still in slumber. He faithfully left the bread on the table every morning – five baps and a loaf of bread. At weekends he left potato and soda farls for the Saturday and Sunday morning fry. He collected the money left on the table and closed the door gently as he departed so that he wouldn't disturb the sleeping inhabitants.

The one place John would not take me to was to see an Elvis film – he just couldn't stand them. He insisted they were for silly females who fantasized about making love to a picture instead of the real thing. "Why imagine yourself in bed with Elvis when I'm willing to bed you in reality." John tried using this remark to his advantage, and cursed his luck when it fell on deaf ears.

"Don't say that, imagination won't get me in trouble, but you could – so belt up and don't even think about it."

"Don't *think* about it! Christ, it's the only thing you allow me to do. We've been going out for a year now and all I get is a promise. I bet Elvis gets more in your dreams." I blushed at this remark – the guilty always feel embarrassed when confronted with the truth.

"See, it's true, isn't it? What's Elvis got that I haven't?"

I stuck my nose in the air and replied in a hoity-toity manner, "Good looks and plenty of money – you lack both." I should not have made this remark, for John told me to stuff Elvis and handed me my bus fare home on more than one occasion.

This became a regular occurrence. John was quite frankly pissed off with Elvis, and told me to make a choice – it was either him or Elvis. Of course I chose John, for even I could see the futility of chasing a dream, and I finally admitted defeat, albeit with a heavy heart.

Chuck was not sending the dollars as often now and my purse was lighter, my heart heavier, my mother nastier, my father even meaner. Mother concocted a plan. She wrote to Chuck asking him to bring me over to America, as her way of getting rid of John. He wrote back saying it was out of the question, because he was not an American citizen, therefore could not claim me. I felt like an unclaimed umbrella in the lost property department of the Belfast Bus Corporation. Anyway, he was joining the American Army shortly as a way of getting round the situation, for two years in the army automatically brought citizenship status. He did say, however, that it might be possible to find me a male pen pal when he joined up.

My heart skipped a beat when I read this. Elvis was in the army

– maybe Chuck would get to meet him. My hopes soared to new heights, only to come crashing down to earth quicker than they were raised. The very same day Chuck joined the army Elvis left it. Chuck did, however, meet a friend of a friend who had cleaned Elvis's boots. Hip hip hooray, I thought, what a lot of use that was. It crossed my mind to write a sarcastic letter, asking Chuck to send me the shoe brush this friend had used, to put under my pillow so I could dream on it. To add insult to injury he sent a photograph of the ugliest man on two feet, who was in the same platoon as himself, with a note attached. It read: "This man is a quarter millionaire and his eyesight is none too good, but for some unknown reason he fancies the look of your ugly gob. Just say the word and he's yours. Signed, Chuck." My letter of reply is unprintable, the only thing I can say is that Chuck's eyes would still be watering to this day had he carried out my instructions!

Mother's ploy did not work. In reality she was throwing me even more into the arms of John and his family. After seventeen years of the Linton institution, the Maher home was like a breath of fresh air. The easy-going atmosphere and normality of family life sucked me in like a vacuum. I now only used my own house as a place to sleep and tried to keep the peace by being in at eleven o'clock sharp every night. John began to buy me my clothes and shoes so that I wouldn't have to beg from my parents, but this caused even more arguments as I was now being accused of prostituting myself for payment.

John was bewildered by my nightly crying fits whenever it came to say goodnight. He still didn't fully comprehend my situation at home, or why I hated returning. He understood my parents' attitude towards him for being a Catholic, even though his parents never got at him for going with a Protestant, but he found it difficult to understand why they were so physically abusive to me. I told him I could not take any more from my parents as I now felt as if my health was starting to go downhill. I could not eat without feeling sick, insomnia had taken hold and I always felt tired. My father's insinuation that I was just a prostitute had felt like a sharp knife being driven into my heart.

He saw red and told me he wanted to meet my father man to man to talk things over. I panicked at the thought. This would mean having to tell John my real age, for he was still under the impression I was over eighteen, and my father would certainly inform him I was only seventeen. For John to carry out his wish I realised he had to know the truth, so I broke the news as gently as possible, fearful he wouldn't want to be labelled a cradle snatcher and tell me to get lost. He was quite shocked for a while but we agreed we were now too involved with each other to end our relationship.

I told my mother the next day that John wanted to have a word with my father, and she flipped her lid. "Why do you do this to me?" she cried, hitting the table with her fist in despair. "I never wanted children, now I'm being tortured off the face of the earth with all their bloody problems. You're not pregnant by any chance? Is that the reason that praying mantis wants to speak to your Da? See if it is, you won't live to see the child brought into this world for I'll kill you with my bare hands, so help me!"

"No, I am not pregnant, I am just sick of being treated like a whore. Sometimes I wonder though if it would make any difference if I were a harlot. I might as well be doing what I'm being accused of, at least we could all be reaping the benefits – you could have half the takings." My face stung all that day from the slap I received from the back of her hand.

At half past seven that evening John knocked on the front door. My heart was beating wildly in my chest when my father pulled me aside and asked, "Why the hell is that bastard coming to the door!" My mother hadn't told him. I started to shake. I could hardly get the words out as everything seemed to be going in slow motion.

"He wants to speak to you," I answered in a low voice as I stared at the floor.

"What the fuck for?" It was the first time I had heard my father use this word and it scared me more than all the bolloxing he had done over the years. Then he did the strangest thing – he turned on his heels and fled up the stairs to hide! Through it all he was a coward!

I let John in and told him to wait in the sitting room. I felt too ashamed to tell him my father had hidden himself in the upstairs bedroom, and made the excuse 'he was at his dinner'. I stood at the bottom of the stairs and pleaded with my father to come down. It was crazy – here was a grown man who a few hours earlier was acting like the lord and master, now behaving like a schoolboy hiding from his headmaster. He poked his head round the corner of the stairs, but refused point-blank to face John, saying he was not going to lower himself. I went back into the sitting room to tell John it would be better if we just left when just then my father meekly walked in, my mother in tow. He then did another strange thing – he shook John's hand and told him he was glad to meet him!

I thought to myself: 'what a hypocrite!' I was even more surprised when my mother did the same. Christ, I thought, now John's going to think I invented all the beatings and abuse – he will think I've gone doo-lally.

"What's wrong, John?" my father asked in a toady manner.

"That's what I would like to know?" enquired John with a look of disbelief on his face. "Valerie says you are hitting her for seeing me, is this true?"

"We never lay a hand on her," my father lied. "It's just that she's only seventeen, we don't want to see her hurt."

I couldn't believe my ears or my eyes. 'Not see me hurt'? Who the hell were they trying to kid!

"I'm not going to hurt her. I just want to see her, with your blessing."

Mother then came out with the most stupid remark I ever did hear: "Did you ever think of going to Australia?"

"What for?" John asked in amazement.

"All young men want to go to Australia," my father joined in, contradicting his own resistance to my mother's efforts to get *him* to emigrate there.

"I don't," replied John, as he looked at me in amusement.

"Well," my father said, rubbing his chin, "even if you went for a year, you could send for her."

Holy God, first America, now Australia! I now not only had the feeling, I *knew* they wanted me out of the country altogether.

"Listen," said John. "I don't want to go to Australia, I just want to go out with your daughter, even if it's only to the pictures, for God's sake."

"Well..." my father answered, this time rubbing his head. "Don't see each other for six months and then see how you feel." It was no use, he was flogging a dead horse. We agreed just to get out of the house.

"I see what you mean," John said outside. "They are a couple of strange characters all the while." He had a befuddled expression on his face, and for one minute I thought he was going to throw in the towel and give me up as a bad job. But no, he just said, "Not a bit of wonder you're confused. If I lived in that house I would be on the drink in order to survive. Just forget about them, we'll carry on as normal."

Nothing changed for all our efforts. I still got a kick up the backside as usual that night plus a red ear from a thump on the side of the head, delivered by father as punishment for putting them in such an embarrassing situation. John's parents were now resigned to having another mouth to feed without cash payment in return, while my parents profited from my wages without having to feed or clothe me in return.

Although John's parents went to chapel every day in life, they were religious in a quiet way. They did not try to ram Catholicism down my throat, and even apologised for the lack of meat on Fridays. John's father, however, was concerned about my age. He often asked me if my parents consented to my going out with John, especially with John being five years older.

He was also curious why I spent so much time with them and very little time with my own family. He didn't wish to seem prying, but he was genuinely concerned about my welfare, and often asked about my parents' attitude towards the religious aspect. As they had been so honest to me I found it only befitting that I should be honest with them. I told them that my parents had no religion, just hatred for those who had. John being Catholic really wasn't of any great significance – even if he had been a Jew or a Hindu it would have been just the same. Sure they didn't even like the local pastor and he was Protestant; they just felt intimidated by religion, full stop. Religion to them meant having to be friendly to their fellow men, and to be friendly meant inviting people into the home which in turn meant having to let outsiders see what a ridiculous and pathetic life they led.

John told me his father had spoken to him about our conversation later that evening, and had warned him against making any demands or trying to persuade me towards Catholicism. According to him I was of a vulnerable age and he did not want to think his son would take advantage of my youth. He told John, "That wee girl doesn't need any more worry on her shoulders. She looks older than her years, but deep down she is still only a child. Think hard an' long about yer intentions, don't hurt her by going with her out of pity. On the other hand, if yer intentions are honourable, take good care of her an' show her a good example. Never deny your faith, and above all never run down hers. We are what we are born – now take heed."

When I next saw John's father I told him that John had told me all that he had said, adding, "I wish I had a father like you." I was taken aback when he then scolded me for saying such a thing.

"Don't ever deny yer parents. Maybe they have a reason for being the way they are. Do ye ever stop an' think about the hurt that ye may be causing them; after all, you are their daughter. Now five years is a big gap when you're in yer teens. To them John is a grown man while you're still a child. John has enjoyed his youth, you on the other hand have been thrown into adulthood before yer time. Maybe you have yer reasons, but yer parents deserve a say in the matter as well. I think the two of ye have a lot to think over, and whatever answer ye come up with, I wish ye both well."

He hadn't a breath after this piece of worldly wisdom, his lips were blue and his chest heaved with the effort of trying to suppress a coughing attack. He had to use his inhaler and I felt guilty for making the remark that had put him in this state. But he had said his piece, he didn't have to repeat it again. There were no back doors to John's father, he told you where you stood and that was the end of it. I loved him all the more for being so honest.

I decided to take lessons in the Catholic faith shortly after this talk, on my own accord. Seeing as I was really of no religion I took it on myself to find one, and where better to start other than where

Christ first instructed Peter on the rock. I went to see Father Arthurs of Clonard Monastery after asking advice from a Catholic friend. John was unaware of this decision and was quite alarmed when I told him after about a month. He said he wanted nothing to do with it – it was entirely my own decision. His mother and father were also concerned and asked me if my parents knew. They were concerned also that I might be contemplating something so important as this just to be acceptable to the Mahers.

"I hope ye are not going through with this idea tae please us, ye have to do it tae please yoursel'. There is a lot tae learn in the Catholic faith, it will not happen overnight. The garden might look rosy at the moment, what happens when the first bloom starts tae fade?"

I assured them that I was one hundred and one percent sure. Anyway, the Catholic church was not exactly alien to me, as I had spent many a childhood day in chapel and had started to feel quite at home in one. John's father wished me luck and promised to help me with my instructions if needed.

He and I spent my afternoons off work watching television and thinking up ways to play tricks on John when he came home. John had a slight stammer and stuttered on his 'b's, so we thought of all the words that started with 'b' and tried our damnedest to devise questions to ask him, for which he had to use words beginning with this letter in his answers. I know it sounds cruel, but we didn't make a public fool of him, we only did it in front of his father and mother. Example: "What did ye call that maun who sang 'White Christmas', John?" "B.b.b.bing Crosb.b.by... shit, you did it again, now b.b.b.bugger off!" He fell for it every time and blushed to high heaven, teasing his father with the threat of hiding his inhaler as punishment. John's father also explained to me how to inflict excruciating pain by grabbing the inside of the upper leg and squeezing, with John always on the receiving end. While he writhed in agony his father tried breathlessly to stifle his laughter and farted involuntarily with the effort.

John proposed to me in November of 1960. It was not a down-on-the-knee job, more a down-in-the-mouth-decision. We were feeling slightly depressed and hadn't much to talk about apart from the latest barney between my parents, who were still bickering on about their wayward daughter. Out of the blue John just said, matter of factly, "Let's get engaged, we've nothing else to do." It was as romantic as courting in a pool of dead fish. I just sighed and answered, "I don't care, whatever turns you on."

We got engaged just before Christmas. John managed to scrape £13 together – the ring cost £12/17/6, the half-crown change paid for our bus fare home. To celebrate we sat in John's house while I made a dress on his mother's sewing machine for the dance on Saturday night. I didn't show the ring to my parents as it would have been like waving a red flag at a bull. John held on to it and every night we met he slipped it on my finger. It felt like getting engaged every other day.

John's father's health got worse over the next couple of months, the doctors unable to do any more for him. On the Easter Sunday of 1961 he almost demolished the kitchen table with his fists trying to suck breath into his lungs, and my heart broke at the thought of losing not only a future father-in-law but a friend and confidant. On the Easter Monday he felt a lot better than he had for years, and told Ellen he felt so well that he would try to make it to chapel the next morning to thank God for the respite. Maybe he would see another year after all. He told Ellen he was going to lie down for a while to regain a little more strength, and she said she would bring him a cup of tea later. He told her not to bother as he had a feeling he wouldn't sleep anyway and would have one when he came down.

He never did come down, and passed away peacefully with a smile on his face. He died the way he lived, with dignity and without fuss. He was fifty-five years old, fifteen years short of the allotted three score years and ten. For the short while that I had known John's father I loved him. Even though he knew his days were numbered he welcomed me the way a father should, with love, with respect and with laughter. I knew him for less than a year when he died, but in that year he showered me with more love than my parents could have shown in a million years. If there is a Heaven, I am sure he will be there, even if it is only to help with the air conditioning, with the quip 'Good aule arse, I thought ye were dead'.

I had known something was wrong when John came to my front door at lunch time that Easter Monday. Even my parents, who were normally impervious to other people's feelings, quickly sensed something was not in order. They did not lose their temper at the sight of him, which was not only unusual but miraculous. As my mother opened the door, I could see over her shoulder that John was crying. He didn't even have to speak, I knew in my heart it was news of his father's death. I pushed my mother aside and looked her in the face, "It's his father, he's dead. Let him in, please." She just bowed her head and somewhat sheepishly told John to come inside.

I lost control with grief and shouted at my father. "Are you going to tell him to go to Australia now? Or perhaps you would prefer to give him a kick up the backside to bring him to his senses. His father has just died, a good honest to God man who never harmed a fly. Tell him he's a bastard now to his face; that is, if you have the guts!" I could hardly see through the floods of tears that were streaming from my eyes. What I could see were two very

110

pathetic and sorry looking sights stuck for words of comfort. I waited for the sting of my father's hand for being so insolent, but instead two small voices said "I'm sorry" in unison. I made John a cup of tea, then we headed towards Belfast to send telegrams to his brothers who lived abroad. He only put four words on each telegram: 'Dad died peacefully – John'.

Chapter 8

MY BOY

Thomas Maher – Tommy to his many friends – was not moved from his home and subjected to the indignity of being laid out by strangers in a funeral parlour. He was lovingly and gently prepared to meet his maker in the back bedroom of the house he had shared for over thirty years with his beloved Ellen. Ellen, whom he had cherished from the day they had met, did not look on his passing as a last farewell, more a parting of the ways until they would meet again in God's paradise.

She did not shirk her duty of helping prepare him for his final journey and assisted Mrs Fitzpatrick, another local handywoman, with the last and final act of dressing him in his Sacred Heart shroud. She clasped his hands together and gently wove his wooden rosary beads between his fingers and made the sign of the cross on his forehead.

"He luks gran', Fitzie, he even has a smile on 'is face. Dae ye think the aule soldier will pass muster?"

"Aye, Ellen, he'll have no problem gettin' passed the gates, sure he's earned 'is ticket ten times o'er. Com'n down an have a drap af tea afore they all start batin' a path tae the dur tae pay their last respects."

"The cup that cheers, eh Fitzie – the cup that cheers."

Later in the day John and I went upstairs to where he was laid out in his bed prior to being placed in his coffin for the wake. John's mother was standing by his side gently stroking his brow. There were no tears in her eyes, just the haunted look of loneliness. My heart went out to her. She had been robbed of a friend as well as a husband; he had been her one and only love just as she had been his, apart from their children.

She looked at the both of us and spoke in a low voice as if Tommy could hear. "I'm lost without him." Her hand slowly brushed over the contours of his face and came to a halt on his chest. "My heart's as heavy as his breast is still. At least he doesn't have to fight the pain of drawing breath any more, that's my only consolation; that and the fact that he's with Jesus and his mother Mary."

I walked over to try and comfort her, and as I lifted my arm to hug her she grabbed my hand and placed it on Tommy's forehead. I wasn't afraid or curious the way I had felt with my gran. He looked so peaceful and young; the lines of years of suffering were gone. I kissed him on the cheek and whispered, "God, take extra care of this very special man." Through my tears I could see John walk out of the bedroom. I understood – he loved his father too much, he didn't want to say goodbye until later.

Although the family were devastated, the wake was not a solemn occasion, and they were spared the charade of people lying to the eyeteeth about how good a person the deceased had been in life. Nobody had to lie, their respects were genuine. Happy memories were shared plus the occasional humorous anecdote of happier days when Tommy used to take pity on homeless flea-bitten down-and-outs and invite them home for a meal and a change of clothes. No matter how much the family protested, it went in one ear and out the other. The fact that the house had to be fumigated after entertaining some of these flea-ridden guests hadn't annoyed him in the least – sure a few fleas never harmed anybody. Or the time he bred canaries and sprayed them with the wrong mixture to stop them moulting, only to find them lying dead with their feet in the air as stiff as pokers the following morning. His only vice was killing out of kindness and smothering with love.

John's mother didn't even cry on the day of the funeral – sometimes grief is so devastating it numbs the brain. She went through the motions as if she was being worked by strings. The rest of the family cried and vented their emotions, which I suppose is a healthy attitude. John's grief was peppered with the feeling of anger. He could not understand why the mourners did not share his anger towards God for robbing the family of their backbone. According to him they would not be the same without his father's words of wisdom, love and sense of humour.

He was also angry with himself, and kept repeating over and over again, "I could have done more for him, why did I close my eyes to the fact that he was so ill? Christ, why did I complain of feeling too tired or fed up when he asked me to perform the simplest of tasks? Such as giving him a quick shave in the morning before I went to work, when even the effort of lifting his arm to do so sapped every ounce of breath from his lungs."

John's anger had also been fuelled by the parish priest who was just about to go fishing when John's mother had first asked him to tend to her husband; nor was the family doctor in any greater hurry to respond. According to them both it was their day off. John had snapped at the priest, "Does Christ take a day off to go fishing! For years my father managed to make it to chapel every day to listen to you say Mass, so that he could thank God for another day – but now you are too concerned about flamin' fishing to spare a few minutes to pray for his soul!" The priest did come to the house and apologised to John, but the damage had been done – it left a very bitter taste in his mouth.

That night after the funeral when John walked me home, we hardly exchanged two words until we were standing outside my house. I was at a loss for words of comfort. I had decided to just kiss him goodnight and leave him to mourn privately when he grabbed me by the hand and asked me to walk up the Lane with him a while. We stopped outside the little shop facing the park. He leant with his back against the wall and pulled me towards him by wrapping his arms round my waist. I stepped out of my stiletto heels and stood in my stockinged feet, put my arms round his neck and snuggled my head in his chest.

"Marry me?" he asked softly. Instead of soaring like a bird, my heart dropped down into my stomach and I pulled back at the suddenness of this question.

"What did you say! Did I hear you right – did you say marry me?" For a minute the sadness left him and he laughed.

"No, I said let's go to the moon. Of course I said marry me. Well, we are engaged." He might just as well have said let's go to the moon, as one was as impossible as the other. You had to be twenty-one years old then to get married without your parents' consent, and no way was I going to get the consent of my parents three months before my eighteenth birthday, especially to marry John.

"Hang on a minute," I said, stifling the urge to laugh hysterically. "Who's going to break the news to Lottie and Bill? You? For I'm not. I've become attached to my backbone, I don't want to see it broke in three places. Anyway, why the urge to get married all of a sudden?"

"I know we just buried my father today but I have a feeling it would be what he would have wanted. He was very fond of you and he did tell me to take good care of you. You've suffered enough in that blasted house, why wait?"

We talked for ages about how we could get the necessary consent from my parents, but there was no way other than if I became pregnant. A hell of a big step just to obtain signatures on a slip of paper, but it was the only option we had. I tossed and turned all night, my brain working overtime as I tried to fit all the pieces of the jigsaw puzzle of my life together.

I was secretly engaged, taking lessens in the Catholic faith behind my parents' backs, and now plotting for a wedding that might or might not take place according to whether or not I got pregnant. Talk about putting the cart before the horse! What course of action would I take? Get pregnant first and then prepare for the wedding or vice versa? And what about the performance I would have to go through to get pregnant?

To add to my troubles I had a row with the manageress of the home bakery the following day and told her to stuff her job, as she wanted me to go to another branch to work. My nervous system was already overloaded, and the thought of making a fresh start in another shop just threw me over the edge. She gave me the sack on the spot. Was I in the shit! I had already told Violet of my wedding plans. She thought I was mental and in need of the twilight home for the mentally bewildered, and when she heard of this new predicament she said she would visit me in the hospital that night after my back had been set in plaster. I told her it would be all right as long as I had another job by the end of the week.

"By Jaysus, I hope you're right. If I know yer Ma she'll ring yer flamin' neck. Good luck, fer you'll need it."

Mother did not take kindly to the news. She broke out in a sweat at the thought of losing a wage and walked me the length of the Lisburn Road by the scruff of the neck until I got another job before the shops closed. I started in Thompson's Bakery in Sandy Row the following day.

Now a new job on top of everything else. We planned a July wedding as then John would have two weeks' holiday owed to him from the builders he worked for, hod-carrying. Better not waste any money by getting married any other time as he would have had to take unpaid leave, a luxury he could not afford. £25 holiday money would go a long way towards the cost of a wedding in 1961; that was three week's wages to John. We decided that I had to get pregnant first, much to John's delight as his honeymoon was now going to come early.

I was in a hell of a dither, not out of anticipation at the idea of losing my virginity, but at how this act was carried out. I knew it took more than French kissing and a quick feel of the aule boobs up the alley in the Lane. We had progressed to this over the past few months, but even that was overstepping the mark in my book, and anything further was completely taboo. In the history of mankind there has only been one immaculate conception, and the Messiah was not going to take a second bow heralded by angels even though the timing was almost right. If I had have conceived at that moment the baby would have been due at Christmas.

And so it was that my sister Dorothy acquired a babysitter overnight without having to ask! Her flat was ideal for the deed that lay ahead. My parents gave me permission to stay overnight after Dorothy had promised to watch over me. As soon as Dorothy and her husband departed we decided to go into action. The attack on Pearl Harbour was probably easier to execute than John's efforts to pry my knickers off.

"You can't do that!" My face went scarlet at John's insistence that this had to be done. "Are you sure?" I asked him, while he rubbed his head in utter amusement.

"Of course I'm sure!" he insisted. I knew I had to remove them, I wasn't stupid, I just wanted to hold on to them a bit longer because of embarrassment and fright. And, once they were off, there was no turning back.

"You've done it before, then?" I asked indignantly. "And you trying to act all holy since the day I met you."

"I have not done IT before – I saw how it was done in books."

"You mean to say you've read dirty books?" The notion of getting pregnant was rapidly going out of my head, in fact I almost broke off our whole relationship at the very idea of John knowing all about the female anatomy, while I knew nothing of the male's apart from my brothers when they were babies.

"Jesus wept!" cried John. "All men read dirty books, now get them off!" So romantic. Whatever happened to the dreamy, starry-eyed man who had asked me to marry him under the moonlight? If he had said 'get them off' *that* night he would have been given his marching orders.

"Our Chuck would be angry if he knew what I was doing." What a stupid thing to say.

"Chuck isn't bloody well trying to get you pregnant, is he?" The veins on John's neck were standing out with frustration, and I burst out laughing. Now, nothing puts a man off sex quicker than being laughed at. He almost tripped as he tried to step back into his trousers but bounced across the room on one leg and whacked the side of his head on the bedroom wall.

"Christ, me nut!"

The whole exercise was rapidly turning into farce, making me choke on my spit, which in turn provoked a fit of coughing, and along with the giggles I turned into a gibbering wreck.

"Will ye shut up!" John sounded hysterical as he bounced up the hall and fell onto the settee in the living room, and huffed until Dorothy and Jack came home. They must have guessed what we were up to as they left us and went to bed, the same bed on which John had tried without success to debag moi.

However, persistence pays off in the end, and after much pushing and shoving, plus cries of "Where the hell do you think you're putting that!" we succeeded in doing the dreaded deed on the rug in front of the fire. Afterwards I started to panic at what would happen if we broke off our wedding plans. No-one would want spoiled goods, the early Sixties not being a good time for a female to be deflowered before getting a wedding ring on her finger. I tried to console myself by thinking I could always say I lost it horse-riding! The worst part was facing mother, who I thought would know by the look on my face that I had been up to no good. I imagined that one somehow looked different afterwards.

But now that we had started we would finish. At every possible opportunity we made love, even if it wasn't all Barbara Cartland and roses. The roses in Musgrave Park might have been witness to a lot of it, mind you, or the trees, or the bowling green, or the ... well, use your imagination!

I knew by the beginning of May that we had rung the bell when I became as sick as a parrot and started boking first thing in the morning; then it was morning, noon and night. John was delighted. I told him, "If you felt as sick as I do, you would not be so joyous." He held me in his arms and told me I would be okay and that he would look after me forever. If only his father had lived to see us married everything would have been perfect. I thought to myself: 'If the man had to get pregnant instead of the woman, it would have been even better!'

I was also baptised into the Catholic church in early May. Those were the small worries out of the way. We decided not to tell John's mother I was pregnant as she had been through enough with the death of his father, on top of which we did not want to give her the impression that we had been having sex on a regular basis and that my condition was a mistake. We just informed her we were getting married in July. Her suspicions must have been aroused when she asked where the money for the wedding was coming from and we told her we didn't have any. She just sighed and said she'd have a word with the Provident man about the possibility of a few £20 cheques to cover the cost.

Now came the hardest part of the plan – getting my parents to consent to our marriage. We explained our predicament to the parish priest of St Anne's Oratory in Derriaghy. He listened with confused interest, telling me to get my father to call at the chapel to sign the consent forms. I told him, "My father will not come to the chapel, we haven't even told him we are getting married yet."

"You haven't told him! You're getting married in six weeks' time and he doesn't even know. This puts me in an awful predicament. By rights I have to witness the signature. It's impossible; don't ask me to even think about giving you permission

116

to marry behind his back. It's against the law for a start."

I started to cry, in fact I nearly went into hysterics.

"But we have to get married, I'm pregnant!"

"You're what! Jesus, Mary and St Joseph, take care of us all – what have I sitting before me? Two raving maniacs?"

I stood up and bawled my head off like a two-year-old. John explained that I had not got pregnant by mistake, it had been planned.

"Holy Mother of God, pray for these sinners!" the priest implored, as he clasped his hands and stared towards the ceiling, tut-tutting and then blessing himself. "The important things such as children are planned *after* a wedding and not before. Babies are not to be used as pawns in a game."

"Please Father", I begged, "I don't want to be an unmarried mother."

"You should have given more consideration to that long before now!" he shouted back, then scratched his head in deep thought. "I'll tell you what I'll do. It's against all my principles, but I will trust you with the consent form as long as you swear to God Almighty you will get your father – no one else now or my head will roll – to sign it. Now swear to the Almighty you will not forge his signature."

"We swear, Father, honest to God, we swear to do as you say."

"Well, take yourselves out the door before I change my mind, and bring that form back as soon as possible, signed by William Linton and no-one else – do you hear now?" He closed the door behind us. We could hear him reciting the Hail Mary loudly as he did so.

"Phew! that's only the first taste of things to come," I warned John, who was turning green at the gills with anxiety. Baby Maher also decided to have a say in the matter and I retched uncontrollably for the next hour.

We made all the wedding arrangements with the help of John's mother and his married sister Annie. Annie had announced that she was pregnant with her third child, it was due the same time as my little secret. I felt sad and alone at not being able to tell anyone of my condition, for the priest and Violet were the only people who knew.

John and I used to sit in Musgrave Park beside the bowling green at night, engrossed in our own private conversation about weddings and babies. I had a feeling from the very first that it would be a boy, and we always referred to 'our son' in our future plans. John wanted to call him Thomas after his Dad, but I remembered my childhood promise to call my first son Kevin. So we compromised – he would be Kevin Thomas.

Kevin Thomas was going to make sure he would not be forgotten about. Twenty four hours a day he sent my hormones into battle; they staged war and sent battalions into every square inch of my body. Even my toenails felt sick and my stomach refused to hold anything other than water. Instead of gaining weight I looked anorexic. The sight of my mother's lumpy porridge had me boking to the point were I thought my stomach was going to come up my throat. How she never cottoned on was beyond me, for trying to vomit without making a noise is impossible. I also felt as if I had a bad attack of flu, another unwelcome symptom of my condition.

As the days passed it got worse. The smell of the bakery forced me to spend half my time bent over the sink vomiting and wiping the tears from my eyes, patting my belly and trying to negotiate a deal with Kevin Thomas. "If you go easy on my hormones now, I will go easy on your ass when you are a bad boy later on." I got some strange looks from the other assistants and wished I had never left the home bakery in Great Victoria Street, for at least there I had Violet to give me sympathy.

We made arrangements with the parish priest of St John's Chapel on the Falls Road to get married on Saturday 8 July after eight o'clock morning Mass, providing that blinking piece of paper would be signed by father. I booked the International Hotel in Belfast for the wedding breakfast, which would cost ten shillings and sixpence per head, plus taxis for the wedding party which cost five pounds and had to be paid up front. This extravagance could not be paid for with a Provident cheque and John had to use up a week's wages. We considered using a Corporation bus to save money but thought better of it, for the cigarette smoke as the passengers puffed away would only make me sick.

John's sister Eileen promised to be bridesmaid while Annie's husband agreed to be best man. As I knew my father would not be giving me away, John's older brother Tommy offered to perform that task. As a wedding present his mother ordered the wedding cake from the local breadman. In the event, Kennedy's Bakery made a good job of it. I went into Belfast on my day off with Annie, armed with two £20 Provident cheques to buy my wedding dress, bridesmaid's dress and going-away outfit. I managed to purchase all this, as well as shoes and underwear, and still had enough left to buy two pairs of Y-fronts and a shirt for John. Finally, my wedding ring cost £3/10/0 and we were all set except for the most important bit – my father's permission – otherwise all this effort would have been for nowt.

In the middle of June my family Doctor confirmed what I already knew. Even though I was aware of the obvious it still came as a shock hearing it from the horse's mouth, and I burst out crying in the surgery. Dr Walker knew my parents well; he also knew I wasn't married and asked me if they knew I was pregnant.

"That's the problem, Doctor. Would you tell them?" He gave me a startled look as if I had asked him to run along Divis Street starkers.

"Do you think that would be proper of me? They might be angry having a stranger give them the news."

"Well, they won't hit you, Doctor," I said shyly. "They will knock seven bells out of me, pregnant or not. Anyway, you're no stranger to our house." He agreed, but only out of pity, for he knew I was not overexaggerating my fears. The fact that he could take a tranquilliser to calm his nerves and I couldn't before facing them probably helped as well.

"Tell you what," he said, standing up and pacing the surgery, one hand scratching his head, the other perched on his hip bone in a fist. I could see he was tense, the knuckles on this hand were white because his hand was clenched so tight. "I will call at half past seven on Monday evening; I have to attend a funeral service first." I thought to myself 'You could be attending another on Tuesday – mine!'

"I will go in first, and when you see me come out, you go in. Stand at the bridge in the Lane, you will see from there." He gave me some iron tablets to build up my strength. According to him I was very badly in need, for I was as white as a sheet. I looked at him and thought *he* was very badly in need of a double whiskey and left. Looking back on the whole affair, I must have been the instigator of many a nervous breakdown.

Monday evening arrived like a long-awaited visit of the grim reaper. You know he's going to come some time in your life, you only hope he will come like a thief in the night and not by invitation. John and I waited at the bridge with bated breath. Doctor Walker passed by at precisely half past seven on the dot. I thanked the Lord for small mercies – at least we were not kept waiting longer than necessary. We watched his every movement – getting out of the car, walking up the drive and knocking the door. There was no going back now, we would soon know the outcome.

Half an hour passed before he emerged, and holy heavens, they were shaking hands and laughing! For one dreadful moment I thought he had taken fright at the last minute and reneged. He waved to us as he passed and gave us the thumbs up, indicating all was fine. 'No', I thought to myself, all is not fine, my parents have been putting on an act, just like the night they put on an act in front of John. It was all a ploy, I was going to get my head kicked in as soon as I set foot inside the house.

Doctor Walker must have told them we were nearby, for the front door was lying open like a gaping hole in the wall. (Come into my parlour, said the spider to the fly!) My father sat with a sickly grin on his face while mother nervously dusted the table with a look of thunder imprinted on hers. They knew all right!

What happened next took us completely by surprise. My father positioned himself comfortably in his armchair and proceeded to talk about the weather. He clasped his hands together, rotating his thumbs, at the same time crossing his legs and peering out through the window as if he was more concerned that the rain would prevent him from mowing the lawn the following day. We sat on the edge of the sofa perched like two budgies ready to lay eggs, my insides rumbling as if I was ready to pass more than an egg, while John wiped the sweat from his brow with the back of his hand and gulped in air by the bucketful.

"That Doctor's a fine man all the same," my father remarked, shifting his position. He now sat on the edge of his seat and stared John in the face. His steel grey eyes and cold Draconian stare would have put the wind up a twenty-five stone wrestler.

"There's no back doors in that man." Insinuating that John's head was full of them. John reached into his inside pocket and pulled out the now dog-eared piece of paper that stood in the way of our plans. My father pulled out a Woodbine cigarette without asking John if he had a mouth, lit it, inhaled deeply and proceeded to blow smoke rings in the air nonchalantly, as if trying to give the impression of someone without a care in the world. John coughed nervously and handed him the form.

"What's this, then?" he asked sarcastically, as if he didn't know.

"It's for your signature so that we can get married."

"And why do you want to get married then?" He was deliberately playing cat and mouse with us, he just wanted to make us tell him what he had already been told half an hour ago in case we thought we were getting off lightly.

"You know why, Da."

"I'm not talking to you, I'm talking to the organ grinder, not the monkey." He inspected the form and sniggered, making my already shattered nerves fray even more at the edges. "I see it's the chapel you intend getting married in then. What's wrong with the church, will a Protestant church burn holes in your feet?" he asked John.

"It was Valerie's decision, not mine," answered John indignantly.

"And it's my decision whether or not I sign this bolloxing form, so don't be so bloody insolent, young man! Anyway, what's your hurry? Sit there while I mull over this for a while."

We sat in silence for what seemed like years, afraid to say anything that would rock the boat. He finally took out his pen but his hand hovered over the piece of paper to torture us that little bit more. Then he signed it quickly and threw it at John.

"Here, take it and get out!" he yelled. He stood up and opened the hall door, but as we passed he grabbed me by the arm and glared at John. "I told *you* to get out, big lad – *she* stays here!" I saw the look of horror on John's face as the door slammed shut behind him. I looked at my mother who had remained quiet during the whole episode. She avoided my stare and scurried out to the scullery, her fat belly and large bosom shaking, the fat of her behind straining to escape from her corset like two pigs in a sack.

I was thrown head first onto the settee and called all the names of the day. "I was dead right, you're nothing better than a whore, after all!" He grabbed me by the hair and trailed me towards my bedroom, then gave me a good sharp kick up the backside, so hard it caused me to arch backward and I fell on my knees.

"Save bowing and scraping on your knees for when you're married to that Papish bastard, for they'll be worn out in a year praying to shrines and idols!" he hissed, slamming the door behind me with all the strength he could muster. My back ached, my head ached and my heart ached, not only for the comfort of John's arms, but for the safety of my unborn child. I prayed to God for guidance. I felt like Christ crucified and asked if he had forsaken me, then cried myself to sleep.

The birds were singing when I awoke the following morning. I remember thinking to myself, 'It is done, I've nothing more to hide. No matter what happens, from now on John will be there to sort things out. Only another couple of weeks and I will be as free as the birds that are singing outside my window.' As I was about to leave for work my mother told me it would be better if I stayed somewhere else as she didn't think it a good idea to be in the same house as my father over the next few weeks. She then remarked: "I'm being paid back after all these years."

I realised what she meant much later on when I found out that she too had been pregnant on her wedding day, the only difference being that my condition had been planned by both John and myself, while hers had been planned by her alone. She went on to tell me my sisters did not want to have anything to do with me ever again – they were all in agreement that I was letting the family down.

"And don't invite them to the wedding, they don't want to go and neither do any of your other relations." Of course she was lying to her eyeteeth, but being naive I believed her instead of asking them to their faces. They in turn thought I was snubbing them, and would not attend my wedding.

I quit work a fortnight before I got married as my morning sickness left me extremely weak. A period of my life had ended and I felt a sadness that I could not put into words. No more would I harp on about the virtues of Saint Elvis to Violet or the depths of depravity some men other than my Elvis would stoop to in order to have their wicked way with us chaste young girls. Violet and I met a couple of times before my marriage, but my sense of humour had all but disappeared I felt so ill. Her last words to me before the

121

wedding were: "Someday, Val, you will laugh at all this. Keep yer chin up me aule Pan Yan Pickle, it's nat the end aff the world, ye know." I tried to laugh but the tears ran down my cheeks instead.

I stayed in John's house until we were married. His mother was under the impression I had been thrown out because I was getting married in the Catholic church. I didn't enlighten her any further, she had enough on her plate. After all, she was still grieving for Tommy; why add to her distress. It wouldn't have looked quite right the bride and groom both leaving from the same house so John stayed with his sister for a few nights.

On the eve of the wedding I went to confession only to be advised by the priest not to go through with my marriage – according to him I was not in a state of grace and he considered my wedding to be merely one of convenience. I chose to ignore him, which possibly meant my marriage would be a sham, but I was not going to start arguing over the matter, my brain could not take any more hassle.

My wedding day did not go smoothly as most weddings are inclined. The flowers, which should have arrived the night before, never turned up, and this led to the police having to get the owner of the flower shop out of his bed in the middle of the night to make up the bouquets. A bad nose bleed threatened to ruin my wedding gown half an hour before leaving for the chapel. To add insult to injury, the flaming limousine looked as if it had belonged to Al Capone, it was that old.

I refused to leave the house and Tommy, who was giving me away and was on the verge of a nervous breakdown at the thought of being late, just shoved a large men's handkerchief under my nose to stem the flow of blood and tears now streaming down my cheeks, then pushed me unceremoniously out through the door.

The wedding itself was relatively free of mishap, apart from my urge to faint after fasting for three hours prior to leaving for the nuptial mass. This was the rule of the church before one was allowed to receive holy communion, which I felt guilty for receiving after having been told not to get married the previous night and disobeying. I worried the whole week afterwards that the priest might later inform me I wasn't really married. God no, I prayed, don't let that happen after all I've been through.

The wedding was rounded off very nicely, I must say, when some old biddy said, "You look lovely, Bridie." Who the hell was Bridie! "Wait till I get you on your own!" I hissed at John. He shrugged his shoulders but looked very guilty. I guessed that 'Bridie' must have been one of his old girlfriends who resembled me. For a brief moment I toyed with the idea of getting the marriage annulled, as I had this strange notion that he had only married me because I looked like her. He assured me of his love with a big kiss and told me he felt as if he was walking on air. Men are such cowards when confronted with the past.

There were forty guests at our wedding reception, forty wedding breakfasts at 10 shillings and 6 pence a head, plus three bottles of champagne to toast the happy couple. The bill came to precisely £25/18/0. That was quite a bit of money in 1961, almost the price of a deposit on a house. Thirty-nine of the guests were from John's side – I felt like an orphan. A very sick pregnant orphan – the Ulster fry washed down with champagne did not stay attached to my stomach very long and ended down the toilet quicker than it took to consume it.

Our honeymoon was a family affair – we spent it touring the South of Ireland with Annie and her husband. We had decided that sharing the petrol money with Eddie would save on travelling expenses. Annie's father-in-law came too for good measure, plus Kevin Thomas who had no other option.

Two hours into our honeymoon my nose started bleeding profusely again, and we had to make an emergency stop at a chemist's where my nose was plugged with half a yard of gauze to stem the flow of blood. I thought this embarrassing until we reached Trim late in the afternoon, when, after a pint of beer, John decided it had been a tiring day and suggested an early night. Of course Eddie knew by the sparkle in John's eyes he wasn't the least bit tired and seized the opportunity to tell everyone in the pub that we were on our honeymoon, hinting that we were not going to bed to sleep. This caused an uproar and we left the pub to a round of applause. I couldn't make up my mind whether to hit John for being so unthinking or transmogrify Eddie for thinking too much. This mortifying incident was only equalled by a slow hand-clap from the residents of the hotel when we made it to breakfast half an hour late the following morning.

Mind you, this was nothing to the cock-up we made in Galway. All the hotels were booked solid and we were offered one of the guest houses attached to the hotel. All these guest houses looked identical and after depositing our luggage John and I went out by ourselves for a walk in the night air. On the way back we stopped for two fish suppers to bring back to our room. The house we had booked into was number 42, but in mistake we rapped the door of number 24. A lady answered and we walked straight past without as much as a by-your-leave, climbed the stairs, entered what we surmised was our bedroom, removed most of our clothes and lay on top of the bed to eat our fish suppers.

A few minutes later we heard a faint knock on the bedroom door. "Excuse me, my dears, what do you t'ink you're doing in my house?" the woman of the house enquired in a broad Irish brogue.

"We are just having a bite to eat before turning in for the night."

"I don't t'ink so, you're in the wrong house. This is a private dwelling, in case you don't know."

There we were in our underwear – John in his Y-fronts, me in bra and panties – eating our fish and chips oblivious to the fact we were in the wrong house. You never saw two people dress as quickly in all your life and hairtail it out onto the street. We spent the rest of the night doubled up in laughter at the thought of that poor woman's face when she caught two strangers making themselves at home in her bed.

After nine months of a very sick and fretful pregnancy plus a lot of false alarms running back and forth to the Jubilee maternity hospital by bus – we couldn't afford the taxi fare – I gave birth to my son.

Kevin Thomas came into this world on 16 January 1962 at twenty past two in the morning, after much puffing and pushing and quite a lot of cursing at the doctor who had been telling me to keep an eye on my watch to see how far apart the contractions were. I ended up throwing the bloody watch down the ward in distraction, shouting at the top of my voice. "Here, you keep count. I'm in flamin' agony!" I turned to the nurse in charge and informed her that if the doctor as much as put his finger near my backside once more I'd ram the effin' timepiece up his rear-end!

Now I knew what John's mother had been referring to when she talked about men hokin' at ye when all ye want is a bit aff pase to get an wi' the job. John's sister gave birth to a girl three hours before I gave birth to our son. I was told she had given birth as if shelling a pea, while I felt as if I had given birth to a baby elephant. Eddie accompanied John to the Hospital later that day, both proud fathers-in-arms. The nurse looked at them as they stood gazing at Kevin Thomas.

The look on her face spoke volumes: it was asking, 'are you not sure which one is the father?' She looked at John and said, "I think he belongs to you, he's your spittin' image." They both laughed at their confusion. John's chest stuck out and he looked as proud as a peacock.

"That's my boy alright, nurse, that's my boy," he said, beaming from ear to ear. My only regret was the fact he had not been born on 8 January, for I would have called him Elvis. My son, though, is very glad he wasn't – living with the name Kevin Thomas is penance enough, according to him.

Our son screamed at the top of his lungs, a foretaste of what lay in store. He would make our lives hell for the first two years of his life. He never shut his gob gurnin' day or night. Was this my penance for disobeying my parents' wishes? Maybe it was!

Chapter 9

THE SOUND OF YOUR CRY

'The hand that rocks the cradle rules the world.' Whoever thought up that saying must have been on the drink. It was three o'clock in the morning, and my right arm had died and was gradually turning blue in my attempt to pacify Kevin Thomas by rocking his pram, which had been sitting beside my bed for the past three hours. I was in no fit state to rule a hen roost never mind the world. I felt as if my eyes were located somewhere at the back of my head and my body was limp with fatigue. I had to dismiss the overwhelming desire to commit infanticide by repeating over and over to myself: 'he will grow out of it'.

After another sleepless night, John got out of bed at half past six to get ready for work, bleary eyed and completely disillusioned with fatherhood. He walked into the wardrobe by accident, he was so confused and exhausted by lack of sleep. We had been living with John's mother since we got married and everything in the garden had been rosy until our son made his debut. Now the little beggar had turned what was once a normal happy home into an argumentative and tired household of nocturnal maniacs who were contemplating suicide as a solution to lack of sleep.

At precisely twelve midnight for the first three months of his life Kevin took colic – a malady mostly afflicting little boys, according to John's mother, which cheered me up no end. "A drap aff cinder tea will get the win' aff 'is wee belly," she advised me in desperation. "Drap a red hat cinder outta the fire inta a wee drap a water and put it in 'is battle; 'is wind will come up ina flash." According to her it was better than the gripe water I had been pouring down his throat by the bottleful.

She had a wealth of old wives' tales stored in her memory bank and doled them out liberally whenever the occasion arose. Once I was about to deposit the contents of Kevin's nappy in the fire when she prevented me. "Don't dae that, the chil' will have diarrhoea for a month if ye burn 'is stools." I felt like answering back, "I'm not burning his stools, I'm burning his crap," but bit my tongue and decided to find out what stools were before making any comment. I was under the impression a stool was something you sat on. Another little gem was her suggestion to rub the baby's tongue with his own urine to clear the thrush from the crathur's mouth. I flatly refused to contemplate such a notion.

She had my chest bound flat with bolster cases for a month after the birth and told me not to walk in the direction of the wind in case I caught the 'weed'. My head was now not only reeling from lack of sleep but filled with worry at the thought of my chest sprouting dandelions whenever I went for a walk. To my relief, I later learnt that the 'weed' was only the breasts filling up with milk because you didn't breast-feed. A drop of Epsom salts would have worked wonders in a few hours.

But her heart was in the right place. She only had my welfare in mind; it wasn't her fault that she had been brought up in another generation filled with superstition. I was to find myself equally guilty of an old wives' remedy when my own grandchild was suffering from the snuffles, and I told Kevin to rub his nose with butter to make him sneeze, only to be told to frig off and butter my own bake. I had to laugh, for it brought back memories of the days when I heeded all these remedies and Kevin was covered in butter, rubbed with camphorated oil, his belly-button held flat with a penny by rolls of swaddling cloth, while his innards floated in cinder tea. Not a bit of wonder he never stopped crying – I would have cried myself at the thought of being so embalmed.

However, we were given an ultimatum – either that child shuts up or we leave home. Margaret, Eileen and Tommy were at their wits' end for the want of a bit of shut-eye. The idea of committing suicide had been discarded as it was against their religion, and they were not prepared to spend the hereafter in Hell just because of a screaming youngster.

We tried to ease their plight by taking Kevin for a walk in his pram at two o'clock in the morning to give them the chance of at least falling asleep. Drunks on their way home from a night's drinking used to stop and scratch their heads in amazement. We reckoned we probably encouraged a few of them to give up the demon drink, for they must have felt they were hallucinating when they witnessed two bug-eyed eejits wheeling a pram and singing lullabies in the middle of the night. Anyway, it didn't make a halfpeth of difference – the wee beggar continued his nocturnal gurnin' right through until eight o'clock, at which time he decided to call a halt to his cat-wailing now that the rest of the house had departed for work.

The look on the faces of John's family's told us we were not wanted, and so we had to move on, across the road to Mrs Fitzpatrick, for she had a room going spare. *She* went 'spare' after a fortnight and told us there was no more room at the inn. Even baby Jesus would have been thrown out of the stable for making less noise.

We moved to my parents' house, of all places. I had been forgiven my sins after my sisters had discovered that my mother had lied to them when she had told them I didn't want them at my wedding because they were Protestants, while at the same time telling me that they did not want to go because of the Catholic connection. They had blown a fuse at any suggestion that they had tried to split up the family because of religion, especially as they had no real interest in religion in the first place. They were raging at the thought of losing a sister because of bigotry and told my parents to catch themselves on – life was too short and hard enough without any of that nonsense.

The attic bedroom in the bungalow almost collapsed as the echo of our son's vociferous wailing rebounded from every crevice. Needless to say, we were again told to move on, as my father got so confused with lack of sleep he said he was thinking of joining a monastery just to get his head showered. Things were bad when father was threatening to join the enemy! Now I knew how Mary and Joseph must have felt when they were on the run from King Herod. The only difference was that I would have willingly handed Kevin over for the sake of a good night's kip.

We packed our worldly goods into a battered suitcase, tied it to the undercarriage of our son's coach-built 'Silver Cross' pram and headed into the big wide world in search of lodgings. We toyed with the thought of drugging Kevin with a strong sedative to keep the wee skitter quiet, just to get past the door of some kindly landlord, only to be brought to our senses by the fear of accidentally overdosing him. After a brief encounter with an unfurnished flat that we furnished on credit, only to have Bannon's Furniture Store repossess the lot for non-payment, we left the kettle that we had obtained from the Electricity Service by quarterly payments to our successors and decided on furnished accommodation.

Furnished accommodation was usually only rented to childless couples, the landlord being concerned with children causing havoc with his furniture. Atlantic Avenue off the Antrim Road was a beehive of furnished accommodation, so we tried our luck there. We stood outside the door of one of the large terraced houses and rang the bell on the off-chance we might strike it lucky.

An old man sporting a Father Christmas beard answered our ring. He peered over the top of his glasses and shuffled onto the doorstep in his carpet slippers. "What dae yous want?" he shouted in a gruff manner, which almost scared the living daylights out of the both of us and woke Kevin up with a start. The motion of the pram on our long haul had rocked him to sleep and we had been enjoying the peace, but now he started bawling all over again. I shoved the dummy teat in his mouth and prayed he would stay silent.

"We are looking for a furnished flat," John said in the hope of being granted a miracle. The Father Christmas apparition peered into the pram.

"Is that a youngin' ye have?" I felt like answering 'No, it's an illusion'. What the hell did he think it was – a monkey? My heart sank, for I was convinced he was going to turn us away, the way dozens had done earlier in the day. I bit my tongue and owned up to the fact it most definitely was a baby, of that I had no doubt, but on the other hand he would be no problem as he was very quiet. When in desperation you would sell your soul to the Devil by lying.

"I've niver met a quiet youngin' yit. Is there someit wrang wi' it?" He looked at the both of us through squinted eyes as if he was reading our minds. "Hae ye nowhere ta go wi' thon chil'?" We owned up to being homeless. What was the use of lying anymore? We resigned ourselves to being turned away again when the Father Christmas lookalike gave us a belated Christmas box. "Com'n ina that, the three aff yous, fer ye luk cowlrife. I jus' might hae a wee place tae put yous."

A large musty-smelling hallway stood between us and the stairs. John and I stood huddled together like a pair of magpies guarding a piece of stolen gold. The gold being our worldly possessions which rested under the pram and the infant who rested uneasily within it. We followed our bearded-faced, carpet-slippered saviour up four flights of stairs, babe in arms, and stood expectantly behind him in another equally large musty-smelling hallway as he unlocked a brown-stained well-worn door that creaked with disgust at being disturbed.

It took a couple of minutes before my eyes adjusted to the darkness of the room that hid behind closed heavy brown velvet curtains. As he opened the curtains a stream of light speckled with dust shone on an old-fashioned mahogany wardrobe that reeked of mothballs and looked as if Dracula had been the previous owner. I surveyed the room and realised the whole decor was brown – the bedspread, furniture, fireplace, wallpaper, carpet, even the few old and chipped ornaments.

We were informed that Kevin's sleeping arrangements were entirely up to us. This was not a problem because we owned a cot that we could get delivered on the back of a Co-op milk float in the morning. The small kitchen off the hallway was, not surprisingly, painted brown – at least everything was co-ordinated. The bathroom that we had to share with the rest of the bedsits was light brown – it made a welcome change from dark brown.

"The rent'll be two poun's, ten shillin's a week, electricity extra. It's yours if ye wan' it." We accepted the offer gratefully. As we descended the stairs behind our new landlord I noticed his socks, trousers and striped jumper matched his carpet slippers – all brown! He was consistent if nothing else. He was also a saint, for on rent day he handed me back a half-crown to put in Kevin's money box. The fact that he was partly deaf endeared me to his heart, for he didn't complain of Kevin's crying, while the rest of the residents gradually left for quieter lodgings.

We stayed there until the summer of 1963, when I discovered I was again pregnant. I must have been a glutton for punishment. There was no way I could possibly hide another baby from the landlord. He had been kind enough to let us the bedsit with one child, and I hadn't the heart to impose further upon his generosity by lumbering him with another noisy mite. Anyway, it wasn't fair on Kevin, who was now running around – the stairs were a danger for starters.

John came home from working on the buses in the middle of August beaming from ear to ear with news of a house on the Falls Road being sold cheap by one of the inspectors. Now this person ate the altar rails and boasted of the fact, and seeing as he was so good-living he would do us a favour. His little kitchen house, according to him, had become too small for his ever-increasing family, but on the other hand would be ideal for our small brood. He played on our ignorance and sold us (without deposit out of the goodness of his heart) this ramshackle of a house for nine hundred and fifty pounds, payable in monthly instalments of £12.

God keep us safe from 'Holy Joes', for the house was only worth three hundred quid had it even been in good condition. But we were young and vulnerable, not to mention desperate, and signed our life away without first giving it a good inspection.

The house in Balaclava Street in the Divis area of the Falls Road was held together with layers of paint and wallpaper, nothing else. The grass was growing up through the flagstones which passed as downstairs flooring, while the scullery was no more than a broom cupboard that held a rusty old-fashioned gas cooker and a jawbox that didn't have a draining board. The outside lavatory was held together with whitewash and the door didn't shut simply because it didn't fit. The stairs leading from the small living area crumbled underfoot; one of the bedrooms was uninhabitable because the ceiling was caving in; the other was only marginally better in that it boasted a small fireplace which could be lit to keep out the damp. The windows could not be opened as they had been painted when closed and were stuck for the duration, which was probably a Godsend. Had they opened a gush of wind could have demolished the house. An old-fashioned cast iron grate, complete with swing-around rings for boiling broth over the fire, completed the picture. I visualised my parents calling to inspect it and saying 'We warned you that this would be the way you would end up', and I cried even louder than the child straddling my hip. John tried to hug me for comfort, but I told him to go and bollocks and cried even louder.

We moved in the following week with the help of John's mother who had given us some curtains, bedclothes, a few plates, cups, pots and some cutlery. She also arranged for us to obtain a few items of furniture and a bit of lino on credit. The first day it rained the house flooded and the lino floated an inch above the floor. But good comes from bad – the grass in between the flagstones flourished, and we now had the luxury of wall to wall grass! We also had the luxury of running water in every room even though it ran down the walls and not out of a tap. The only thing left was my sense of humour. I prayed for the strength to hold on to it, to prevent me from murdering the sod who had conned us into buying this bloody millstone. May the hairs of his head turn into drumsticks and beat the brains clean out of him, I thought to myself.

Still, we had to be thankful for small mercies. At least we had a roof over our heads even though a quarter of it lay in the back yard. Pregnancy did not make my hair shine or put roses in my cheeks, or for that matter make me throw out a certain radiance, or any of those things mentioned in the advice books. According to them, pregnancy was a natural state, yet I was in one hell of a state – it could only be men who live in a world of fantasy who write such books. If a woman gave birth to the first child and the man gave birth to the second, the world would only be filled with two-child families, for the man would soon put a halt to the proceedings, having been put off procreation for life. Men are not known to suffer pain gladly.

I had put my first experience of never-ending morning sickness, plus zombie-like appearance, down to family pressures. My deathly appearance I now put down to the poor state of my home surroundings. Having to boke up one's guts in a smelly outside loo with half the street listening in, as well as having to rinse out the contents of an eighteen-month-old's nappies in a bucket of cold water, does not exactly turn a twenty-year-old female into a model housewife.

'Elvis! Elvis! wherefore art thou, Elvis!' I thought to myself as I looked at my reflection in the mirror hanging over the cast iron fireplace. 'Why the hell didn't I send you that photograph!'

John tried his best to turn our hovel into some semblance of a home with a new layer of wallpaper and paint, but first we had to remove the old wallpaper, which looked as if it had been hung before the Second World War. By the time John had stripped the walls, and the plaster came off along with the paper, he was demanding that capital punishment be brought back.

"That effin' bleeder who sold us this bloody house should be hung from the neck until he's proclaimed dead. Take a look at this, Val. Remember the lumps we thought were only air bubbles? Well, its flamin' rolled-up newspaper shoved in these holes in the wall!" He was frantically pulling screwed-up paper out of the walls and trying to make out the date at the top of the pages so as to find out when the house had last been decorated. He couldn't quite make out the date but Hitler's photograph was staring out from one of the pages.

"Here, take a juke at this, Val. Would you believe Mein Führer is the only thing between us and the aule doll next door. If it wasn't for Adolf we'd be shakin' hands through the wall." There were only two options, one was to cry, the other to laugh. We chose to laugh; had we cried there was every possibility we would have been brought up for murder. The house resembled a building that had been bomb-damaged from the inside. The plaster dust hung in the air like a cloud and when it settled John and I lay huddled together in self pity, covered in grey. It was akin to a scene from Pompeii after Mount Vesuvius had erupted, with our bodies preserved in hardened ash for posterity.

There was a knock at the door, and when we answered, still enveloped in grey matter, a small voice asked, "Are yous all right in thor? Fer there's a helluva racket goin' on; I wus beginnin' tae wunder if the house wus fallin' in."

It was Mrs O'Brien from next door, the opposite side to the aule doll who shared Hitler's likeness with us. "Come on in and sit down if you can find a seat under all this rubble." John held the door open while she tentatively stepped over the plaster-strewn floor. Kevin could be heard crying upstairs in his cot. Mrs O'Brien looked towards the top of the stairs, then at us.

"My God, it's childer rearin' childer!" she exclaimed with a look of disbelief on her face. "What are yous doin' – tryin' tae build a new house?"

"Almost," I answered in disgust. "By the time we've stripped the rest of the house, the place will need rebuilding." I then burst out crying like a baby.

"Ack, don't annoy yersel' chil' dear, sure a lick of paper an' paint will have it lukin' gran' in no time." She opened a tiny tin box and with thumb and forefinger extracted a pinch of snuff and put it in between her thumb and fist of her left hand and sniffed it up one of her nostrils, then repeated the action for the benefit of the other nostril. After a few seconds she sneezed into a brown hanky and remarked, through floods of tears and bloodshot eyes, "God bless all here. By Jaysus, that fairly clears the head." I thought to myself, 'It's a pity it wouldn't clear the house.' At least it made me laugh, for it was the first time I had ever witnessed anyone taking snuff. I had only read about it in Charles Dickens's novels.

I watched in fascination as a brown dewdrop formed at the end of her nose, then it was promptly sniffed up and the sneezing started in earnest. With one hand she wiped her nose on the brown-stained hanky, and with the other she wiped away her tears using the end of her apron. Mrs O'Brien was to become a good friend over the next few years and often pulled me out of a tight spot with the help of the local money-lender, who for the loan of £5 demanded £2 interest in return. We were not in any position to argue and even ended up borrowing to pay back the loan. With the aid of one such loans we decided to go the whole hog. John pulled out the dratted cast-iron fireplace and replaced it with a modern tiled surround. He built up the front doorstep to keep out the rain and plastered the walls with a spoon and a knife, a trowel and plaster skimmer being well beyond our budget.

And so our tiny abode was made more or less habitable with the aid of basic kitchen utensils. Together we slapped on a bit of wallpaper and gave the paintwork a lick and a promise with odd colours of gloss paint. Youth has its benefits, and worries soon run off you like water off a duck's back. We settled into our first home, albeit humble, and prepared for the birth of our second child.

I didn't have fond memories of Kevin's hospital birth and Mrs O'Brien's suggestion of a home birth greatly appealed to me. The fact that we didn't have hot running water or a bath or inside toilet didn't deter me one little bit. The thought of breaking the news of my condition to mother frightened me more than giving birth to triplets on the back of a bike. Marriage had not strengthened my nerves when it came to facing my parents – the echo of 'You will be bogged down with children at the insistence of the Catholic Church, and haggard before you're thirty' kept rattling through my brain. I dreaded the day I would have to tell them and kept putting it off until I could no longer hide the fact.

After one of my visits to the 'bungalow', as my mother would call it when in a polite mood, I relayed the news to her by shouting, "By the way I'm expecting again", when I was about fifty yards up the Lane and out of her reach. I watched as she fled down the driveway to tell my father while I dashed out of sight with Kevin and his pram.

My parents didn't visit us much anyway as the Lower Falls was not up to their standards. Mother had a short memory – she had forgotten about her own roots when she too lived in a small kitchen house and had to pee in an outside toilet. I can fully understand that I must have hurt my parents the way I got married and in the religious aspect, but had they been more understanding and accepted John for what he was – a good, clean, hard-working individual who held no animosity towards his fellow man regardless of creed – we would not have hurried into marriage, and perhaps we might have been able to save towards a better life. As things worked out, their bitterness towards John only made me more determined to prove them wrong. The only things I ever asked from them were love and respect, and as they could not come up with the goods, I was fortunate to find someone who could.

Fortunately too I was able to love and respect John in return, or I might have been accused of marrying him in order to get out of the house. I didn't have to take the drastic step of marriage and motherhood at the age of eighteen to get out of the family home if I had not wanted to. My brother Chuck had offered to bring me over to America before I got married even though I would have had to stay with friends, and if the prospect of living in the same country as Elvis did not put me off, nothing would.

Love and respect do not pay the bills, however, nor do they put food in your belly. John found himself working all the hours God could send. The house might not have been up to standard but we had good neighbours who were concerned about each other's welfare, and our front doors were never closed during the day. I was never stuck for company and we shared our problems without fear of ridicule. We didn't have the problem of keeping up with the Joneses, simply because the Joneses did not exist in our books. Fridges, washing machines and wall-to-wall carpeting were only to be found in glossy magazines and not in the humble homes of ordinary working-class citizens. A new fireside rug was cause for celebration, and the furniture was rearranged about a dozen times to show it off to best advantage. A new ornament was usually the spoils of a charabanc trip to Omeath organised by the locals as a respite from the dull environment around Divis Street where the sun never seemed to shine and the streets were so narrow.

Yet while the streets might have been dull, the insides of the houses, especially Mrs O'Brien's, often jumped to the point of raising the roof whenever there was a 'sing-song'. The hearty singing of 'McNamara's Band' and 'You're drunk, you're drunk, ye silly old skunk', echoed up the street. Mr O'Brien would strangle 'Danny Boy', and to please me they sang 'The Sash' at the end of the night and no-one complained. Needless to say, we transmogrified a few Elvis songs as well, and the rendering of 'All Shook Up' by Mrs O'Brien's son Brendan had us in stitches.

Every street had its corner shop, and ours was no exception. Annie and Minnie, two elderly spinster sisters, owned the small Dickensian shop facing us. Minute weighing scales for snuff, liniment decades out of date, and remedies for maladies I thought only existed during the Boer War, kept company with rusty tins of peas, Blackjacks, Spangles and bars of Frys Chocolate Cream. The old mixed with the new only added to the eccentricity of these two individuals who obviously could not throw out anything under fifty years old. Stepping into that shop was like stepping back into history. The darkness and the fusty smell of decades of accumulated dust – complemented by the appearance of Annie or Minnie – was surely akin to a scene from *David Copperfield*. This picture was completed by the arrival of their brother, who had decided to retire amidst the clutter, for he resembled Mr Micawber. They were handy all the same for the more than occasional packet of cigarettes on the slate, which the Mr Micawber lookalike entered with precision in his log book in pen and ink.

Although the two sisters were old maids the news of an imminent birth in the street fuelled their curiosity and filled their humdrum life to the point of utter distraction. They kept a vigilant eye on the local midwife as she made her weekly visits. Annie peeped through the downstairs window while Minnie peered through a chink in the yellowed lace curtains of the upstairs bedroom. As soon as the midwife left I felt it my duty to inform them of her verdict and waddled over to the shop to put them out of their misery. It was always the same reaction – they patted my swollen belly like two schoolgirls and enquired in a fit of giggles if the ba was almost cooked. I envisaged a scene of cannibalism as soon as the baby made his debut, the glint in their eyes conjuring up a vision of hungry wolves. I almost scanned the shelves for evidence of bottled babies amidst the pickles!

Kevin was by now talking fluent Irish – by that I mean 'pub Irish'. As well as having a shop in every street we also had a pub on every corner, the punters of which were none too polite after a jar or two. Mind you, they were none too polite before it so you can guess what condition they were in when inebriated. As Kevin sat on his swing, which hung from hooks at the front door, his bud-like ears missed nothing. His first words were not 'I love you' or, to be more babylike, 'I wuv you'. It was the 'F' word. He looked like an angel but swore like the devil. People often stopped to talk to him only to be told to 'Fuck off'. I hid behind the door, watched the look of disgust on their faces as they fled up the street, then walloped him round the legs, only to be told to 'Fuck off' in response. I just held my head in my hands and screamed with frustration. The angelic-looking mite had the mouth of a drunken sailor. I felt like 'The Mother of Sorrows' as I looked at him and thought, 'Is this the same child John and I talked to for hours on end when he was only an embryo? Our son, the one I decided to name after a shy, introverted gentle little boy I went to school with? God, where did I go wrong?'

Mrs O'Brien and her daughter Margaret catered for my every need as my confinement loomed on the horizon, and Margaret went with me to the health centre to collect my delivery box. A brown sealed parcel that held all the paraphernalia for a home delivery, a label with the words DO NOT OPEN, UNLESS BY MIDWIFE in bold letters stuck firmly in place on the front. It only added to my curiosity, as it sat like a time-bomb beside the bed and made what time I had left pass by very slowly. What on earth did it hold anyway? The bright red warning had my mind running circles around itself. Did it contain some medieval form of obstetric torture perhaps!

"When do you think this child is going to make up its mind to enter the land of the living?" I asked Dr Walker, in the hope of him answering 'This very night, Valerie.'

"It will come when ready and not a day before." Dr Walker helped me off the examination couch and told me to be patient. I buttoned up my skirt which had been let out with a piece of elastic, pulled my smock top over my bump and sighed.

"It's a week overdue, Doctor, is there anything I can do to hurry it up?"

"Just content yourself. In a few weeks' time you will be wishing you had your bump back. At least it's not crying for attention in the middle of the night."

Mrs O'Brien suggested a bottle of castor oil to hurry up the proceedings, omitting to tell me not to take it in bed. "Mix it wi' a drap aff orange an drink it down quick. You'll be away in the mornin'." Like a fool I took it in bed, forgetful of the fact we had an outside toilet. I didn't think it would work quite so fast. I was away in ten minutes and I don't mean in labour. My stomach went into a vice-like grip and my bowels told me to run like hell. I jumped out of bed and made it to the landing at the top of the stairs where my bowels decided to evacuate of their own accord. By the time I reached the outside loo the evidence was left on every other step of the stairs. After ten exhausting minutes perched on the cold seat of the outside toilet on a bitterly cold March night, I weakly made my way through the back door wiping the sweat from my brow with the tail of my nightdress to find John almost crying his lamps out at the thought of having to clean up the mess. He cursed Mrs O'Brien in and out of hell for not warning me that it would work within minutes. I cursed the oil for not doing its job. I did not go into labour, I spent the rest of the night with the wind whistling round my ankles in the coldness of the outside toilet, John's bus conductor's overcoat wrapped around my shoulders and my backside on fire. All I could do was curse or peruse the bits of *Belfast Telegraph* which hung in squares from a piece of cord. I had splashed out on the luxury of two shiny white toilet rolls, but they had been safely tucked away, along with the baby's layette, only to be used after the big event.

Wednesday 18 March 1964 started off without much of a fuss and ended up with an extra addition to the population of Ireland. Exactly a week to the day after the great oil rush my body decided to become two human beings instead of one misshapen lump. At exactly half past six in the evening I had a twinge followed by another twenty minutes later. I sent for Mrs O'Brien who knew I was well and truly ripe by the flush on my cheeks.

"Oh, you're away, all right; you're ready fer the aff." I felt like a race horse in the Grand National. This feeling became stronger as Mrs O'Brien and her daughter Margaret started placing bets as to whether it would be a boy or girl. "It's a wee lad, alright, she's all tae the back." Mrs O'Brien had made one of her few but profound statements, and awarded herself with a few pinches of snuff to clear her head should she have to think of another later on in the night.

John went into a panic and convinced himself things would go smoother in hospital, only to be told to pull himself together as he wasn't the only one about to become a father in the land. I reminded him that he had been there at the beginning and was most certainly going to be there at the end, even if it meant tying him to the bedpost. He was told to make himself useful by putting the teapot on, to start boiling pots of water, light the fire in the bedroom to warm the room up and then bugger off to the pub.

He obeyed the first three orders but declined the offer of going to the pub as he needed to stay sober to look after Kevin who by now was effing and blinding in his high chair with all the excitement. Margaret went to fetch the midwife, who arrived armed with gas and air and the tools of her trade in a small black bag. Annie and Minnie, who were determined not to miss any of the action, positioned themselves by their windows and Mr Micawber took control behind the counter. The rest of the neighbours in the street started arriving with plates of sandwiches and buns and took over the house while I went upstairs with the midwife. All they needed was an Irish fiddle-player, a few bottles of whiskey, a couple of story-tellers and they could have had a ceilidh to round off the festivities.

I had an easy labour compared to Kevin's, so easy I even wondered whether I had been mistaken – perhaps it was just a dose of wind. At three minutes to midnight my dose of wind came into the world crying at the top of its lungs, and a round of applause plus a cheer wafted up the stairs, followed by John holding Kevin in his arms. He was told, or should I say ordered, by the midwife to stand outside the bedroom door until mother and baby were cleaned up.

After the midwife had laid the baby in my arms she told John to enter. I told him we had another son and informed Kevin he now had a brother. I told Kevin to give his new brother a kiss. He bent down, pursed his little rosebud lips and gently kissed him, then told him to "Fuck off". Stephen Paul slept like an angel with a tiny smile etched on his little face. His expression said it all: 'My day will come, big brother, my day will come – looks can be deceptive!'

Chapter 10

T-R-O-U-B-L-E !

The front doors of Balaclava Street in the early Sixties only closed when the residents retired to bed, during the day being open house to all and sundry. This made personal hygiene a work of art, and a quick wash under the oxters was performed with extreme difficulty. The only thing between you and whoever else was in the house was a curtain that hung at the scullery entrance. You had to be very careful not to be caught in your knickers by the insurance man, the coal man, or the binman, who usually collected the bin through the front door.

Once a week I went to the Falls Baths to pay for the luxury of a hot bath, armed with soap and towel. Some of the people should have been provided with scrubbing brushes to remove the layers of dirt, for it seemed as if the last time they saw water was when they were baptised. The thought of having to get into the same bath after one of these individuals was nauseating but nevertheless a necessity. The attendant filled up the bath to the permitted level, then proceeded to read out the rules in a Hitlerite fashion: "Do not attempt to use any more hot water. Clean out the bath when finished. Vacate the cubicle when you hear the rap on the door." You were in and out of that bath so quickly your body hadn't realised it had got wet. Most of the old folk didn't believe in taking a bath, because it destroyed the oils of the body, leaving you open to all sorts of ailments. Instead, they spent their lives smelling to high heaven.

Talking about the lack of bathroom facilities reminds me of an incident the memory of which can still bring tears to my husband's eyes. Whoever designed a bus conductor's uniform must have had a sadistic streak for the material was as rough as sack cloth. It was a warm July evening, shortly after Stephen was born, when John came into the house after a hectic day on the buses. Racing up and down stairs collecting fares, he had ended up with a severe case of adult nappy rash – in other words his wedding tackle had endured a bit of a bashing due to sweat and the friction of this ghastly material.

When I recommended he use some nappy cream to ease the

pain, he vanished into the scullery to apply a dollop or two. I didn't give it a second thought for it was a simple enough operation, when this agonising scream reverberated through the house from the direction of the scullery, followed by a torrent of foul language, then the sound of running water. He was yelling at the water, "Will you get out of that tap effin' quick, I'm ruined for life! Come on, ye bleeder, before me cobblers drop off!"

He pulled aside the curtain that separated the scullery from the living area. His trousers were round his ankles and he was hopping up and down, at the same time fanning his manhood with a broken piece of linoleum.

"What kind of friggin' cream was that! It's burning like bloody blazes!" I was feeding Stephen and unable to just jump to his assistance. He disappeared back into the scullery, the splash of water plus an immense sigh of relief echoing through the curtain. Curiosity got the better of me and I went to see what all the fuss was about. The sight that met me is imprinted on my mind to this day. John was sitting with his backside in the sink, up to his waist in ice cold water, his legs dangling over the edge, trousers round the ankles and sweating cobs.

"Jesus, Val, I think I've done myself a terrible injury. Will you take a look at that tube and see what kind of flamin' cream I've just rubbed on me knackers."

I lifted the tube and in bright red letters the name 'Deep Heat' stared me in the face. I burst out laughing, not only at the sight of John sitting perched like a fairy in the sink, but at the thought of him rubbing embrocation for a sore back onto a very sensitive part of his anatomy. I'm glad to say he was not in a position to grab my throat or I might have been six feet under the clay today.

"Why the hell didn't you tell me which tube to lift, stupid cow!"

"Why the hell didn't you read the label, you big pockle!" I answered. I thought to myself, 'Well, perhaps we are going to be a two-child family whether we like it or not.' I pictured Elvis in this predicament, and the thought sent me into a fit of giggling. I had a image of him singing a duet with Jerry Lee Lewis, the song being 'Great balls of fire!' I made the mistake of telling Mrs O'Brien, who in turn told her next door neighbour. Before the week was out the whole of the Street knew and poor John, who still couldn't sit with his legs crossed, had to endure an endless stream of jokes.

This incident, although painful, was not life-threatening, unlike one of John's hair-brained experiments that went terribly wrong and charged him with enough electricity to light up Las Vegas. The outside lavatory light would not work, and John inserted bulb after bulb, only to discover on closer inspection that the bulb was not making contact with the light fitting which hung precariously from the crumbling ceiling. He scratched his head and prowled the yard in deep thought. Eureka! – the gormless git in his infinite wisdom decided to use silver paper to make the connection. Of course, I was not completely blameless, so have to admit to my part in what happened next. The switch for the lavatory light was situated inside the house, and unbeknownst to me John inserted the bulb at the exact moment I flipped this switch in mistake for the scullery light. A blue flash lit up the yard closely followed by John who flew through the air feet first, his hair smouldering and standing on end – this being before he lost it!

Of course the whole house was thrown into darkness as all the lights fused. The only sound he was capable of making was the death rattle of a dying man, as he lay in a heap, shaking from head to foot.

"It works in theory you know, bbbut bbbby God, it doesn't work in practice," he stuttered, still shaking uncontrollably from the shock. Well, what can one do in a situation like this, other than double up in nervous laughter, especially when confronted by a blithering idiot stupid enough to use silver paper while tampering with electricity. He got no sympathy, only a tip to stick to conducting a bus and to leave the conducting of electricity to those trained for the job. Poor John, he never tried that experiment again. However, it had been a close call and really no laughing matter.

We were a friendly lot in our street, friendship being the only commodity we could afford, apart from the offer of a cup of tea or the lend of an ear to listen to each other's problems. The strange thing was that our problems were small compared to today's. As long as we had food on the table and coal in the hearth nothing else really mattered. Money was in short supply, but this applied to most homes in that area. We shared what little we had, and thought nothing of asking our next door neighbour for the loan of a mop or a shilling for the gas. Nor was it unusual to borrow the odd cup and saucer when visitors were expected.

Monday morning was pawnshop day, and anything that wasn't nailed to the floor was in danger of finding its way to Uncle Tom's around the corner. Tuesday being family allowance day, the eight shillings I received saw me through until pay day on Friday. The only item worth pawning, apart from my engagement ring, was John's suit, which went in and out like a yo-yo. John was unaware of the fact his suit was going out the front door every Monday minus his body. He did not approve of stooping so low as to pawn the very clothes we wore. He never went out anywhere during the week that required the use of a suit so I felt safe enough in committing this dastardly deed, until one Tuesday night when, feeling somewhat depressed, he decided to go out for a drink with a few mates.

I tried to talk him out of it with the promise of an early night in bed, but by God he must have been depressed alright, for he refused.

In the few years we had been married I never once knew John refuse an offer of a night of passion, so things were indeed bad. I watched in a state of panic as he searched the house for his suit, my mind working overtime for some excuse as to why the item was missing.

"Have you seen my suit?" John shouted from the bedroom.

"What suit?" I replied timidly.

"*What* bloody suit? The suit that hangs alongside my dinner jacket, tuxedo, morning suit and pheasant-shooting outfit!" he answered sarcastically.

"Oh that suit! It's in the cleaners." Well it was the only excuse I could think of on the spur of the moment.

"Well go and get it out of the bloody cleaners." I had already spent the 17/6 the pawnbroker had allowed me on the accursed garment as a down payment on six rolls of wallpaper, a few tins of paint and a new knocker for the front door.

"Give me the ticket for the cleaners and I'll get it out myself. I don't know why the hell you put it in the cleaners in the first place – a rub down with the clothes-brush would have been sufficient."

The hunted look on my face must have given the game away and I thought he was going to burst a blood vessel or take a coronary – his face was puce with rage.

"The friggin' thing's in the pawn shop sittin' beside some tramp's flea-ridden outfit, isn't it! Could you tell me what in the name of God I'm going to wear tonight apart from my bus uniform?" I did the only thing that came naturally, my bladder being close to my eyes – I burst into tears, ran up the stairs and flung myself onto the bed. I did this so often I could have won an Oscar as Miss Scarlet in 'Gone with the Wind'. John's heart ruled his head as often as my bladder ruled my tears, so he ended up consoling me while I sniffled into the pillow, now and then peering up at him with Betty Davis eyes, trying to convince him I only did it to brighten up our dull home. I'm not sure who I was trying to convince, him or me, but it worked a treat. It is known as female manipulation – we closed the front door and stayed in that night!

Evening outings for John and I were limited to the occasional visit to relatives with the two boys in tow, or, if lady luck sent us a surprise in the form of a baby-sitter, we went out for a drink in one of the many lounge bars situated on either the Falls or Shankill Roads or else a game of bingo. I still went to see Elvis films, although John declined on principle, for he had not been getting his conjugals as often and the sight or sound of Elvis made him cringe. Whenever I refused him his oats he would turn his back to me and mutter: "If it was Elvis, you would jump on his bones without having to be asked." I must say I had to agree into myself.

The early Sixties had not as yet been subjected to the hostilities of bigots bent on destroying the love one had for one's neighbour. I can say this having had the fortune of seeing both sides of the fence. Living in a mixed area had broadened my outlook as far as religion was concerned. Even my parents' attitude towards John stemmed as much from pride as it did from bigotry – had he been a man of wealth the religious side might just have been overlooked. When Chuck had sent the photograph of one of his army pals, stating he was a quarter millionaire, they did not ask his religion but were impressed by the size of his bank balance. The fact that he resembled something from outer space did not alter their opinion either – as long as he had the spondulicks, looks and religion could have been conveniently overlooked.

People then were more concerned with building a home rather than building bridges of hate. Even though the Falls Road was predominantly Catholic, while the nearby Shankill Road was Protestant, the people of both communities treated each other's views regarding religion with a certain amount of respect.

It has always appeared to me that religion is too often encumbered by intolerance and fear. It's a situation pertaining in most countries, and Ireland unfortunately is no exception. It's a pity really, for we Irish only argue on home ground – put us anywhere else in the world and we love each other to death. We are among the friendliest and most hospitable people in the world, and will spend our last penny feeding and watering others – as long as they are not fellow Irish of the 'wrong' denomination. No matter where you go in this world every other person seems to have Irish roots, even if it is only a third cousin of a third cousin twice removed who was deported for stealing a lamb. The Irish would also appear to be born fighters, and if they don't have a problem they will go out of their way to find one. Religion and politics are two topics each capable of starting an argument in an empty house. Put the two together in Ireland and you will easily start an argument that has no hope of ending peacefully.

My own religious belief is limited to the acceptance that there must be a God – what would be the meaning of life if we are only born to die? And if there is no such thing as God why would we constantly beseech his help in times of need? Religion is belief. Whatever you believe in – that is your religion.

Most of the world is under the impression that the present troubles in Ireland started in 1969, when in fact the natives were feeling restless as early as 1964. The proletarian tribes of different persuasions were getting too friendly, frequenting each other's huts of mud and straw, offering gifts of understanding and love. A few hard-liners got together for a bit of a chinwag and decided to put a halt to this practical Christianity. You can love thy neighbour – depending on what month of the year his celebrations fall on. If it is

July paint his colour orange, if it be August paint it green. Try to mix these two colours and the end result either offends or pleases, depending on the eye of the beholder. I am glad to say these two colours mixed together are very pleasing to *my* eye.

A bingo session in a hall in the middle of Divis street on an autumn night in 1964 started out with the friendly banter of Protestant and Catholic housewives bent on winning a few pounds for a few luxuries. It ended up with the caller who had earlier been shouting "two fat ladies 88, and two little ducks 22", now appealing for calm as we made our way out of the back entrance so we could hasten home without having to pass the rioting which had erupted on Divis Street and the Falls Road. Some of the people in the hall had heard what sounded like gunshots earlier in the evening, but with the windows being at ceiling level we could not see out and dismissed it as merely a car backfiring. What with the normal noises in the hall and the fact that the building was situated a little way off the main road we didn't even hear the commotion being made by yelling protesters.

Apparently it all started over a tatty green, white and orange tricolour that lay rolled up behind a dirty window which itself was covered with a net curtain. John and I had passed that window on numerous occasions, but had never once laid eyes on the flag. Yet some individual hell bent on trouble decided to start a bit of a fracas by demanding that the police remove it. One punch led to another and then another, and before long a crowd had gathered, which soon degenerated into a mob. Within an hour a full scale riot had gripped the heart of Divis Street and its surrounding arteries, clogging all routes in or out.

Terrified was not the word for how I felt as I made my way through the maze of streets leading to home. Mrs O'Brien's mentally handicapped son Brendan, who was then about twenty-five years old, held my hand like a child and cried for his mother, for the sight of grown men fighting in the streets had him very agitated. A few women from the Shankill Road side were also in hysterics, as it was impossible to cross over the main road to get to their homes, but we all clung together as the mayhem continued. Words cannot express the fear that gripped the residents of this part of town. They stood at the doors of their tiny homes, young and old, in utter despair and disbelief at what was happening. The previous hour peace had reigned, people had been minding their own business – now they asked questions no-one could answer. On making it safely home, I was met at the door by Margaret O'Brien who had Kevin by the hand and Stephen in her arms.

"John's out looking for you!" She was distraught with fear. The first thing that came into my mind was the thought of John making his way towards the bingo hall in his bus uniform.

"He will be mistaken for a policeman in the dark! In the name of God is he right in the head, he will be killed by that crowd!" It was my turn to go slightly hysterical.

"Jesus, Mary and Joseph!" cried Margaret. "Get in aff the street. They're throwing paving stones an' manhole covers at each other!" John turned into the street at that very moment, soaked to the skin, a slab of concrete missing his head by inches as he entered the house, followed by an onslaught of verbal abuse.

We quickly slammed the door shut on a group of youths who were calling, "Throw that fuckin' peeler out, or the door gets kicked in!"

John shouted back, "I'm not a bloody peeler, I'm a bus conductor, for Christ's sake! Ask the neighbours in the street!"

Kevin and Stephen were crying at all the shouting plus the banging on the door. I prayed they wouldn't start on the window, the only thing holding it together being paint and putty. I could just about make out the sound of a few of the neighbours trying to convince the youths that John was indeed a bus conductor.

"Come out and prove it then, or the fuckin' door goes!"

"For Christ's sake, open the door!" I yelled at John, who obeyed without having to be asked twice. Those yobbos were making no idle threats, they were hungry for action – the type who looked for trouble at the drop of a hat; rioting just gave them extra fuel. They most likely didn't even know what the rioting was about, and probably didn't care. They were disappointed John wasn't a policeman, but they did not make any apologies. In their thirst for action someone suggested they beat him up for the hell of it anyway, but thank God one of them had the sense to tell the others to catch themselves on, and they proceeded to slouch up the street in search of someone else whose face was not to their liking.

I had just enough time to breathe a sigh of relief when Brendan came dashing into the house crying and running from one person to the other like a child who has just lost his mother in a crowd. Because of his affliction Brendan was inclined to talk very effeminately and mince when he walked. This might have stemmed from mixing with women rather than men. He delighted in going to the launderette for all the women in the area, their chatter being softer to his ear than that of loud-mouthed men. He spent the better part of the day in chapel lighting candles for lost souls, my soul among them.

"Me Ma's not well, she can't breathe! Oh God, please don't let her die, she's the only mammie I've got! If she dies I'll be put in a home!"

Poor Brendan was beside himself with fear, his eyes darting around in their sockets as he searched frantically for help. The sight of a grown man acting like a five-year-old through no fault of his own is heart-rending. We did not know whether to believe Brendan. Perhaps he was overreacting, his childlike mind not being able to comprehend why everyone was so distraught. Of Mrs O'Brien's two mentally handicapped sons, Brendan was the lesser afflicted. Josie, the older son by about five years, who could hardly join two words together, spent his time wandering the Falls Road smoking. He never removed the cigarette from his lips between puffs and took full advantage of his Woodbine until it was no more than a few strands of tobacco held together by spit.

We knew something was badly wrong when Josie came running in close on Brendan's heels. He was crying and holding his head tightly, trying to block out the noise. Josie did not like noise, it was as if it invaded his own little world where the word hate did not exist. Unfortunately the only word Josie could get out without effort was the 'F' word, and whenever roused or anxious he repeated it over and over again. On this particular night a torrent of 'F' words came tumbling forth, ending with an anguished 'Me Ma!'

Mrs O'Brien had indeed taken a heart attack in the middle of all the furore, and she sat clutching her chest. Her lips were blue and she was fighting for breath. The only person in the street who owned a telephone happened to be the bank manager of the Northern Bank, situated on the corner of Balaclava Street. Luckily for us he lived in the flat above and John suggested we use his phone to call for an ambulance. The street by now had turned into what could only be described as a battlefield, and anything that could be thrown was flying up the street – bits of kerb stone, bricks, manhole covers, bottles, plus the occasional human whose face didn't fit in with the revolting masses.

John tried to zigzag his way across the small span of road that separated us from the other side of the street, but without success. He pleaded with the crowd to let him cross, explaining that a woman was dying and in need of an ambulance, but mob rule had taken over and not even an ambulance was going to be let through. What kind of person can stand by and decide another's fate just for the thrill of a fight? It doesn't take bravery to confront defenceless sick women; I am sure there are not many medals handed out for cowardice. On top of it all the police had decided to use water jets in their effort to control the situation, and armoured jeeps trundled up the main road spraying everything that moved. They aimed the jet in the direction of our street, and to add insult to injury, for the second time that night John was sent flying through the air under the force. It had happened earlier when he had tried to make his way to the bingo hall, proving that you can be mistaken for a protester when in actual fact you are only an innocent bystander.

However, he managed to make it to the bank's side door with his coat protecting his head against missiles. He hammered the door with his fists, at the same time kicking it with his feet. The door opened a few inches and the barrel of a shotgun poked through the opening, with a faceless and very nervous voice attached to the other end. "Clear off or this gun will explode in your face!" The bank manager thought he was being robbed in the middle of it all and was taking no chances. John very nearly lost control of his bowels as he shouted back in fright. "For frig sake, don't pull that trigger, I need an ambulance for Mrs O'Brien! She's having a heart attack!"

"I said clear off, do you think I came up the river in a bubble! I know your sort, any excuse to get through this door and you're in like Flynn. B...b...bugger off, or by Christ your head will keep company with your feet, for that's where it'll land when I blow it off!" The bank manager was beside himself with fright, and the barrel of the gun was pushed a further couple of inches out the door.

Taking his life in his hands John pushed the door open in the hope he would be instantly recognised. Luckily the ploy worked and the bank manager realised who it was – otherwise John would have been done for. The bank manager was ashen and shaking like an aspen leaf, while the shotgun was locked in his hands with fright and John had to prize his fingers open to get him to release it. They rang for an ambulance only to be told it would be difficult getting through to any of the side streets; however, the ambulance service would do their utmost to get there.

It arrived about half an hour later with horn blaring. Not that it made any difference whether the horn blew or not, for the thugs starting stoning it, and when this failed to stop it they set upon it, rocking it back and forth in an attempt to topple it. I could not believe my eyes. Holy Mother of God, what kind of human beings would prevent aid reaching an old woman – and this supposed to be a civilised country! I am convinced humans are the lowest species. That's why I can't for the life of me understand people calling such hoodlums 'animals'. Animals don't deserve such an insult.

It was just as well it wasn't a serious heart attack or Mrs O'Brien would not have survived. I often wonder how those thugs would have felt if she had died. Would they have boasted about their bravery when they read the newspapers the following day to learn that the only victim of the night's fighting happened to be a defenceless mother of two handicapped sons who had been frightened to death.

Protestant and Catholic alike suffered that night, all because of faceless people who came out of the sewers like rats on the rampage in the hope of spreading disease. I am sorry to say they germinated the first cells of the cancer that exists today. If the malignant cells had been destroyed in the early stages the secondaries might not have developed. We had a five-year relatively trouble-free remission, which uncannily is what you can achieve with a malignant condition.

Perhaps God is trying to tell us something – if only some people would take the time to listen!

After a fitful night of snatched sleep amidst the noise of sporadic rioting we decided for the children's sake to clear off for a few days. With ours being a mixed marriage we were just that extra bit scared. The thought of a petrol bomb landing in our small home – which had no rear escape route – felt more intimidating than any hostile crowd. As far as we were concerned they could pillage what little we had or burn the bloody thing down – as long as we were not in it at the time.

We gathered together a few belongings – nappies, baby bottles, clothes and baby food – put them in a box and a couple of carrier bags and made the hurried decision to flee to John's mother's for sanctuary. As for going to my parents, well, their first words would have been: 'You made your bed, lie in it, we knew nothing good would come from a mixed marriage in this damned country. You always end up living with the Catholic side whether you like it or not.' Conveniently forgetting the fact that hoodlums from both sides of the religious divide had been involved.

The front door of 7 Balaclava Street closed behind us early in the morning. I felt as if I was leaving an old friend behind. Be it ever so humble it was still our home. The memory of Stephen's first cry after he was born in the small upstairs bedroom came into my mind, and the fragrant smell of his sweet newborn innocence, which I prayed he would never lose. The peace and tranquillity of holding new life close to my breast, surrounded by smiling faces and the feeling of being my own person for the first time in my life, filled my emotions. I could feel the tears welling in my eyes. Was this all to be lost in the space of a day? I cursed those faceless people for ruining my new-found happiness, for trying to take my memories without permission.

John and I were two very frightened people as we made our way up the Falls Road pushing a pram that held one small sleeping baby in it plus another not so small toddler perched on the end, our few possessions tucked underneath. We weaved our way through the debris of the previous night's battle – bricks, broken kerbstones and shattered glass – and prayed our home and memories would not be violated in our absence.

After a couple of days we returned to find our street back to normal, the debris cleared, and our home just as we had left it – humble but welcoming. Brendan was first on the scene to greet us. He told us his 'mammie' was alright, she would be coming home from hospital in a few days, for according to him 'Her wee heart hadn't had a bad sickness, it was only a wee fright.' Josie tapped me on the shoulder from behind, and indicated he wanted a light for his cigarette butt by miming a smoking action. I lit a match and held it up to a butt no longer than half an inch. He cupped the match with his hand to shield it from the wind. God only knows how he managed to light it without scorching his nose, but he had it down to a fine art and puffed away in a flurry of smoke. Without a word of thanks he strolled off, the 'F' word tripping off the end of his tongue with clarity, the butt firmly held between his lips and both hands shoved down his trouser pockets.

Brendan sighed, and like a mother hen shook his head from side to side, tut-tutting. He informed us, "I don't know what to do with thon big lad, he's an awful worry to me mammie and meself. He's goin' to go up in smoke one of these days with them aule fegs, but sure it's all he's got, God love him."

He never mentioned the trouble that had earlier frightened him half to death. His innocence shone through sparkling eyes as he took Kevin by the hand and said, "Com'n son, let's go in an' make your wee Ma a cup of tea, she's the only mammie you'll ever have and she loves you, just the way me mammie loves me an' Josie."

I had come home, to the people who mattered, the Brendans and Josies of this troubled land, to friends from both sides of the community who tried in vain to work hand in hand before that final curtain call and Ireland became the stage for maniacal players trying to play God.

Chapter 11

THE FAIR IS MOVING ON

"Well, that's that bloody thing off!" John had just beheaded the wooden ball perched on the end of the bannister rail with one fell swoop of a hatchet. He had decided the time was right for a little bit of do-it-yourself to modernise our tiny home. Seeing as the stairs led into the living area he came up with the bright idea of boxing them in so that the rickety stairway would not be visible to the eye. His tools had now been upmarketed from spoon and knife to a hatchet and half a hacksaw blade. His use of the hatchet to chop a few sticks for the fire had obviously gone to his head – after all, Iron Age man had worked wonders with one of these tools, why ruin an age-old habit just because of progress? The offending round wooden object rolled across the floor before the rim of the hearth halted its progress and it lay forlornly on the fireside rug. I had a feeling it should have been heralded with a drum roll. I felt like Madame Guillotine at the beheading of Marie Antoinette, as I too had been knitting at the time.

"Put that on the fire, Val, one ball's no use to anyone." John was in a cheerful mood, and when John was in a cheerful mood he had a very colourful imagination. I reminded him of the incident with the embrocation and how near he had been to joining the banisters. "That's enough of that now, there's no reason to get personal," he joked back. "I'll go up the Shankill tomorrow morning to get a sheet of plywood to finish the job. I hope there's no rioting on the way over, one well-aimed brick could finish off what the Deep Heat tried to do and failed."

I giggled at the memory and threw the ball onto the fire. The layers of paint that had gathered over the years quickly ignited and started to spit flames up the chimney, and within a couple of minutes the chimney had caught fire. From their shop across the street, Minnie and Annie, who never missed a trick, saw the sparks shooting into the sky and took it upon themselves to warn the neighbours of the impending Great Fire of Balaclava Street. The last time a chimney had caught fire in the street it had spread through the lofts of three houses, so the residents had been warned to be extra careful in future. Had it spread any further there was every possibility the street would have had to be demolished. We doused the fire with wet tea leaves and listened for the roar that usually accompanied a chimney fire, but were relieved at the silence.

That silence was broken when half the street suddenly appeared through our front door, almost bursting our small home at the seams. Our ears were bombarded with the raised voices of people curious as to what the hell we had been burning.

Brendan minced through the crowd of anxious neighbours and starting flapping his arms around as if conducting an orchestra on Proms Night. "Oh God, help us! We cud all have been burnt to death! Are those wee childer all right upstairs?"

Mrs O'Brien calmly retrieved her small tin snuff box from the pocket of her wrap-around pinny, tapped the lid with her index finger to settle the contents and slowly went through her snuff-sniffing ritual. In between bouts of sneezing she told Brendan to pull himself together.

Annie and Minnie, having had the opportunity to set foot over the door, took it upon themselves to have a bit of a nosey. Like Tweedledum and Tweedledee they held hands and peered into every nook and cranny. Aggie from number 11, who weighed somewhere in the region of eighteen stone, was sweating profusely in the scullery after her mad dash up the street, and was busy wiping the sweat from her brow with a cold dish cloth. Her girth completely filled the small room, which made refilling the teapot with water an impossibility, so it was just as well the fire had been quenched before she arrived. Josie put his head round the open door and, butt in mouth, effed at the speed of light for a full minute without pausing to catch his breath, then ambled off into the night scratching his head in bewilderment.

Mr O'Brien just happened to be making his way home from his nightly visit to one of the many local watering holes and, duncher cap askew, enquired in an inebriated voice, "What's all the bloody fusshh about, has someone kicked the bucket?" He teetered unsteadily at the door as he tried without much success to light a cigarette. Mrs O'Brien sneezed into her hanky for the umpteenth time and guldered, "Go inta the house, Paddy, an' lie down for Christ's sake, afore ye fall down." He doffed his cap and, swaying back and forth, replied, "I washh only ashkin', fer God's shhake! Ishh there a law againshht it?" He stumbled out into the street and landed on his back, his short legs shooting straight up into the air and thrashing about like a heavyweight boxer in his efforts to get up again.

"Will ye luk at the state aff that, Ma, that man's goin' to kill himself one af these days," Brendan shouted at the top of his voice. Mrs O'Brien wiped the brown dewdrop from the end of her nose, pointed towards the stairs and hissed, "Get upa that an stap yer nyammerin'. Haule yer whisht, there's childer tryin' tae get ta sleep up them stairs, ye drunken aule scut!"

Brendan started his orchestral manoeuvres all over again and went to his father's assistance. "Com'n Da, me Mammy's sick of you comin' home in this state; you're makin' an eejit of yourself." He helped him to his feet and as he led him into his own house called over his shoulder, "I'll only be a minute, Val, don't worry your wee head; sure men are all the same." He said it in such a way you would have thought he had sole rights to quelling any situation.

What a carry-on – all this fuss caused by John decapitating the staircase! When the drama of the burning ball had subsided and peace reigned once again over number 7, John finished his masterpiece, much to the admiration of the other residents. The end result was that John developed bannister madness. Anyone foolish enough to pass the remark, 'Mind you, I wouldn't mind having my bannisters boxed in', found John on their doorstep, hatchet and hacksaw blade in hand ready for action. In the space of six days he beheaded six banister rails, wreaked havoc in six houses, and no doubt would have been responsible for six chimney fires had the occupants not had the presence of mind to dispose of each ball in the bin. On the seventh day he rested, not only to regain his strength, but because his hatchet and hack saw blade were knackered. I prayed to God it wouldn't go to his head, prompting him to put in an application to renovate the stairs of Belfast City Hall, or somewhere of similar grandeur. Once John was praised for some menial job he performed, his brains ran amok and he thought he could become a genius in whatever he had been doing.

I can honestly say, hand on heart, that my stay in Balaclava Street saw the happiest years of my life. Apart, that is, from that dreadful night in 1964 when insanity grabbed a very small part of the population by the throat and throttled it into semi-consciousness. Thank God sanity eventually prevailed, even though it was only to be a short time before the light of human kindness was eventually to be dimmed to the point where it resembled the flickerings of a melting candle.

I look at my surroundings today – the trappings of modern-day living, such as central heating, wall to wall carpeting, fridge, freezer, microwave, and of course the family car. Or should I say cars, as I watch my eighteen-year-old daughter swan out the front door enveloped in a haze of expensive perfume – the price of which would have kept a family of four for a month in the early 60s – jump into her own vehicle, turn on the radio cassette player and race off with the thud of Heavy Metal or some other inaudible clap-trap ringing in between her nine carat gold earrings – and all of it taken for granted.

No more do I have to sit on an outside toilet with the constant fear of a rat disappearing up my rear end, and hoping the coalman would not make a delivery and catch me with my knickers round my ankles. I have the comfort of deluxe toilet tissue, gentle on the bum yet strong enough for mischievous puppies to trail around the house without fear of it falling apart at the perforations. I can luxuriate up to the armpits in my peach-tinted bath, soaking myself in Marks and Spencer's bath oil. Or pamper myself with creams and lotions, the names of which match the decor of the bathroom – peach, magnolia and forest fern.

Neither do I have to rinse dirty nappies in a bucket of ice cold water in the back yard on a winter's morning until my fingers have turned purple and feeling has left my hands. Or bundle clothes into carrier bags and traipse to the launderette, watch my knickers and John's Y-fronts tumble round in full view of the public only to suffer the indignity of accidentally losing a pair to someone else's wash. Then sit in embarrassment as the entire establishment is brought to a halt while everyone turfs out the contents of their laundry bags to find the missing undergarment. Today, if I do mislay a pair of my knickers, it's probably to the mysterious knicker-snatcher who lurks in the dark depths of my own washing machine, the same ogre who has an appetite for odd socks.

150

Yet I often yearn for those days to return, when you were a name and not a number on a computer, when any cups lucky enough to have handles and be devoid of cracks were kept safely tucked at the back of the kitchen cupboard for use by special guests. Special guests – I'm afraid not too many of those spring to mind except for my mother and father who made the cursory visit in their precious car. I can't for the life of me understand why they bothered, for my mother tried to act as if she had been born with a silver spoon in her ever-open gob while my father stood at the door to make sure none of the peasants touched his precious car.

My sisters visited quite often, Betty's son David once enquiring with a puzzled expression on his face, "Auntie Valerie, why do your cups not have handles like ours?" "We can't afford the handles, son, we'll get those when your Uncle John works some overtime," I replied jokingly.

Betty had blushed with embarrassment, but not quite as much as on the night she helped me carry home a carpet from my other sister's house in Newtownabbey. Never look a gift horse in the mouth, especially when the gift is something you have longed for – in this case a twelve by ten foot carpet. It would not only cover the living room floor but the stairs as well. By a stroke of luck Dorothy happened to be disposing of this item of luxury. I asked Betty, or should I say I beseeched Betty, to help me carry it home before someone else snapped it up. I had the audacity to ask the bus conductor if we could put it on his bus. He took one look at the carpet, then looked along the interior of his bus. "Oh, go on then, lay it in the aisle," he answered resignedly. He spent the journey straddled over the blasted thing trying to collect fares and ended up extremely cheesed off.

When we were alighting he started gurning about the length of time it took us to get the offending item off his bus. Betty looked all flustered and informed him I was to blame, for one had only to say 'Do you want it?' and I would snap up whatever was going. He gave me a look that would have withered an iron rod and pressed the driver's bell twice, an indication to take off again at the double. As the bus roared off up the road I yelled at the top of my voice, "You're bloody lucky it was a carpet and not a bedroom suite, mate!" We had to laugh, and he gave us the two-fingered salute in disgust.

I had good neighbours, some of whom had their little idiosyncrasies (but then don't we all) – all those quirks and foibles that make us human. Especially 'Mr Micawber' across the street, who had taken to wearing carpet slippers and a waistcoat. All he needed was a top hat and the picture would have been perfect.

Annie, the elder of his two sisters, decided to bow out of this world without first putting in a bit of overtime so as to add a few shillings to the kitty, and thereby enable her brother and sister to close for the couple of days normally expected for mourning. In the event, they took the drastic action of closing the business for a period of one whole hour while her remains were hastily ushered out of the shop to be sent to their final resting place in that big grocery store in the sky.

Minnie shed a few tears and blessed herself as the coffin bearing her sister was hastily bundled into the back of a big black limousine more befitting a bride, an honour Annie had been denied in her life. The tears dried faster than spittle on a hot iron, and Minnie and Mr Micawber shuffled back into premises that had been caught in a time warp and declared business as usual.

It is characters like these who add a little spice to our lives. Indeed, if we were all the same it would be a very bland and colourless world to live in. The Divis Street area might then have been achromatic with its many drab-facaded buildings, but it did not lack colour within its kaleidoscopic populace.

Their easy-going attitude towards living, compared to my parents' never-ending rantings and ravings, made me feel optimistic for the first time in my life. My childhood days where safely tucked away in the furthest corners of my mind, apart from those happy memories which we all seem to keep as a safety valve lest we forever feel sorry for ourselves. I doubt very much if there are many people who can look back at their childhood and say in all honesty, 'My childhood was one long happy holiday.' Still, I had enjoyed myself outside the home, being lucky enough to live in a very pleasant part of the country, and I would have been far worse off had I have been in a wheelchair or deaf or blind. I thank the Lord I could claim my cup was half full and not half empty.

Kevin was almost five years old and Stephen almost three when I decided to help out with the financial side of things. John had a steady job on the buses but the wages were low, so another few pounds in the kitty would not go amiss. However, I didn't want to take a job that would entail leaving the children to child-minders. That would have meant breaking my promise of always being there when needed, especially as Stephen was of a nervous disposition. I put this down to the turmoil we all went through when the troubles erupted just outside our home, for until that moment he had been a placid child. After that unsettling experience he started having fits, in the middle of which he would pass out for a few moments. The doctors in the hospital (where he was known as the 'little angel' because of his looks) could find no physical cause and recommended tender loving care rather than medication.

In the end I decided to open a ladies' hairdressers at the top of the street, above a grocer's shop. My friend Carol, she who had turned my hair bright red by accident, now owned her own hairdressing salon. I often helped her at weekends and had picked up quite a bit about styling and cutting hair. Now, a little bit of knowledge is a dangerous thing, and I thought I could become the female version of 'Mr Teazy Weazy' on the Falls Road.

On surveying the premises at close quarters my heart sank. The downstairs living area was falling apart, and the kitchen area was leapin' and badly in need of a new cement floor and proper cupboards. The ancient sink was mingin' with dirt but it did boast an old gas water heater which was attached to the wall – just about! At least it provided hot water at the touch of a match, a little bit of luxury which blinded me to the fact that the rest wasn't fit for human habitation. Not only would it need to be gutted, but John and I realised how much it would cost for renovations. Being broke we had to traipse from one bank to another in search of a loan, with one bank manager after another refusing our request with a curt, "No, I'm afraid not, my dears."

We had almost given up hope, and our dream of owning our own same business was crumbling as fast as the floorboards of the accursed shop. The bank manager who lived above the bank facing us, the same one who had threatened John with the shotgun, was our last resort. He resembled a pit bull terrier and would have scared the crap out of a constipated horse with one of his glares, yet turned out to be an angel in disguise.

Armed with a £200 loan that the bank manager had given us without a quibble, we purchased enough cleaning agents and disinfectant to stock a hospital, rolled up our sleeves and proceeded to renovate what soon became known as 'Valerie's Hairdressing Salon', pensioners half-price. The hairdryers, sinks, mirrors and sundries were all purchased on the never-never. We were up to our eyes in debt and danger but held great expectations. The first six months were fine but we should have taken a leaf from one of Charles Dickens's books. Mr Micawber, for example, and his saying: "Annual income £1, annual expenditure nineteen shillings and sixpence – happiness. Annual income £1, annual expenditure £1 and sixpence – unhappiness." We suffered the latter.

The staff I had employed in good faith soon took advantage of my inability to give orders, and took it into their own hands to come and go as they pleased. As I tried to raise a family in the flat below, as well as helping out as best I could in the shop, unbeknownst to me they were turning customers away so as to get resting their fat asses, with the result that more money was going out than coming in. My nerves started on the downward slope to nowhere, and John had to take an extra job at nights just to help pay the wages of those useless girls. As my health prevented me from taking overall care of business we had no option but to keep them on, and yet no business can really afford to employ passengers.

I started taking to my bed at the same time as the two boys – around seven thirty at night – with depression, and then the panic attacks started, soon to be followed by migraine headaches. I closed the front door to all my friends and pretended to be out. My mind started to play tricks on me, and my parents' warning that 'You will end up living in poverty and praying to idols' kept echoing in my head. And indeed the flat was as near to poverty as one could get. The toilet was not only outside, it was about thirty yards from the flat, dirty and doorless. The men who worked in the grocer's below used it as well which led me to buy a chamber pot to avoid having to use the toilet until they went home.

I stopped visiting my friends in Balaclava Street, while my friends from the Shankill Road, who usually came to get their hair done at the weekends, started to drift away when the political climate began to heat up.

I felt alone and helpless. I was also behaving more and more in a manner reminiscent of my mother, turning in on myself and neglecting the two boys who I had sworn would never want for love. While they pleaded with me to play with them I would lose my temper and put them to bed only to lie alongside them out of self-pity. I even lay in bed one evening listening to my parents knocking at the front door, refusing to answer out of pride. The flat was in one hell of a mess, with me being in a bigger mess as I had completely neglected myself and now resembled a waif badly in need of a good feed and grooming. My parents' words were coming true – I *was* living in abject poverty, it just so happened to be in a Catholic area, and the holy statues in many of the windows stood out as if to torture my brain even further.

I had no reason to feel so despondent. The last time I had such a feeling was when I had been eight years of age and standing in a shop listening to two men criticise me for something I had no control over. They spoke sarcastically about the shabby clothes I wore and how unkempt-looking I appeared, as if a child my age had no feelings. But I did, and ran out of the shop and hid behind a hedge in Musgrave Park and cried. This time, however, there was no hedge to hide behind and cry, only a fusty bedroom that overlooked a grey factory wall and the walls of glass that separated me from reality.

I looked in the wardrobe mirror and didn't like what stared back – a twenty-three-year-old hag in a torn dressing gown with two small children at her side crying out for love. My mother shouted through the letter box, "We know you're in there, open the door! Are you all right? Answer me this instant or your father will get the police!" I then heard her shout hysterically at my father, "Bill, do something for God's sake, I think she's been done in! There's no sound, even from the children!" I heard the car door shut, while my father's voice smothered my mother's ravings with his own frenzied utterances, "For Christ's sake keep your voice down, woman, half the bloody road can hear your maniacal rantings! That's that bollocksin' git she married. I knew no good would come of it; him and his 'I'll take care of her'. He's probably in there with her, holding her against her will."

The tears were streaming from Kevin's eyes as he cried "Open the door, mommy, Granny's shouting." I was crying too, but my feet were rooted to the floor. 'No!' I thought to myself, 'open that door and all's lost. Just a few more minutes and they will be gone. Let them in and they will rule your life all over again, girl.'

Their voices then seemed to disappear into the distance. I felt as if I was drowning as my whole life passed before my eyes. All the bad memories came flooding back: the constant arguments, my mother telling me she never wanted me, the beatings I had to conceal from my father, the fear of being left alone with my mother, that bloody cupboard under the stairs where I used to crouch listening to the mice scurry in the corners, waiting for her temper to subside until she thought it time to let me out. I remembered the look on my father's face as he called me every bad name under the sun, some of which I still didn't understand the meaning of even after being married for six years.

I was brought back to reality by the children's crying. I hugged them close and told them to be quiet. Stephen's sweet little tear-stained face, surrounded by a halo of fluffy blonde hair, looked up at my equally tear-stained face, his bottom lip quivering and his big blue eyes reminding me of a scared rabbit. My heart ached and I lifted him in my arms. I hugged him to my breast and wiped the tears from his cheeks with the palm of my hand. I sat on the edge of the bed with Stephen on my knee, while Kevin jumped up beside us. Children instinctively know when things are not as they should be. They sat as quiet as mice as the hammering and shouting at the door began again unrelentingly.

Just then Mrs O'Brien's familiar voice floated through the bedroom window: "What's all the fuss about, Mrs Linton?"

"It's our Valerie, do you know if she's in? They wouldn't be out with the kids at this hour of the night." It was only eight o'clock. My God, you would have thought it was midnight the way she was carrying on.

Mrs O'Brien came to my rescue like a knight in shining armour. "They're away to the park for a walk, and then they're going to John's mother's."

She was no idiot, Mrs O'Brien; I knew she was deliberately lying, but for why! This placated my parents; they told her to tell me they called and then drove off. After a few minutes she rapped the door and called through the letter box, "Open the door, girl, I know you're in there."

I did as I was told as I trusted Mrs O'Brien. She slipped past me and closed the door behind her. "Now just what are ye playin' at? I haven't seen sight nor hair of ye for weeks. Those kids are not gettin' out, for Kevin hasn't been up to his usual tricks of openin' my front door an' cursin' me up an' down like a trooper." She removed her snuff box from her pocket, a sure sign she was staying for a while.

"He *is* getting out, he's going to school." Well, it was half the truth.

"Ah, he might be going to school, but what happens when he gets home?" she asked, looking me straight in the face. I found it extremely hard to look someone in the eye and lie, so I stared into the fireplace and tried to change the subject.

"Luk at me, my girl, it's me talking, not the bleedin' fireplace." She put her hand on my shoulder and twisted me round to face her. The bladder near my eye had filled up again, and tears of self pity rolled down my cheeks.

"What the hell is this all about, you've changed completely since ye left number 7. Ye were fulla life, now it looks like the dead lice are droppin' aff ye, you're that slow an' gaunt lukin'. Now, I lied to yer parents deliberately, I've sinned to protect ye. It's only fair of ye to at least gimme an explanation as to why you're actin' so strange."

It all came tumbling out: my childhood, all the hassles over getting married, the problems concerning the shop, and the fact that John never seemed to be there when needed.

"Well now, who's feelin' sorry fer themselves then? I don't know fer the love a me why ye moved outta that house in the first place. Pull yersel' together fer the sake o' those childer, and wash your face fer heaven's sake. Tell John he's needed here in the home an' get ridda thon gabshites that are supposed to be runnin' the shop. In fact, get shot of the shop altogether, it's a millstone roun' yer neck."

"Don't blame John, it's not his fault for not being here, we need the extra money," I answered in his defence.

"Don't flatter yersel', it's not John I blame, it's you. Forget about yer past, it's gone. History. Those two childer are yer future plus any others ye might have."

Her words were still ringing in my ears hours after she left. They were indeed words of wisdom, wisdom gained from years of hardship rearing two handicapped sons. I felt very humble and small as I compared her life to mine. I had two healthy sons, I was young and had a good husband, even though my parents thought otherwise.

We sold the shop, just about breaking even and moved back to my parents' house. We couldn't have moved to John's mother's, for it had become overcrowded – with his sister Margaret, her husband and children staying there. John changed his job – he had managed to get work in a car factory, and his wages almost doubled. Our life had started to look up again.

We could live with my parents' arguments, but the straw that broke the camel's back was the day my mother called John a bastard for taking a day off work with the cold. She couldn't have chosen a worse name as John hates it. His own parents never let it pass their lips, and in no way was he going to let my parents use it on him. It was the first time I witnessed John in such a rage. He grabbed my mother by the throat, informing her he had a mother and father but they cared for their children. Now you would think my father would have stood up for my mother in this situation as she begged for his assistance. Not on your nelly – he hid in the bedroom, the yellow streak up his back almost protruding from the top of his head.

"She's bad with her nerves, John." His toady voice could just be heard coming through the keyhole.

"Bad with her nerves! She has the whole effin' house bad with their nerves, mine included! She should be in a friggin' lunatic asylum! Findin' one with the balls to take her would be the only problem."

He let go and my mother scarpered into the bedroom to join my father where they had a lie down to calm their nerves, both gobsmacked by John's reaction. For the first time in their lives someone had stood up to them.

But our lives were still made a misery, even on Christmas day when father handed out the sherry. One glass was filled and passed round like Holy Communion, each person having a sip except for John, who was deliberately left out. We took the hint and decided to move on once again.

After a brief stay with my sister Betty in Dunmurry we were soon settled in a Housing Trust house close by – our first real home with an inside toilet and the luxury of a bath. We nurtured it like a baby, painted it, wallpapered it, hung white lace curtains, and, as a special gift to ourselves, bought our first radiogram on credit. A special offer of £10 worth of records accompanied the purchase.

My boat had come in at last, for £10 bought an awful lot of Elvis records in 1968. Heaven is not the word I would use to express how I felt. Elvis's singing echoed through every room as the volume was turned up full. Had I died and gone to Heaven or what? I was thirteen all over again, only this time no-one told me to turn him off or made fun of me. Not only that but new songs I hadn't heard before were now sending me into another dimension. I thanked God for my new-found happiness, and prayed it would never end.

Chapter 12

MAKE THE WORLD GO AWAY

In August of 1969 the 'Troubles' started with a vengeance. Thankfully the outskirts of the city were relatively free from conflict, but the fear that had been sown in my mind from our 1964 experience had me panicking to the point where every news bulletin gave me the symptoms of the dreaded irritable bowel syndrome. There is no fear like ignorance, the topic of politics not being top of my list of priorities. Catholic married to Protestant became more of an issue to outsiders than the families concerned. My immediate neighbours were very friendly and understanding, but outside influences soon took control as Catholic turned against Protestant and vice versa. The estate we lived in being predominantly Protestant had no other choice other than obey the wishes of the majority. A lot of Catholic families occupied homes in the area but the constant worry of majority rule hovered over one's head like a time bomb.

Indeed, a cloud of civil unrest hung precariously over the heads of everyone at that particular time. Yet the ordinary Joe Soap in the street asked for nothing other than a few shillings in his pocket, or to be greeted with a smile from his neighbours regardless of religion, and to hell with bigots. Maybe if they had thrown all those trouble-making bastards into a field right at the beginning, and let them beat the crap out of one another, it might have been nipped in the bud.

The added worry of being labelled a turncoat did not help my already fragile disposition. Being four months pregnant at the time did not contribute to my wellbeing either. I certainly knew when to pick the most inopportune times to get pregnant. Someone up there must have been at their lark when feeling bored and had the idea: 'I know, let's get Valerie pregnant again. We'll let her get the first few months over with to lull her into a sense of wellbeing, then we'll let all hell break loose.'

On this occasion, it was the beginning of the daddy of all senseless and futile strife over a piece of land the size of a postage stamp which was going to play havoc with my latest attempt at motherhood. I decided to concentrate on self-discipline and willed my brain to disregard thoughts of everything other than getting on with the job of creating new life. I had miscarried six months earlier and I was adamant that this time nothing or no-one was going to interfere with the life that I could just about feel growing within my body.

My mind filled with thoughts of baby clothes, especially little girl's pink dresses, frilly knickers and bonnets. After having two boys, a little girl about the home would have been a welcome change. Not that another son would not have been loved just as much, but a daughter would be the icing on the cake. This was also supposed to be a home birth, but after many false alarms the doctor decided that apart from a stick of dynamite nothing was going to shift this child out of the comfort of the womb, and he sent me into the Jubilee Maternity Hospital.

My much-wanted daughter was forced into this world in the early hours of Tuesday 12 January 1970. The tiny mite took her time in making her first cry, unlike Kevin and Stephen who had exercised their lungs within seconds. Through the haze of pethidine-induced euphoria I could just make out the nurses frantically trying to get that first precious intake of air into my daughter's lungs. The transfiguration a woman experiences after giving birth, the feeling of wellbeing combined with the release from pain, was now replaced with that sixth sense that tells a mother all is not well with her offspring.

The drug-induced stupor lifted as the seconds turned into minutes, panic gripped me and two nurses had to prevent me from jumping off the delivery bed to rush to my daughter's aid. Then, just as I was about to hit out with frustration, she gave a small cry, no louder than a kitten's miaow. I fell back onto the pillow with relief and thanked God she was alive. A nurse placed her in my arms. She was beautiful, her dark swarthy complexion and jet black hair resembling John's father to such a degree she could have been spat out of his mouth. Memories of him flooded my thoughts, and his words 'take good care of her' came vividly back to me. I could almost feel his presence and said a silent prayer, asking God not to forget to tell Thomas Maher he had a new grand-daughter. Somewhere at the back of my mind a tiny voice told me she would need that little bit of extra care.

Nothing could stop the tears of happiness I shed as her delicate little form snuggled against my breast, and I wished that John could have been there at that moment to share the feeling. The novelty of having a daughter led me to change her nappy every hour whether it needed changed or not, just to make sure it hadn't all been a dream. The absence of dangly bits kept reassuring me she was indeed a girl. I was twenty six years of age going on four trying to play house. John laughed at my exuberance when he came to visit me, but I knew in my heart he was every bit as excited as myself. Men feel like heroes when their wives give birth to sons, while for some reason the birth of a daughter has the ability to turn them into soft-hearted teddy bears. John was no exception. When I asked him if he wanted to hold her he almost had a fit. "God no! I will only hurt her, you hold her and I'll look."

"Don't be so daft, you silly bugger! Don't think for one moment this lets you off having to get up in the middle of the night to feed her." Those words were to haunt me for ages.

I was really only booked into the hospital for twenty-four hours – the rest of the confinement was to be spent at home with the family around me, for Kevin and Stephen needed my attention just as much as the new arrival.

On the Wednesday morning the paediatrician had a concerned look on her face as she lingered that bit longer with the stethoscope on my daughter's chest. She left the ward only to return with a second doctor in tow. They took it in turns to examine her, then turned their backs to me, as if in deep conversation. I knew then that tiny voice had been right.

"Mrs Maher, we'll have to keep your baby in hospital for tests."

"Why, what's wrong?" I asked as my heart jumped into my throat.

"Her heart has a murmur." The doctor didn't look me straight in the face as she said it and I instinctively knew it was only part of the truth.

"What does that mean?" I enquired through misted eyes. The background chatter in the ward faded as the sound of my heartbeat filled my ears. I wasn't ready for the answer she gave, not that I could ever have been ready so it didn't really matter.

"It means, I'm afraid, that your daughter might not survive. We just don't know."

Within minutes the little girl I had prayed for was removed from me by a complete stranger without even an explanation as to where she was being taken. I tried to shout 'Please don't take her away', but the words were trapped in my heart just as firmly as those three little words 'I love you' had been held prisoner through lack of love from my parents. But it wasn't any lack of love for my child which held those words back, my heart was breaking from love so overpowering words were totally inadequate.

John entered the ward beaming from ear to ear, carrycot in one hand and bag of baby clothes in the other. I told him through floods of tears what had happened. He turned on his heels and fled out of the ward in search of our child. He came back after what seemed an eternity, crying. He held me in his arms and asked, "What name do you want to give her?"

I couldn't comprehend – why did he want to know her name so urgently? "Why?" I asked.

"I've asked the hospital chaplain to baptise her. They told me the same thing they told you – they said she might not survive the night."

"Call her Heather, Heather Kirsten." I don't know why I picked those names, they just seemed to suit her. Heather grows in the wilds, it's a hardy little plant – maybe it was an omen.

I left the hospital without Heather. I could have stayed with her in a side room just off the intensive care unit, but watching her lying in the incubator and not being able to hold her would have torn even deeper into my heart. I wanted her to be with my family, people who cared, not left sitting alone in a small room listening to the bleep of a monitor as it ticked off every second of my baby's life.

Leaving hospital without your baby, as any new mother facing the same situation can verify, has the same effect as losing a limb. You feel helpless, part of you is left behind, the part that is invisible to the naked eye of others. Yet you need this part to function as a mother to the children at home. Your physical being is all very well, they can see the physical you, but they want to share the loving you, which is impossible when you can't be in two places at the one time. I found it very difficult to function at all and neglected the two boys yet again, depriving them of a mother's love as I sat upstairs pining for my daughter like a cat that's lost its kittens.

My parents called at the house that night expecting to see Heather, my father angry at me for not coming down the stairs to welcome them and wanting to know what all the fuss was about. Betty and John told him I was very upset and wanted to be left alone. They were dumbfounded by his response: "I always think if a child's meant for this world it will live. If it isn't it won't, so what's the use of worrying." John's anger was so intense he had to leave the room, either that or kill my father on the spot. Betty told my father he wasn't worth hanging after making such a remark.

The hospital rang the next day to tell us to come up as they needed our permission for tests which had to be carried out on Heather. Had I known then what the tests were for I doubt very much if my nervous system could have handled it all. I later learnt they had tested her for Down's Syndrome as well as for being spastic. Her thick black hair, and enlarged tongue, which I had not noticed, were cause for alarm, and the fact that she had a heart murmur only added to their suspicions.

After performing a lumbar puncture they were able to discount the first two suspicions. They did, however, say her heart was definitely not as it should be. I wept at the sight that met me the following day when we went to visit her. Heather lay naked, her tiny arms tied to the sides of the incubator to restrict her movements, and she was lost in a sea of wires and patches that were monitoring her heart. Her beautiful shock of black hair had been shaved off as she had to have a drip inserted in her head; she was being fed through a tube inserted in her nose; and she was covered in plasters where they had taken blood. It was impossible to hold her, and I watched helplessly as her tiny chest heaved with every breath.

God! how she resembled John's father, I thought, even to her laboured breathing. The doctors still couldn't say whether she would live and that night as I lay in bed I prayed to God. Please God, spare her, her life is in your hands. I wanted the world to go away, and yet where there was life there was hope. I even took it into my head to let on I was buying a pram to test the doctors' reaction. If they said I could it would give me a hint as to whether they felt she would survive. I didn't give a damn if I had to wheel her in a cardboard box as long as she lived – I was clutching at straws. I thought to myself that the day they said 'Go buy a pram' it would be a sign of hope.

On the tenth day of her life they finally said those four precious words and it felt as if she had been reborn. I couldn't have given her a better name. Like the hardy heather that grew wild in the fields, she battled all weathers. They diagnosed a hole in her heart the size of a sixpence. However, they refused to operate unless her health deteriorated to the point where it would be an absolute necessity. We were told that if she got through the first year of her life she would stand a better chance of survival.

For that first year John and I hardly slept, with Heather close beside our bed while we took it in turns to watch her every breath. She attended a heart specialist every week and then fortnightly. He was amazed at how healthy she looked and couldn't understand why she wasn't breathless or cyanosed, as the lobes of her lungs were congested. She did take a lot of chest infections but otherwise she was a mystery to the medical profession.

To us she was a little miracle, a miracle we prayed for night and day, and with the help of the Almighty she made it to the age of nine when they closed the hole after a seven hour operation. Today this operation is relatively safe, but in the early 70s heart surgery was pretty much touch and go. It was a very traumatic time for all concerned.

When Heather was seventeen months old I gave birth to my third son, Peter John, on 28 July 1971. His was a difficult birth – he too had obviously decided to continue this family tradition. Just to keep us on our toes he was born with a congenital hip defect and had to lie in a frog splint for five months. One of the most distressing aspects was having to listen to people's exaggerations or fend off nosey parkers, some of whom had exaggerated Peter's hip defect to the point where he apparently had no legs.

So here I was running from one hospital to the other – one week the Belfast City Hospital with Heather, the next the Royal Victoria with Peter. Thank the Lord I was young and fit, otherwise I might have ended up in the Mater Hospital with heart failure. John would then have had to run around like a blue-arsed fly as he ministered to all three of us. The only hospital left would have been the mental institution where, more than likely, he would have been finally admitted suffering from exhaustion.

Through it all we still had the bigots objecting to our religious state. We just couldn't win – being a mixed marriage, even though I had turned a Catholic, was an uphill battle. We had the Protestant bigots at our throats and the Catholic bigots up our backsides. Trying to stay neutral was almost an impossibility, but we managed it. It wasn't the people who had lived in the estate for a long time who started this business of discrimination against Catholics. A lot of hard-line Protestant families who couldn't stand the thought of trying to be friendly to their Catholic neighbours had moved from other areas in an attempt to wreak havoc among those who could. This also happened the other way round, making one side as bad as the other, and the people who suffered in the end were the innocent.

One business to prosper at that particular time was that of the flag maker, and the Twelfth of July celebrations became an excuse to suss out the orange from the green. Flag madness gripped the nation by the short and curlies; like a Rottweiller it clamped its jaws round the balls of sanity and any Protestant or Catholic foolish enough not to purchase either a Union Jack or Irish Tricolour found themselves being labelled a traitor.

My sister Betty, who lived in the same estate and who had never flown a flag in her life, was ordered by complete strangers to hang out a flag or else join her Lundy of a sister. I felt bad that day – my sister and her family were being penalized for my sins. Apologies were no comfort. Anyway, my concerns for Heather and Peter were more immediate than having to worry about hoodlums hell bent on disrupting the community. These hoodlums most likely led very boring lives – a few family problems thrown their way might have prevented them from taking to the streets simply for the thrill of adding a little spice to their lives. At least I could sleep in my bed at night with a clear conscience.

The Seventies for some reason brought on a hunger for earthly possessions, credit facilities escalated and whatever one desired could be obtained by a simple stroke of the pen. Catalogues filled with offers of everything from socks to Chesterfield suites took pride of place in every home worth its salt. Payment for a candlewick bedspread, sheepskin rug, plus a set of loose covers for the three-piece suite, could be spread over twenty weeks. We became obsessed with material belongings as a substitute for neighbourly kindness, and the day of the ever-open door was fast becoming a thing of the past. Television took precedence over loving thy neighbour and visitors were subjected to watching the box rather than enjoy good conversation. Indeed, the good old days of conversation and consolation were rapidly disappearing for good.

John's signature made me the proud owner of my first washing machine after the birth of our fourth child. With the help of my Burco boiler, rows of brilliant white nappies now blew in the wind, a far cry from the bucket of cold water in the backyard that served no other purpose than to cause chilblains and turn the nappies grey and hard. We bought our first car the same year, and part of John's hard-earned wages was signed over to a finance company for a period of three years. It was a ludicrous thing to do as there was only about a year's life left in the rust-encrusted jalopy. It sat outside the door more often than found itself on the move, for we couldn't always afford to buy petrol. It did have its uses, however, in times of crisis. One of these emergencies involved ferrying my mother to the hospital when my father took a heart attack. For all John's faults he did come in handy when the time suited.

I am aware a heart attack is not an excuse for frivolity but in this case what would have been cause for concern for most families turned out to be a farce for mine. John sat outside the City Hospital in the car while my mother visited my father. An hour passed and John didn't know whether to go in to see if all was well, when mother finally appeared. Her face had a hunted look and she was on the verge of tears. John almost felt pity for the old battle-axe and opened the passenger door to help her in, words of comfort tripping from his tongue, for he thought the way she was acting meant Bill was close to death.

"Don't distress yourself, now, he will be all right, the doctors can work wonders these days. Where would you like me to take you? Maybe a wee drink will settle your nerves?"

She glared at him, the tears ceased and a wild expression replaced the hunted look that had just a few seconds earlier been imprinted upon her face. She yelled in exasperation, "For Christ's sake, hurry up and get this car up the road! Take me to the nearest phone 'till I have a word with the Prudential man. I want to make sure Bill's insurance policies are up to date!"

John asked her if he was going to be all right. She gave him a look that would have sent shivers up Dracula and shrieked, "He will better be all right! If he dies without insurance he'll just have to go into the bin!" Bill did, however, survive and her thoughts of a spending spree on the proceeds of his insurance were short-lived.

In 1973 we moved to Lambeg, after saving the deposit for a house of our own, to escape the intimidation and threats that were being directed our way by individuals acting in the belief they were doing their duty in the name of God and Ulster. At the same time,

Protestants doing nothing apart from minding their own business were being forced out of their homes by people who didn't know who the hell *they* were fighting for, other than it was somehow in the name of Ireland.

A two-mile move up the road in Ireland can have the same effect as emigrating. We were living in another world where people of all religions could mix without fear of being petrol-bombed or labelled.

Our fifth and last child, Shauna Louise, was born to us in Lambeg on 20 June 1974. Anyone who tries to say that the more you have the easier the birth, is talking through their backside. I pulled the knickers off the midwife in the final throes of labour in my efforts to bring this child into the world. I meant to grab hold of the hem of her uniform just to hold on to something while bearing down, but missed and my hand went up her skirt and I grabbed the leg of her knickers by mistake. If every labour ward had a swear box the proceeds would most likely keep the Health Service's head above water. I cursed John in and out of hell, along with all the rest of the world's males for being so sex-orientated.

When Shauna was born, the nurse placed her in my arms. Her eyes were wide open and I swear I could almost detect a stifled giggle as she looked me straight in the eye with a Donald Duck look imprinted on her tiny face. I thanked the Lord she was perfect but added: no more, Lord, no more.

Paying the mortgage and feeding the family were our main priorities – the added luxuries of modern-day living were a bonus. Central heating and ceiling-to-floor curtains plus the now almost obligatory wall-to-wall carpeting enveloped and cossetted us to the point where we imagined life wasn't worth living without them. A piece of *objet d'art* strategically placed for the benefit of friends and relations lulled us into a false sense of wellbeing and we became complacent. Our priorities were up the left and when John's job collapsed it felt as if we had been hit with a ton of bricks.

Our complacency was now replaced with uncertainty – we had become the victims of our own naivety. We had bitten off more than we could chew; the economic climate was not going to stay at the same temperature just to keep John and Valerie Maher up to the standard to which they had become accustomed, gained out of more signatures than sense. The end result meant having to sell.

We moved to Antrim in 1975 in the hope of starting a new life in a new town. Had I had the powers to see into the future I would have gone down on bended knee to the building society to keep our home in Lambeg. I would have happily scrubbed floors, brushed streets – I was going to say 'sold my body' only that would be going slightly over the top – anything to stay where we were, for over the next thirteen years I was to make a slow journey to hell and back.

165

Chapter 13

LIFE

If someone were to stop me in the street and ask directions to Antrim, I would be tempted to remark, "For Christ's sake don't sneeze when you hit the top of it, for you'll miss it as you drive out." On the other hand, don't be misled by its size – small *can* be beautiful. Unlike larger towns, the air is clean and fresh, free from pollution. The people of Antrim are proud of their little piece of green, and rightly so. I myself find that the longer I reside in this part of the country the more it reminds me of Elvis's song 'K-u-i-po', which means 'I love you' in Hawaii. The words being: 'I love you more today, more today than yesterday; but I love you less today, less than I will tomorrow.' Corny perhaps, but as Antrim is inclined to grow on you, nevertheless true. After a lock of years, as the locals would say, you begin to blend in with the surroundings as the tranquillity envelops you like a cloak of green velvet.

The Antrim born and reared folk are on the whole friendly but clannish. This could be a throwback to an earlier time in our history when the town was ruled by clansmen. Of course, this could apply to almost anywhere in Ireland when at one time we used to beat the brains out of each other with clubs and shillelaghs. We never really stopped, the weapons have just became more sophisticated.

Eighteen miles separate Antrim from Belfast, yet the dialect of Belfast-born people stands out like a sore thumb compared to the fast, almost Scots-like tongue that is evident in Antrim and its surrounding areas. Your first ten years in Antrim could be described as the revision years. The following five years are spent passing the examinations. You know you've passed with distinction when you can talk to one of the natives for half an hour and you've understood every word that has passed their lips. When that pockle from Ahoghill could almost be yourself, the wan who lives a wheen o' miles up the road.

When we first set up home in 1975 the Housing Executive was building estates on the periphery at such speed Antrim town was like a pot of rice which had boiled over. We were allocated a house in one of these estates. As soon as I set foot over the doorstep, for some unknown reason my heart sank to the pit of my stomach.

It felt as if it had no soul, not helped by the fact it had been built ass about face – the 'front' door being at the 'back', an anomaly which had visitors bewildered to the point of distraction. Whenever we opened the door to their timid knock we found them scratching their heads, wondering why the dustbin had been keeping company with the letter box and the kitchen, instead of the living room, was pointing into the garden.

Compared to our bright and cheerful semi-detached home in Lambeg with its dawn chorus and panoramic view over pastures where cows browsed contentedly upon lush grass, the grey sombre rows of colourless boxes which passed for houses in Antrim were, to say the least, disheartening.

Life appeared to be taking on the momentum of a yo-yo. Two years up, two years down – it was beginning to grate on my nerves. Some people might say that at least it wasn't predictable. One thing's for sure, it was never boring. Taking into account the times we lived with relatives, this was our thirteenth move since the day we walked up the aisle. Unlucky for some you might be tempted to think, and you would be right.

The notion of buying a mobile home and taking up a life as nomads had entered our minds on more than one occasion. I knew in my heart this stay would not be the last, but tried to make the best of a bad deal. The house served its purpose. It was exactly that – a house, but not a home. In fact it was haunted – yes, haunted. If someone had told me that a new house could be inhabited by the departed from this earth, I would have told them to take a hike. Ghosts and ghouls maybe only existed in horror films, but I can swear, with hand on heart, that that house was home to the unknown.

It all started one hot summer's evening when the house went as cold as an ice box. John and I had retired to bed after a long exhausting day, a day when cold drinks and ice lollipops had been doled out to the kids in an effort to keep them cool, especially the youngest, Shauna, who had whinged non-stop since early morning. We were the last to retire, the rest of the family having gone to bed early and now fast asleep – though not for long.

"Mum! Heather's standing at the bottom of my bed, will you come and tell her to go back to her own room, she won't go for me," Kevin shouted from his bedroom.

"Oh, bloody Nora," moaned John, who had almost been on the verge of falling asleep. "Just tell her to get back to bed – I'm exhausted."

"I did, Da – she must be sleep-walking."

John got out of bed, albeit unwillingly, and went into Kevin's bedroom.

"Where is she?" John asked, scratching his head and yawning.

"She's vanished!"

"Where to?" asked John.

"I don't know, she just disappeared!"

John went into Heather's room and found her fast asleep, the bedclothes unruffled.

"You must have been dreaming, you half wit, she's fast asleep!" he hissed at Kevin, for he did not appreciate playing games at twelve o'clock midnight.

But Kevin insisted that a girl Heather's age had been standing at the bottom of his bed, crying. What little hair John had stood on end as he listened to Kevin's description of the girl, and the long white dress he insisted she was wearing seemed to indicate that Kevin had not confused her with his sister, for Heather had been wearing pyjamas. At first we thought Kevin had imagined it all, but as the weeks went by he saw her several times, always in white and always crying. On another occasion, there were three loud raps on the front door, followed almost immediately by three loud raps on our bedroom door. When I say loud I mean loud – they shook the house to its foundations. John and I lay in bed terrified after the booming had stopped. The children told us the next morning they had heard it too but had been afraid and hid under the bedclothes.

We told no-one as we thought they would have labelled us nuts, and just accepted our mysterious guests, even though we were scared witless on many an occasion. Lights went on and off for no apparent reason, the toilet flushed on its own, cupboard doors opened and slammed shut, cups flew through the air – one almost took off John's ear as it whizzed past his head. Ice cold water was poured over us as we lay in bed, soaking us to the skin.

Somehow, the family got used to the 'happenings', as we called them, and we even joked about asking 'them' for rent. We had more ghostly visitations than I care to remember, but then again I suppose no life is complete unless you have had a good haunting. It always goes down as a good party piece. We tell the story but not everyone believes us, and yet I swear to God it is the truth. We do have a couple of outside witnesses, but they too feel stupid when people don't believe them, so they keep it to themselves rather than be laughed at.

A couple of years later, on the very day we vacated the house, whatever it was within that dwelling departed with us, for the glass on the front door exploded outwards. It left a perfectly round hole, so perfect it seemed that nothing natural could have made it, for it was done with the precision of a glass cutter.

John's mother's health deteriorated. Her stay in this world had lost all meaning since the death of her beloved Tommy. However, she had managed to endure fourteen years of heartache. She had no fear of death, she looked forward to being with her husband for eternity and prepared to meet her maker. I knew she had finally lost the will to live by her attitude. The hearth that used to shine with glittering brass was now strewn with ashes as she spent her time staring into the flames with lifeless eyes. She often told me she had visions of Tommy when she was on her own, that he had been beckoning to her for quite a while now. I often remarked, "Don't talk like that, Ellen. I don't want you to leave us, I couldn't bear to say goodbye to someone who has been more of a mother to me than my own kith and kin." Sometimes I held her hand as she spoke like this and she often added, "It'll be you that's goin' tae be haulin' my haun when it happens, Val."

"For goodness sake, Ellen, catch yourself on, I would pass out with fright. Anyway, you're not going and that's that." The way I said it you would have thought she was a child asking for permission to go outside.

"It's nat the dead ye shud be afeerd aff, it's the livin' ye have tae watch, sure the dead wudne harm ye." Words of wisdom. I remembered my ghosts and shuddered.

"For Christ's sake, Ellen, give over."

"That's enough a that, nye, don't take the Lord's name in vain." I felt small in her presence and slapped myself on the back of the hand as a sign of punishment.

In August 1975 she suffered a stroke and went into a coma. While in the coma she deteriorated, and a second stroke left her as helpless as a newborn babe. The hospital staff were insistent we talk to her as if she was conscious; we were not to assume she could not hear even though every other bodily function had ceased. The family took it in turns to sit by her side night and day, it being bad enough that she had to leave the comfort of her own bed without being left to suffer on her own.

Finally the doctors realised the end was near. The curtains were drawn around her bed as a final act of respect, to hide from public view the distress of a dying woman's last intake of air. The bedside lamp that shone directly onto her bed only served to add insult to injury by shadowing her pitiful condition upon the curtain.

My mind wandered back to Tommy's death and how he had been spared the indignity of losing control over body and mind. Ellen was being denied this final graceful curtain call. She did not deserve it and for a brief moment I felt angry with God, only to be brought to my senses by the memory of her words: "Tommy's beckonin' me, it's time tae go."

When she drew her last breath I felt no sadness, I felt no fear. I felt honoured and thanked God for having given me the privilege of having known her and to have been there to say goodbye before her soul left her body. I looked down. I was holding her hand and it was the most peaceful experience in my whole life.

Cancer. This word has the ability to strike fear into the bravest of men. My father was not brave, so when my mother was informed of his condition she made the family promise not to tell him or even mention the word 'cancer' in his presence. He had been diagnosed as having cancer of the stomach which then spread to his oesophagus – in other words it was inoperable, and he was given six months to live. I had just got over the death of Ellen when my mother told me of my father's illness.

Somehow Ellen's death, apart from having to watch her lying so helpless in a strange bed, had not been a frightening experience. Her spiritual strength was a comfort and lesson to all the family. My father on the other hand had nothing to lean on, he did not have faith in God – well, if he had it didn't show – but he was no fool. I am convinced he knew of his condition, for all of a sudden my mother became his strength. Ever since I had been able to understand my parents, my father had made it perfectly clear that he considered my mother nothing other than a nuisance whom he tolerated through gritted teeth. Now he would hardly let her out of his sight as she catered to his every whim. Of course she took this as a sign of affection and boasted that Bill could not live without her, as if it had been this way all their married life, while behind her back he gave her venomous looks which spoke volumes of bitterness. He was silently thinking: 'Why is that bitch so healthy while I feel so ill and helpless.' I know he was thinking this as he often let his guard slip and said it under his breath.

Such a contrast to John's parents. There is no law that states you must 'love' your parents; until a certain age the law only says you must 'obey' your parents. The Bible tells us to 'honour thy father and thy mother', which obviously means to accord them proper respect. As my parents never accorded me much respect, or for that matter demonstrated any love or affection, I found it extremely difficult to show any in return. I felt pity and anger over my father's illness – pity for the suffering he had to endure, and anger at myself for not being capable of telling him the truth.

Why could I not bring down the wall of glass that protected me, why could I not smash it and tell him? Perhaps I was as big a coward as he was. Trying to pretend all was in order when in his company was a terrible strain. He kept asking us why he didn't appear to be getting any better, especially if it was seemingly only a stomach ulcer. My mother convinced him that this was the reason he couldn't keep anything in his stomach for more than five minutes. They had moved from the bungalow in Stockman's Lane the year before in somewhat of a panic. My father was penny-wise and pound-foolish, and had not made provision for his retirement years. Never in his life had he thought a big strong healthy man could succumb to illness – in his mind he would work forever. His heart attack three years earlier had put an end to his high position in the organ works. He was not as indispensable as he had thought. Where business is concerned the weeds are soon plucked out to make way for young healthy shrubs, and he was plucked and thrown by the wayside.

As he owned the bungalow outright he sold up, paying cash for a smaller home. My mother found herself back where she started – in a two up, two down terrace house. Not only had my mother lost her pride and joy – the bungalow which nestled with the crème de la crème of society – she now had a new set of neighbours to fight with, only this time they told her to go to hell and shut her gurny gob. Who in blazes did she think she was anyway, they told her, trying to act all hoity-toity when the ignorance was hanging out of her?

Her mind started to work overtime. She knew Bill wasn't long for this earth and began to make plans for her future. A trip to America to visit her three sons (who had all emigrated by now) after his death was arranged in her mind. She would sell the house and, armed with a few thousand quid, plonk herself on one of her three sons. She hadn't taken into consideration the fact that none of her offspring was fond enough of her to let her live with them – the seeds of contempt she had sown when her children had needed her were now bearing fruit. Her children quite frankly couldn't give a damn. Indeed, the reason the three sons had emigrated to America in the first instance was out of frustration and of feeling worthless in the eyes of their parents – not the call of the Wild West. The three daughters had found love outside the Linton household and were making up for lost years by giving their own children a taste of the honey of which they themselves had been deprived.

As for my father's upper crust friends, they had now ousted him from their lives since he was of no further use without his health. The hands that were once supple and capable of fashioning out of wood luxuries such as wall panelling, solid mahogany dressers and whatever else made a home into a showpiece, were now weak with fatigue as his cancerous condition worsened. The heart that used to soften at the prospect of creating masterpieces was now as hard as stone as he watched the friends he once thought more of than his wife and children, carry on living life to the full without ever once enquiring about his health. They had used him, sapped everything he had to offer and now discarded him.

Mother squeezed what little love he had for life clean out of him by constantly reminding him that he had been used all his life by these so-called friends – but not to worry, for she would take good care of him. He didn't need friends, he had her. He despised her even more, but couldn't show his disdain outwardly, and instead tapped into her strength, picking at her continually. He convinced her he had been a good husband and father by emotional blackmail, repeating over and over, "You're my strength, Lottie, you always have been," until she actually believed it, and lifted and laid him, mistaking need for love. This was all more emotionally painful for the family than witnessing two people genuinely in love hold each other for comfort when one partner is dying.

The bitterness he felt knew no bounds. He was filled with rancour to the extent he even begrudged his sons and grandsons their youth. He openly expressed this hostility towards youth by putting the blame for all the troubles in Northern Ireland on everyone under the age of twenty. This included his own grandchildren, none of whom would have harmed a hair on your head.

"Curse the lot of them," he would say, "they should all have been drowned at birth." And he meant it. To yearn for lost youth, when one has led an active and healthy life up until the ripe old age of seventy, to the extent of cursing your own flesh and blood is not only amoral it is surely a mortal sin. I prayed to God to forgive him, for I found it impossible to turn the other cheek.

The doctor's prognosis of a probable six-months life expectancy passed and a further year went by. Mother became a trifle impatient but yet still jumped to attention when Bill cracked the whip. The neighbours tried in vain to win Lottie over to their side with offers of help in her time of need. Lottie was too proud to accept, she became a martyr and one would have been forgiven for thinking she really cared about Bill's wellbeing. The truth of the matter was that she had Bill where she had always wanted him – relying on her alone and by her side constantly. It is a sorry state of affairs when after forty-two years of marriage it takes a terminal illness to make two people share each other's company, albeit out of necessity.

She was just about at the end of her tether when Bill was admitted to hospital in the latter half of 1976 after taking a turn for the worse. Being thankful for the respite she went on the rampage with Bill's cheque book, treating herself to a new wardrobe of clothes for her forthcoming visit to Uncle Sam which would follow when Bill finally kicked the bucket and made his way to that big organ works in the sky.

Her new finery was carefully hidden away – old dresses were placed over new on clothes-hangers, shoes were left in boxes or placed on top of the wardrobe and covered with blankets. She became as secretive as a drug addict and her stash of forbidden fruit was guarded with all the cunning of a fox. After every visit to the hospital she returned home sweating with relief, for during these visits she was not only under the strain of having to avoid any mention of the dreaded 'C' word, but she had to keep the state of Bill's bank balance from his notice. His body may well have been deteriorating but his brain was firing on all cylinders and he still guarded his money with prudence – there just might be a few pockets in *his* shroud.

Of course she shed the obligatory tear expected of a woman who would soon be losing her husband. The family were not impressed or taken in by this pretend grief – we told her to save her 'sorrow' in case a miracle occurred and Bill survived. Her crocodile tears soon turned to tears of unmitigated fear when the doctor informed her: "For some unknown reason, Mrs Linton, your husband has taken a dramatic turn for the better. We just can't understand it. He has the constitution of a horse – any other man with his condition would have died a year ago."

Had I not witnessed her reaction to this remark, I could be forgiven for calling the person who described the ensuing scene by the name 'Hans Christian Anderson', for only someone with his vivid imagination would have been capable of making up the story. Her face turned puce – had she had a face-lift the day before it would have dropped to her feet with the fright. In an indignant and breathless voice she snapped back, "What do you mean a turn for the better? Only yesterday he was staring death in the face. No! no! no! The man's dying, you must have made a very grave mistake. Bill just can't be on the mend, he's got cancer, you know!"

"I'm quite aware he's got cancer, Mrs Linton, but the man has a will of iron. In cases like this no-one knows what goes on in the human body."

She heched and peched up the corridor swinging her handbag in the manner of a demented trouser-presser. After a few seconds her strength was spent, she faintingly made her way back into the side room that the doctor used for discussing the patient's progress and plonked herself down on a seat in a state of self-inflicted exhaustion. The tears welled in her eyes and she opened her handbag, pulled out a well-used hanky and wiped the sweat from her brow. Her large bosom heaved with her efforts to regain control of the situation and the same hanky was used to soak up the moisture that had gathered in her cleavage. It was only when the doctor had mistaken this melodramatic act as a sign of relief – and not the actions of a woman fraught with fear at the thought of being caught out forging her husband's signature on his cheque book – and patted her on the back with words of what he thought to be comfort, that she broke down completely and cried tears the size of which would have filled a spirit measure.

"Now, now, Mrs Linton, good news can sometimes have a strange effect on the mind. Go and see your husband, he's looking forward to seeing you."

That did it! There was only one reason Bill would be looking forward to seeing mother – not out of love, but out of curiosity, to see how the finances were faring in his absence. She glared at the doctor who was now smiling at her with a saintly expression imprinted on his face, as if it was he himself who had miraculously brought Bill back from the grasp of the grim reaper. His smile soon disappeared when she glared at him with the eyes of Medussa, and the poor crathur turned the colour of stone and backed off as if he had just witnessed the coming of the Antichrist.

Betty, who had also been witness to this embarrassing scene, tried to make apologies for my mother. She steered mother out of the door by the elbow and once out of earshot of the doctor told her to get her backside up the corridor and into the ward, pronto.

"I don't want to go in on my own, your father's going to ask questions."

"That's your problem, mother," Betty hissed. "I'm going to have to make excuses for your bloody ignorant behaviour to that doctor. I don't want him thinking we're all raving lunatics in the family."

When we made it back to the side room the doctor was sitting with his head cupped in his hands. He looked up when he heard us shifting about in the doorway and I could detect a quiver in his voice when he enquired what our return visit was in aid of.

"That woman's not right in the head," Betty told him, pleading in my direction with her eyes for moral support. "The fall she had from a tram when she was young led to concussion and she has been suffering flashbacks on and off ever since."

Looking back we should have made our escape while we were still ahead, as it only added fuel to his already bewildered state. He shook his head and said, "Well, God does work in mysterious ways, his wonders to behold. And if you don't mind me saying, but that mother of yours could well be the eighth wonder of the world – most people would be elated with the news I gave her."

We beat a hasty retreat and toyed with the idea of hanging mother with the strap of her handbag whenever we got home. Serving a life sentence in jail soon put that thought out of our minds – we had already served more than a life sentence being reared by her.

Following his return from hospital father sat huddled by the fireside wrapped in layers of clothes in an attempt to hide his weight loss. He had always been proud of his well-built physique and often boasted to those of puny stature of having a forty-four inch chest measurement. Before his illness he frequently insulted his sons-in-law by removing his jacket and, throwing it in their direction, make the snide remark, "Here, try that on, I bet it will hang on your shoulders like a tent. You young ones now are built like kippers, a bit of hard work would kill you stone dead. Take a tip from a man who's never been on the dole in his life. Start graftin' and stop mollycoddlin' your wives." This last remark was spat out with venom, as the very idea of spoiling mother with love would have been anathema to him. He always looked in her direction when he said it and screwed up his face as if he had swallowed a mouthful of vinegar.

The layers of clothes did him no favours other than accentuate his emaciated body. His features looked even more Draconian now that the flesh on his face had all but disappeared, and his nose had a pinched look about it. The steel grey eyes that once put the fear of hell into me were now lifeless – they appeared to be searching his own mind for answers and were clouded with the film of tears that he always seemed to be holding back. The mouth that was once capable of spewing forth dirty-minded remarks was drawn back and his false teeth defied the law of gravity, giving him a fixed sickly grin that unnerved a person to the point of almost making them beg him to remove them. His long bony fingers were stained yellow with nicotine from the cigarettes that he almost smoked – half the time he forgot he had lit one and absent-mindedly let it burn down to the cork tip, only to stub it out in the ashtray and automatically light another as if he were worked by strings.

He must have known he was dying. He only had to look in the mirror – which he avoided doing. He sat in his chair by the fire when using his electric razor and shaved by touch. He became even more cantankerous than usual with mother, and, for all her faults, she took all his crotchety remarks with a stiff upper lip and martyred herself to the point of no return. The family begged her to tell the man the truth. We thought it was his right to know, to come to terms with the fact his life was almost at an end, so that he could put his life in order and make his peace with God.

"Your father doesn't believe in God," she would snap back. What she really meant was that *she* didn't believe in God, and anyway no minister of the church was going to get his foot through the Linton door. The only thing ministers were good at was sitting like vultures waiting on their prey to die in order to get their name included in the will when the aule mind wasn't thinking straight.

"They are a load of sanctimonious parasites – all dog-collar and mouth. Take the dog collar off them and they are just like any other men, in fact they are worse. Wolves in sheep's clothing; they would leave a widow woman begging in the street just so long as their cassocks were lined with the hard-earned cash of honest men who have kicked the bucket."

"How long do you intend keeping it from him?" Betty enquired after one of these outbursts.

"Right to the end. His name has been put down for Beaconsfield

Hospice, the staff there see they don't suffer." *'They'* ? Did she think people were dogs and not humans? "He will be drugged to the point of not knowing whether he's coming or going, so I've been told. If he asks out straight what's wrong with him when he goes in, tell him it's to build up his strength."

"If he asks, I'm telling him, he's begging with his eyes for help. He mightn't have been the best father or husband in the world but he is human. In the name of Christ he's got a bloody brain and he's not stupid. Do you intend going round the other dying patients warning them: 'Oh, whatever you do, don't tell Bill you're dying. If you feel like snuffing it shuffle out to the toilet and go quietly'." We were all in complete agreement with Betty on this point, but mother was adamant and used the excuse of her nerves giving in as blackmail.

In the middle of January of 1977 he was readmitted to hospital. This time he had no remission. His gullet had almost closed and he was literally starving to death, his diet consisting of nothing other than liquid nourishment. A few spoonfuls of clear soup plus a sip of water was just about all he could manage. Why he never questioned the reason for this abnormal eating disorder remains a mystery. Nothing will convince me he was unaware of his impending departure from this earth.

Mother was present at every visit. No-one was allowed to be left on their own with him for fear that a slip of the tongue would make him suspicious. When the time came for him to be transferred to the hospice, the delicate task of breaking the news tactfully added an extra burden to what was already a major dilemma. Who would be the most capable of handling the situation with tact? The three sons living in America made it even harder for those left behind to cope. Had we been a close-knit family, visiting relatives might have helped ease the burden mother had put on our shoulders. As for friends, well, it would have been easier to extract blood from a stone than to get them to even sit in the same room as my mother, for she had drained the sap of kindness out of those who genuinely cared for my father. By rights the eldest son should have been brought over to see my father for the last time, but mother dug her heels in even further. No way could one of the boys come over – such an act would definitely put the cat among the pigeons.

To add to our problems Dorothy had taken a cancer phobia to the point were every pain or ache meant taking a trip to the doctor for a full examination to ease her mind. Nothing or no-one could convince her that cancer wasn't contagious. Her body went into sympathy with my father's, she took on his symptoms, her stomach refused to accept food and she lost weight through lack of nourishment. In normal circumstances families pulled ranks in a situation such as this, but normality in the Linton home was as elusive as bottling the wind. Trying to keep hold of one's sanity, never mind trying to act normal, became a battle in itself.

My own life had been one battle after another. Heather's heart condition had to be taken into consideration. Her life was virtually only beginning, and the prospect of a nine-hour operation with a fifty-fifty chance of survival was a constant worry to John and I. How my mother had the bare-faced cheek to ask her children to be compassionate towards her husband after he had previously been so dismissive of Heather's right to life was beyond comprehension.

In the end Betty told him he had to go to Beaconsfield Hospice. She dutifully informed him against her own better judgement it was in order to build up his strength. His eyes spoke volumes after she had finished relaying this fairytale mother had concocted. He gave her such a piercing look it chilled her to the bone, as if to say 'You lying bitch, why don't you tell the truth? You're putting me away to die.' A single tear rolled down his cheek. He wiped it away with the cuff of his pyjama sleeve and, shrugging his shoulders in resignation, lay back on his pillow and stared at the ceiling.

He never looked Betty straight in the eyes again. Betty was sent to Coventry over something she had been made to say against her will, and what little feelings she had held for my mother were now torn from her. The love/hate relationship changed to indifference, to no feelings at all, which in a way was worse.

The hospice was set among beautiful gardens, where the birds sang and the gardens flourished with evergreen trees and bushes, even though it was winter. The entrance to the main building did not appear clinical, in fact one would have been forgiven for mistaking it for the lobby of a hotel with its emerald green carpet, potted plants and reclining chairs. This look was not confined to the entrance for the benefit of visiting friends and relatives, or to camouflage what lay beyond – the bright airy atmosphere continued throughout. The staff were not austere or unapproachable, they were warm and gentle. Your surname was put to the side after your first visit and you were greeted by your Christian name as if you had been a friend for life.

My own worries over how to act or what to say in a hospice were soon dispelled when a young lad in his early teens came prancing up the corridor in full disco gear, flared trousers, fitted jacket and platform shoes – the full works. He grabbed a nurse round the waist and asked her to run away with him for a fortnight of passion. It was only when she accidentally knocked off the trendy headgear he was wearing and revealed his scarred bald head did I realise he was a patient. Yet here he was full of the joys of life, a young lad in the springtime of his years enjoying what little time he had left. The sound of his laughter echoed in my ears and for a few minutes I thought of my father's embittered attitude towards the youth of that time, and while my heart prompted me to tell him to thank God for reaching at least the autumn of his years my head told me to bite my tongue.

The duplicity of feelings within the immediate family did nothing to help my father's pathetic fight for life. Oh, he smiled at the nurses, all right, he even managed the odd joke and convinced them he was the life and soul of the ward. As soon as they were out of sight he became his usual self and the sound of silence was almost deafening as he picked our brains with his eyes.

As each day went by he became increasingly frail until he was no more that seven stone in weight, less than half the man he used to be. Through his drug-induced stupor he still managed to instil fear into his wife and children without having to utter a word. As his death became imminent his hands appeared to be grabbing at invisible ropes, unseen images. It was so distressing I had to leave his bedside. I prayed to God to take him, to free him from his misery, and unashamedly I asked God to give the family back its freedom. The freedom to carry on with our lives without the feelings of guilt at having our own health and strength.

I stood at the door and put up that invisible wall of glass, this time to protect me from reality. As long as it didn't shatter I felt like an outsider looking in. Whatever lay behind could not touch me even though I could see and hear it. Each second of his last hours he inhaled life and fought for it, holding on to it as death's grisly form cast a shadow of darkness over his hospital bed. With every last ounce of strength left in his cancer-ridden body, he clung to the one woman whose strength was unquestionable.

"Lottie," he gasped, hoping that her touch would inspire greater strength for this, his last fight. Tragically this was not to be and slowly he began to lose his battle – he was slipping and his drugged rasps finally turned into a shocking silence. I felt nothing but pity for a man who had so frantically fought to hold on to life. His death was not dignified or peaceful.

It was, in many ways, both traumatic and unemotional for a physically and emotionally drained family – a blessed relief. Mother did not shed a tear and arranged his funeral with military precision, even managing a bit of shopping in between visiting the coroner and the funeral parlour where he would be laid out for those wanting to pay their last respects. She even had the bare-faced cheek to ask a minister to attend the funeral service after all her talk of them being nothing more than vultures.

The poor man said all the niceties expected of him and my brother Alan, who had come over from America for the funeral, told me he had the urge to look into the coffin to see if the minister was talking about the same person we had called 'father'.

After his cremation on a cold grey day in February my mother made the remark, "I'm glad your father was cremated, it's such a cold day." To this day I cannot for the life of me see what difference it made, but at least it put a smile on the faces of the mourners who had been trying their best to put on a show of sadness. This chapter may appear depressing and indeed the title 'LIFE' may not be the word that would spring to mind when talking of death. But as the words of Elvis's song 'LIFE' imply – life is love and love is life, love would make us all, while hate would surely make us fall – I think it appropriate. Life is everlasting, God saw to that when he breathed the breath of life into our souls. He also professed to making the perfect man who understood, yet he must have lost his way in the people factory when he produced William Linton.

My father's death marked the passing of a man I can still see standing there with his Draconian stare, laughing at other people's misfortunes, calling everything and everyone a load of bollocks – and yes, sometimes I see a funny man in long-johns making me laugh. In life not everything is bad, people do have a good side to their nature no matter how small. If you take the time to open your eyes, to ponder on life now and then, you will find that good side and smile.

This period was also the prelude to probably the most tragic part of my own life – when I had to fight to hold on to my sanity, my family and ultimately my life.

Chapter 14

EDGE OF REALITY

On the morning of Tuesday, 17 August 1977, the sun shone over Antrim. The dull grey barrack-style houses were bathed in a warm yellow shroud, giving the estate an almost Mediterranean glow. As I dandered slowly home from the primary school where I had just deposited Heather and Peter, I felt the urge to give the house a bit of a belated spring clean. It's amazing what a little sunshine can do for the soul. Especially one that's had its fair share of life's battering ram thumped in its guts. Since my father's death earlier in the year, depression had become an unwelcome lodger in the Maher household. This situation, however, was not solely the result of my father losing his pathetic fight for life. No, fate had conjured up a special challenge for me – a challenge that would wreck me physically and leave very deep emotional scars – scars that will never heal.

Despite losing his job in the car factory, John was determined to put clothes on our backs, bread on the table and pay the bills that five fast-growing children incurred. Northern Ireland, however, was not the best part of the world to be living in at that particular time if you found yourself out of work. A man had to take work where he found it, and for those with the will to work the prison service offered good employment.

It was open season for gunmen and bigots, who at the slightest excuse would stalk their prey, to dictate with the gun just who had the right to live and who had not. We now had all the ingredients of a recipe for disaster: a mixed marriage, John's new job and a desire for peace. The latter did not gel too well with those people who demanded justice with the fervour of frenzied head-hunters, no matter if it meant killing innocents who got in their way.

The only politics we believed in were the politics of living. Life is beset with many pitfalls; adding a few more for good measure on your own bat is not only foolhardy it demands a prompt examination of the brain to find out if it is in full working order.

Shauna was helping me clean the house the way only a three-year-old is capable of – by moving the dust around rather than actually removing it, using a piece of old shirt as a duster. To help soothe my nerves I turned down the sound on the television, put my favourite Elvis L.P. on the record player and turned its volume high. Elvis's voice was still salve to a troubled mind after twenty-one years, when he first came into my life at the age of thirteen and my nervous system was being bombarded with worries that now appeared almost trivial compared to the problems married life and unseen forces had thrust upon me. The news on television only annoyed me further by adding fuel to my fertile imagination. Death and the starving millions in the world were two topics I couldn't handle without feelings of guilt. I felt powerless over both and often took the coward's way out by not listening – what you don't know won't upset you.

I had been miming to the words of 'Wooden Heart' with Shauna, at the same time vacuuming the carpet in pace with the beat, when Elvis's face appeared on the television screen.

The first thing that entered my mind was that it was news of him coming to England for a concert tour, and I excitedly turned up the volume, my heart beating wildly at the thoughts of the one and only Elvis Presley gracing the British Isles with his presence. I managed to hear the tail end of the newsflash – "Elvis Presley died at the age of forty-two at his home 'Graceland', yesterday, the 16th of August."

The vacuum cleaner was still humming, Elvis had just finished singing 'Wooden Heart', and the next song 'Surrender' soon replaced the light-hearted side of his voice with the more dynamic tones with which we usually associated him. The newscaster, the vacuum cleaner and Elvis all intermingled with each other and time stood still while I stared transfixed at the television, the news of his death refusing to register in my brain.

"Mommy, dance." Shauna was pulling at my hand in her impatience to start our little dance all over again.

"Shushh love, Elvis is dead." I picked her up in my arms and sat down on the settee, without turning off the cleaner, the television or the record player. The poor child didn't know what I was gabbling about but sensed something was amiss and burst out crying. This brought me to my senses and I hugged her tight and smoothed her blonde hair. "It's all right, love, mommy's just being silly."

All of a sudden the sun didn't shine anymore. The day that had begun with the kiss of summer sunshine, the same sun that had temporarily dispelled the cloud of depression which hung over my head like a veil of black lace, had now been replaced with the dark shadow of disbelief. I switched off the vacuum cleaner and the television set but not the record player. Elvis's voice echoed round the living room, contradicting the news that had just a few minutes ago made my heart sink to the pit of my stomach. It felt very strange, to say the least, as if someone had just told you a member of the family had died, yet there they were still talking to you. No, they must have made a mistake. Elvis dead? Never! Sure the man radiated life? Even those who didn't particularly like him had to admit, albeit reluctantly, that he had a certain something no other entertainer could buy – how could that have been taken away? As yet the world was unaware of his illnesses and prescribed drugs, though of course there had been rumours. There was talk too of a book written by three of his so-called friends, detailing his sordid life and drug-taking, but his fans had dismissed it all as the idle gossip of jealous contenders. And, anyway, weren't they all at it, dabbling with the happy pills and wacky baccy – if you were to believe all you heard.

The 16th of August – but sure this was the 17th? How come a dedicated fan like myself could miss news as important as this. I had forgotten to take into account the time difference and the fact that America was at least five hours behind us. By the time the news would have reached us it would have been in the evening. As I had retired to bed early last night, without listening to the news, I had been left completely unaware.

I looked out of the window for signs of life, to ask somebody, anybody, if the news I had just heard was true, my mind still refusing to accept it. Apart from a few children engaged in a game of football the street was deserted. I couldn't settle, I had to confirm the news one way or another. The telephone rang just as I was about to pick up the receiver to call my sister, and even before I answered I knew what the person on the other end was going to say.

"Did you hear the news, Val?" Sophie, one of my friends from further up the street, asked in a cautious voice. I knew she was being deliberately cautious just in case I hadn't heard.

"I can't believe it, Sophie, just don't say those three words." She knew I meant 'ELVIS IS DEAD'. As I replaced the receiver a light drizzle transformed the previously sunny morning into a very grey midday, this sudden change in weather matching my altered state of mind. The man who had kept me sane through times of stress just by the sound of his voice had gone, the dream of someday seeing him in the flesh was shattered. Tears of self pity streamed down my cheeks. My mind wandered back to the days when I thought he was singing for me alone; now I felt as if I was the only person in the world mourning his demise. By the end of the day my eyes were as red with crying as my voice was hoarse with talking. Everyone I met that day had their own special memories of Elvis. The teenagers' reminiscences were of a young romantic Elvis, who always got the girl in the movie; while those of my own ilk – who had been present at the birth, you might say, when he grabbed the youth of the middle Fifties by their drain pipe trousers and duck's ass hairstyles and put rhythm in their souls – had their own memories of seeing him transformed from a shy blonde-haired pimply, but otherwise handsome young man who threw out a childish innocence, into a dark-haired handsome Greek God radiating sex appeal and confidence. And just like the day President Kennedy was assassinated we would all remember what we were doing when we heard the news of Elvis's death.

Humanity has its fair share of cynics, and it was inevitable that some of them would come up with the jibe, 'It was a great career move, he's selling more records now he's dead than when he was alive.' And indeed his records and tapes now began to disappear from the shelves like snow from a ditch. But sure this happens in all walks of life. Authors, artists, actors, pop stars – many of them don't become famous until they are six foot under the clay. Eddie Cochran, The Big Bopper, Buddy Holly, Ritchie Valens, and now Elvis – legends who will never grow old. We had a wake for Elvis but we never buried him, he lived on in our minds and life went on as if he had never died at all. His presence was sorely missed but the memory lived on in our hearts – we would always love him tenderly. Your life does not grind to a halt every time someone important to you dies, even if they have been a beacon of light when your own candle of life has at times barely flickered, but it is still traumatic. My father's death had left me physically and mentally scarred; Elvis's death had now ripped apart my emotions.

The world was not going to become a better place to live in to suit Valerie Maher, the terrorists in Northern Ireland were not going to turn hippie overnight and resort to flower power and plant tulips instead of bombs. John's job had my nervous system so uptight my nerve ends were fighting their way through my skin and I found myself starting arguments at the slightest provocation. Instead of comforting one another when the going got tough we were at each other's throats like pit bull terriers.

The job itself was not the problem. As soon as John was behind the gates I knew he was safe, for his attitude towards the inmates was strictly non-biased. As far as he was concerned he was neither judge nor jury. It was not his job to say who was right or wrong, he was only there to look after their welfare, to protect them from each other. No, John had put his life on the firing line to feed his family; he never complained, unlike most of his so-called friends who had now deserted him as if he were contaminated with a deadly disease. As with many of his contemporaries he could not voice his inner thoughts, his constant feeling of being like a hunted fox. If he did let his guard slip he never got any sympathy, only remarks such as 'Well, that's the price you have to pay, you shouldn't have joined in the first bloody place.' No, it was not the job, it was the people who objected to his job who were the problem.

My blood boiled when his family or friends avoided him like the plague. Of course, there were those who had no option other than avoid him, people he knew who lived in troubled areas. Prison officers were looked upon as the lowest of the low by those who sympathised with the extremes, be it loyalist or nationalist. As John looked after both sides he was a traitor according to his friends of a nationalist persuasion, and a Fenian informer to those of a loyalist persuasion. It was a 'no win' situation.

Crises can sometimes bring people closer together. In our case it drove a wedge between us. John earned good money all right but he had to put in the hours, and being left on one's own to rear five children without a father to keep them under control was tantamount to being a single parent. I felt piqued and was easily provoked into outbursts of resentment at how other wives could be taken out for the night to the cinema or to the pub for a drink, while *our* social life was non-existent, apart from mixing with other prison officers who were in the same boat. And so a vicious circle formed around us. I was on a short fuse and so was John. We grunted at each other like cavemen. That was on the good days – on the bad days we yelled. Stress leads to tiredness, and the time he spent at home invariably saw him lying exhausted on the settee, snoring his head off, while my frustration and temper knew no bounds.

Most husbands are met with a gentle kiss on the cheek and words of endearment on their arrival home from work, but John had to duck flying crockery plus the language of a fishwife, lest he wanted to feel the caress of a plate wrapped round his head. Our sexual relationship was more akin to that of the black widow spider who eats the male's head after mating, and as John was fondly attached to his head he decided it safer to avoid making sexual advances in case I took a cannibalistic streak and ate the bake of him. Our marriage had now almost reached the point of no return – we did not look at each other, we only snarled at each other.

The arguments were also having a detrimental effect on the children, which was very wrong – I should have had the wit to realise the effect continuously arguing parents have on their offspring, and exercised more decorum. Wrapped in our cloaks of self pity we forgot to take into account that children are very quick on the uptake. They detected the atmosphere of uneasiness, the younger ones became fractious and their little quirks and foibles, which once made us laugh, were an irritant to our now nervous dispositions, while the two elder boys became openly rebellious. Refusing to follow house rules they took to staying out late at night, giving back cheek and behaving obnoxiously as their act of defiance.

Kevin, who was now at grammar school, really needed our support as he was continuously studying, but had to do so without the help of loving parents. As a backup to his frustrations he took to motorbike racing in an attempt to vent his anger at our inability to cope as parents. He became an angry young man and frequently lost his temper whenever anyone didn't agree with his motorbike revving at midnight and the pools of black sticky oil in the driveway. He painted his bedroom deep purple. For good measure he deposited bits and pieces of an oily motorbike under the bed and littered the rest of the room with whatever wouldn't fit underneath, a Freudian attempt to make a statement about how he viewed life in general – dark, depressing and cluttered.

Stephen took to mitching school and drinking beer while he hid in the local forest, safe from the prying eyes of the teachers, or so he thought. He was soon caught out and became defiant when challenged. He adopted the stance of a boxer, jutted out his chin and, looking me straight in the eye, protested, "So! What are you going to do about it?" Giving him a good hiding would not have solved the problem. Even though my mind was in turmoil I had the sense to realise this. In a roundabout way they were screaming for attention. With hindsight I can't blame them, we were unintentionally ignoring them as we fought for our own sanity.

We tried to rear our children with the belief that everyone has the right to live regardless of whatever their religion may be. I thought I had made a good job of this when one of my children asked if Ian Paisley was the Pope – at least I knew they were not interested in the politics of Northern Ireland, a sign they did not want to be involved in the religious divide. It was a comfort to me to know that through all our ups and downs we had managed to safeguard them from the grasp of bigots.

"Australia!"

I woke up with a jolt to see John pacing up and down the living room like the Pink Panther.

"Australia, that's the place to be – it's as far away as one can get from this bloody country. Bar-b-ques on the beach, permanent sunshine and gorgeous girls in bikinis."

I had been having a welcome doze in the armchair after bathing and bedding three young children, who had earlier been putting me round the bend with their incessant bickering over who should have the last chocolate biscuit. I rubbed the sleep from my bleary eyes and in between yawns informed John, "If you don't stop acting like Phileas Fogg and Walter Mitty rolled into one I'll ram this poker up your ass."

"I'm telling you, Val – Australia, it's the only answer. We'll sell everything and bugger off."

I was perplexed as to how the hell we were going to work that idea into our hectic life and enquired, "How in the name of all that's holy could we get to Australia?"

"I've already seen to that," John said, balancing on his toes as he perched beside the chair, looking like a hen ready to lay an egg. "I was on the phone to my brother and he said to come over on a return ticket. If we get there we can claim emigration status once we land. It's a lot easier than applying for it over here."

"What about Heather? She has to have her heart operation." I must admit I felt a little excited at the prospect and all signs of tiredness left me.

"There're hospitals over there, it's all been taken care of, Val. Come on, give it a go. We've nothing to lose and everything to gain." Famous last words. "Sure it will be better for the kids, it'll get them out of this hell-hole."

I foolishly let myself be carried away with the excitement of the moment and agreed to everything. My spirits lifted, we even started to joke. "Maybe your boobs will grow, Val; everything grows bigger in the sun they say."

"In that case you had better stay off the Ozzy beer, in case you get a beer belly – nothing grows in the shade."

"Well, I'm a big boy now, Val, I'm sure there's no growth left down under."

We felt elated at the thought of breaking free. For the first time in ages we laughed together instead of biting the heads off one another. Now and then doubt raised its ugly head but my brain was tired and my resistance was low – anything for a quiet life. We put the wheels in motion and applied for visas. The visas were granted but they must have smelt a rat – John's had 'NO WORK PERMITTED' stamped in large letters across it.

In our naivety we took misguided advice – that once there we could fight bureaucracy, it was only a hiccup. Everything we owned was either sold or given away. We said our farewells to family and friends through tear-filled eyes, gave up our home and left Ireland with six suitcases and the clothes we stood up in.

Once in Australia we walked the vast streets of Melbourne in search of accommodation, but with five children no-one was interested. Neither was bureaucracy. They were not in the least concerned with our plight – no Green Card, no work.

A hasty decision had to be made – take our chances and begin a new fight in a strange country or go home to an age-old conflict and a country we knew. We chose the latter – the devil you know is better than the devil you don't know. Twelve days later we were back in Ireland, the shortest emigration in history. The so-called land of milk and honey was soured by no jobs and no future, the sight of so many nationalities thrown together made us feel like refugees – as indeed we were.

The Antipodean experience cost us dearly. We never even got the opportunity to wear a cork trimmed hat, John never had the chance of drinking a XXXX beer, and we were now much worse off than before. The house we had left in Antrim had not been re-let so we managed to get it back, much to the amusement of those people who only a handful of days before had waved us goodbye and bon voyage. What little self-esteem we had left soon disappeared out the window, hastened by the snide remarks of so-called friends and neighbours who delighted in making fools of us by asking 'Did you only go over to see the time?' John had to tuck his tail between his legs, and cap in hand applied to regain the job he had given up in the vain hope of making a new life for us in more peaceful surroundings. He had a good work record, so they accepted his application. He would have been better signing on the dole or accepting charity, for his desire to better our lives by working all hours God sent to rebuild our home almost cost us the ultimate sacrifice – his life and mine.

No-one offered to hand back the items we had given away before we set out on our journey of disappointment. Our only remaining possessions apart from our clothes were two packing cases filled with a few of the necessities of life we had packed before going to Australia. Luckily for us the warehouse had not shipped them out or we would have had nothing.

£180 – that's what we had in the kitty towards rebuilding our home; this bought us a few beds to sleep on. Two of our friends managed to salvage an old chesterfield suite from a rubbish tip and very grateful we were at that. We cooked on a borrowed gas picnic stove and stew became our staple diet. The children never set eyes on their father as he worked around the clock, until within the year we were back on our feet and our worldly possessions had been replaced, though at a price. The up and down momentum of our life had gradually weakened the string of the yo-yo. Something had to give and unfortunately it was our marriage.

Today it happens to the best of families, but then it was still a stigma to admit to a marriage breakdown, and the neighbours had a field day at our expense. I was glad my father had died otherwise his words of 'It will never last' would only have made the situation worse. There are none so blind as those who cannot see – we were both to blame and yet each tried to blame the other.

I accused John of tricking me into emigrating to get me away from my family and friends so he could have me all to himself out of jealousy. Because I had lost interest in the sexual side of our marriage he took it as being personal, and assumed I didn't want him anymore. The truth of the matter was that I had been left alone for most of the time and had retreated into a shell. I now wanted to be on my own, in fact so much so I would have been happy living in the cupboard under the stairs to escape the realities of life. My mind refused to accept the obvious – he had given up all he had worked for because of my neurotic state, to save me from cracking up and to save our crumbling marriage.

. We separated. The whole affair was messy and embarrassing. Not an experience to be undertaken lightly. Arguments from old are brought to the fore and exaggerated out of all proportion; you cast aspersions and you use the children as pawns. Your whole life becomes a goldfish bowl as solicitors pick your memory for something to use as grounds for separation. In our case nothing could be found other than incompatibility.

A marital separation brings out the worst in people and they do stupid things, though funny moments can also come to the fore. I can still see John racing out of the house after the court case with his mother's china coffee set and standard lamp tucked under his arm. Luckily for him the milk bottle I had thrown after him just missed his head.

We spent six months apart, six months of hell that could have been prevented if we had only taken the time to think. We were not to blame for the breakdown of a marriage, we were simply among the lesser victims of this country's campaign of bitterness. The bigots who couldn't stand to see two people of different religions live in harmony had won a tiny battle and laughed behind our backs while we stood by in ignorance and let them. The pathetic sight of five children suffering for our stupid behaviour and the sound of two adults acting like children in a game of 'I don't want to play house' finally brought us to our senses and we decided to start all over again. This time we would beat the system, prove to ourselves and others that we had the strength to overcome all the odds.

Heather had been used to hospitals over her short nine years, so they held no fear to her, which I suppose was a blessing. Needles and X-rays were part of her life; she posed for X-rays as if she was just having her photograph taken, and when the results were shown to her her eyes lit up. "That's me, inside out," she informed the doctor as if he didn't know.

"Is that right, Heather? I think it's a bag of bones."

"There's a hole in my heart, you know. Here, put your hand on my chest and feel."

She laughed and giggled when he felt her wee heart buzzing away like a bumble bee trying to escape. An adult would have been petrified, a child on the other hand hasn't the sense to worry – nature's sedative.

Signing the form to give permission for the surgeon to operate felt like signing her life away. The seventy/thirty chance of survival were not the greatest of odds. On the other hand, if she didn't have the operation her life expectancy, plus the quality of her life, could not be assured. Hobson's choice! At half-past two in the afternoon on a wet Tuesday the phone rang, exactly the time the surgeon told us he would ring with news.

"The operation was a success, Mrs Maher."

I couldn't reply I was so pent-up with emotion.

"Mrs Maher! Mrs Maher, I said the operation was a success, your daughter's out of surgery and doing well."

"Thank you, Mr McClelland, I did hear, I'm just so relieved I can't speak."

"I understand Mrs Maher, we are as relieved as you are. The operation lasted six hours."

I cried with relief. John, who had been standing beside me misunderstood my tears of relief as tears of sadness and his face turned the colour of clay. "She's over it and well, our daughter's well, our daughter's well." We held each other and wept with joy.

The sound of artificial breathing and the heart monitor was deafening as well as frightening. Her life depended on machinery and I wouldn't have bet twopence on her recovery at the sight that met us the following day. An uncovered scar the length of her chest was held together with clips. Wires and tubes were attached to almost every part of her body and the bleep of the heart monitor was the only indication of life other than the slight rise and fall of her tiny chest. The nurses quietly and deftly went about their duties, changing drips and replacing tubes with confidence. They tried to allay our fears with words of comfort as they sensed our anxiety.

"Wait 'till you see her in a day or two, it's not as bad as it looks.

188

Children have a built-in resilience to operations and illness. They don't fight it, for, unlike adults, they are not so afraid of dying. Maybe you would be better going home and coming back tomorrow." Just as I was bending down to give Heather a kiss before leaving she regained consciousness.

"Take me home, mommie." This was heart-rending.

"I would if I could love," I answered through misted eyes. I tried to hold back the tears for her benefit, but she went back to sleep as quickly as she had woken.

"It's all wrong," I said to John. "This is not the order of things, parents are supposed to die before their children. It should be you or me lying there, not our daughter."

"Heather's not going to die, Val. The nurse just told us we won't know her in a day or two. It looks worse than it is. She's a fighter, she always has been."

I could see the tears in his eyes, but he held them back.

"It's still all wrong, even if she was 50 years old and I was 76, it would still be wrong, she is our child and always will be."

I looked over my shoulder as I left the ward, my heart feeling the same way it had when the nurse took her away from me when she was a day old. Her nine years had flown by as if it were only yesterday.

On the Friday Heather was in the main ward, sitting up and playing with her dolls. She looked as bright as a button and was ordering the nurses around. Once again she had lived up to her name – children are indeed resilient. She never looked back and today at the age of 24 is travelling the world with the energy of two people and the determination of four. She goes trekking, horse riding, plays squash and tennis and manages to hold down a demanding job in between. A credit to the dedication of the nurses, doctors and surgeons who are so often taken for granted.

Shortly after Heather came out of hospital we moved house yet again – we were delighted to be finally leaving the back to front house. We bought a house in 'The Folly'. We should have looked up the meaning of the name before buying, as the word 'Folly' suited it down to the ground. My nervous system never got a long-enough break between crises to heal on its own. I was born on a Thursday, and 'Thursday's child is full of woe'. By God, whoever penned that line was dead right. I could have spent my entire life repeating 'Woe is me, woe is me!' Thank God my sense of humour comes to the fore or I would have thrown myself under a bus long ago. It was going to take one hell of a good sense of humour to get me over the next eight years.

We were in fits of laughter, laughter that makes the body ache, on a ladies' night out (a sexy underwear party to be precise) at the

Newtownabbey home of a friend of my sister Dorothy. A toothless hag of elephantine proportions had been modelling a see-through nightie for the amusement of those present.

"By Jaysus, the man that gets the haule a that on a dark night wud have his hauns ful, plenty to haule on tae. Thon's nat love handles, thur like the dur handles af Belfast Castle." An elderly woman who had come for the laugh was being the life and soul of the party; she had even brought her own carry-out of wine, for to her a cup of tea and a biscuit were more for a Women's Institute night out on the art of flower arranging, not for a night where everyone was having a bit of a geg at the sight of peep-hole bras and sexy knickers with the gusset removed.

The door bell rang and the elephantine female made a bee-line for the kitchen to hide, her large backside taking a good two seconds to catch up with the rest of her anatomy as she disappeared round the door. The laughter almost drowned out the loud knock that followed.

"In the name af heavens, it's the polis!" cried the elderly woman as she hid her wine behind the settee. This made us laugh even louder and we reminded her there was no law against having a drink.

"Aye I know that, but it might be agin the law tae run aroun' the house in yer drawers. Maybe there wus a chink in the curtain an' they cud see in!"

"For frig sake, Aggie, give over, will ye! Wouldn't it be worse if you were the one paradin' about." Phylis, who lived in the house, opened the door and Jack, my brother-in-law, rushed in, and for some unknown reason I knew it was news for me. Call it second sense but I knew it was about John and my laughter dried up.

"You've to go straight home, Val. John was on the phone to me just now. He said to lock the doors and pull the curtains and make sure the lads are in."

An awful silence replaced the sound of laughter and we just stared at Jack as if he had told us World War III had started.

"I think you had better go, it seems there's a bit of bother."

"He's been shot!" I fell back into a chair with the feeling of weakness that had now crept into my legs with the shock.

"You don't know that now," Jack said. "Anyway, he couldn't have been shot – he was the one that rang, for heaven's sake!"

"Well, what's the spot of bother that entails having to lock all doors, close all curtains and get the boys in!" I was hysterical by now as I knew rightly what it meant. My brain took on a sense of unreality and the sea of faces that were looking in my direction all seemed to merge together.

"I'm sorry, Jack, I don't mean to shout, but what exactly did he say?"

"That's all he said, apart from saying he'd ring you when you got home."

I don't remember leaving that girl's house apart from breaking a glass shelf in her hall as I ran out the door. The car journey home is also a blur in my mind. I went up the motorway at the speed of light. How I didn't have an accident God only knows. John's instructions were carried out to the letter. I sent the babysitter home, tried not to show any signs of stress to the children and sat patiently waiting for the phone to ring. As soon as it rang I grabbed the receiver and yelled down the phone.

"John, what's wrong?"

"This is the police barracks, Mrs Maher. We have your husband here."

"Well bloody put him on, then!" In my highly-strung state I forgot to be polite but didn't care. John came on the phone and I breathed a sigh of relief, though the relief was to be temporary.

"Val, don't worry, I'm safe. Did you do what Jack told you?"

Don't worry! You'd have to have had your head chopped off not to worry in a situation like that. It turned out there was a bullet out with John's name on it. By whom and from what source no-one would tell. He had been told to take it seriously, to be thankful the information had fallen into the right hands at the right time or he wouldn't have made it home that night. To this day I don't know and don't want to know who was going to carry out the killing, it could have been either side.

All I know is that whoever had planned it had no right – John would not have deserved it, he had never harmed anyone in his life, he was just an easy target. Like so many others who have lost their lives in this bloody awful conflict. He would have been a name on a gravestone and remembered by no-one other than his family, and for what – for trying to earn a living?

"I have to go back to the jail, Val, the police won't let me come home. It just means lying low for a while."

It just means lying low for a while? Christ, this was something you hear in a gangster movie, not over the telephone in an ordinary working-class home.

"For how long, for Christ's sake?" I yelled down the phone.

"For a week or two, that's all. Just keep the boys in at night and don't open the door to anyone – now I mean no-one who can't identify themselves."

He tried his best to reassure me that as long as he was away things would be all right. I was not convinced but I had to be strong for the family, so I put on a pretend front while my inside fell apart. I lived life on the edge of reality, the glass wall that usually protected me shattered and fear became a constant bed companion. During the day the shadows followed me and the nights didn't set me free

191

with the relief of sleep. In retrospect I should have been counselled and maybe I might not have been caught up in a world of prescribed drug addiction, but then the world is full of maybes and mights. I went to the doctor for help. He was very sympathetic to my situation and could well understand my inability to sleep. He prescribed 'Halcion', now more commonly known by its generic name of Triazolam, and for the first time in weeks I slept. At last my mind could rest, albeit at night with the help of a drug. It never entered my mind that a prescribed drug could destroy one's life in the way that little blue pill could. An innocent-looking tablet not much larger than a matchhead would now control my life. I courted insanity with every one that passed my lips.

John's couple of weeks away from home turned into months, and the longer he stayed away the longer I had to take the pills – until I was finally hooked. The doctors themselves, I am sure, were on the verge of nervous breakdowns listening to other people's problems. I absolve the doctors from all responsibility when they prescribed me those pills; they were acting in good faith. The drug manufacturer is to blame for not testing them properly. For eight long years I walked the halls of surrealism as I frantically fought to hold on to life for the sake of my husband and children – I literally lived on the edge of reality.

Chapter 15

HELP ME (To help you forget)

'Not tonight my little blue beauty, back into the bottle you go. I don't need you anymore, I'm going to make it on my own.' I was talking to myself again, usually a sign of money in the bank or the onset of madness. It could only have been the latter, for our bank statements made a laughing stock of the former. The bank manager had stopped sending demanding letters, now being at the pleading stage. It wasn't a case of 'With humble heart on bended knee I'm begging you please Help Me'. More a case of 'Please Pay Me'. Fans of Elvis will recognise lines from his song 'Help Me'. The words of this song were to hold special meaning for the way I would feel for years to come. I thought I could make it on my own that night – I was proved wrong.

John's three month stay in the prison had passed, a three month sentence imposed on him for not committing a crime. He had no sooner got used to lying in his own bed at night when his refresher course meant another fortnight away from his family. I pleaded with him not to leave me and the children on our own again so soon after the horror the previous months had inflicted upon us. The politics of life are always unfair and the long road I had travelled had had its fair share of tragedy, laughter, tears and smiles, but I had reached this new crossroads and did not know where to turn. I needed some respite from the constant fear that a gunman lurked round every corner. I needed John to comfort me, even if it was only at night, and now this small comfort was again being denied. He had no choice in the matter. When the powers-that-be call, you have to jump to attention. His mental strength was much greater than mine, he couldn't understand my need for moral support and unwittingly said all the wrong words.

"Pull yourself together, woman – fight it." I turned on him like a rabid dog, my saliva hitting him in the face as I screamed, without stopping for an intake of breath. "Pull myself together! DAMN YOU, Mr Psychologist – since when have you been an expert on the workings of the mind! If I could 'pull myself together', as you so calmly say, I wouldn't need the help of bloody drugs!"

He wiped the spit from his face and gave me a disgusted look.

"I'm the one whose life was threatened – why the hell are *you* goin' to pieces. If I can cope, why the friggin' hell can't you?"

"I'll tell you why I can't cope. I'm the one who has to stay in the house, worry about the boys, watch the bloody army jeeps pass the house six times a day and answer the flamin' door to strangers while you are tucked safely away behind bars as if you were a criminal. Go on, get out, leave your wife and kids to the fate of maniacs!"

"The only maniac about is you! For Christ's sake pull yourself together, I won't tell you again! Living in this house is worse than hell itself. Sure you have a look of the devil imprinted on your face."

It was true. I had changed, my whole personality had taken a horrible twist. My sense of humour was non-existent, I didn't want friends to call anymore, and my day was spent pacing the house crying. The metamorphosis from happy-go-lucky to drug-crazed had started to take form like a thief in the night; my brain had laced up its trainers and gone walkabout.

John left the house and I was so incensed I failed to see the hurt on his face. In my state of self-induced pity I couldn't understand it was safer for him to be out of the house – at least the intended prey would not be there. I mockingly laughed at his words 'Pull yourself together'. If a person could pull themselves together half the mental hospitals would not be needed. Those three words had angered me to the point of almost turning me inside out with exasperation.

I again felt piqued that I should be left all alone to protect our five children while John was once more tucked safely away from the horrors of living and constantly looking over one's shoulder. I knew the hunters were still on the loose. Seeing as they had missed their intended target they just might turn their attention on another member of the family. I was not going to pretend to act all saintly, turn all wifey-wifey and stand by my man. Women who put their husbands on pedestals, or for that matter let them walk all over them, are definitely not my kind of women.

John was a good husband and father, that I couldn't deny, but he was human, and humans have failings. He failed to comprehend how terrified I felt that day and so I became very angry. In my anger I made the decision to try and make myself a stronger person. One of the ways of achieving this meant going without my little helpers, as I now called my pills. 'What are you, anyway? You're small and insignificant. What could possibly be so strong as to make a little pill such as yourself make a tormented mind calm down? No, it's all in the mind.'

I put the small brown plastic bottle on the top shelf of the kitchen cupboard and went to bed. But then, as I lay in the darkness the strangest sensations took hold of my body. My hair felt as if it was standing on end, my body felt as if it had been put in the fridge then taken out and placed before a raging fire. My skin felt as if it was going to shed like a snake discarding its outer coat. My heart started to skip beats, the air that I breathed felt as cold as ice and my mind began to play tricks. Did I live in Dunmurry, Lambeg or Stockman's Lane? What did you call my children? For that matter, how many children did I have?

I turned on the bedside light with trembling hands and jumped from the bed. The light did not bathe the room in its usual soft pink glow, it hurt my eyes as if a torch had been aimed straight into my face. A newspaper lay on the floor beside the bed, and out of curiosity I looked at its date, hoping it would help fit the pieces of the jigsaw together.

The date meant nothing to me, but the headlines – 'Two people shot in West Belfast' – made me tremble. This has something to do with the way I am at the moment, I thought, but why? My body was shaking uncontrollably and I tried taking deep breaths to get some oxygen into my brain. I felt as if I was having an 'out of body' experience, as if I was looking back at myself.

Slowly my life fell into place. I remembered I had five children, even though I had to go through the alphabet to put names to their faces. The mirror on the dressing table, the glass that tells no lies, reflected a shuddering wreck of a human being. Eyes with huge black rings underneath stared back, set in a skeleton thinly covered in a white sweaty skin. This was not the reflection of a thirty-eight-year-old woman, it was a surrealist painting of an eighty-year-old hag. The sweet sickly smell of body odour filled my nostrils, a cold sweat enveloped my entire body, and I realised I was the source of the awful stench and felt sick to the bone. These were withdrawal symptoms and I was terrified. I had read about things like this in horror stories about junkies withdrawing from heroin. But I wasn't on heroin – this was a prescribed drug, for heaven's sake! I refused to accept that I, Valerie Maher, a respectable housewife of twenty years, could have sunk to the level of a quivering junkie.

No, I tried to convince myself, it was the fear of fear, that's all – in the light of the morning it would all become clear. But sleep would not release me from the nightmare. What felt like hours ticked by. I went over to the bedroom window and drew the curtains. Perhaps there would be signs of life in the street, people going to work, anything to distract my attention from my predicament.

I looked at the alarm clock – it was two o'clock in the morning, the night had only begun! The houses looked as lifeless as the inside of my head felt numb. Neither light from the houses nor signs of life disturbed the solitude. Except for the stars in the sky and the glow from the street lamps, the street appeared dead. How would I get through the long hours of the night, why do problems appear so magnified in the small hours of the morning, especially when you're on your own?

I got down on my knees and prayed. Every prayer I knew was repeated over and over again. I spent the next few hours on my knees begging God to remove the chains of darkness, to miraculously take away the craving for the drug that was now making me feel so ill. By half past four my body had almost collapsed with the withdrawal symptoms. I could take it no longer and crept down the stairs.

My hands were shaking as I unscrewed the bottle of pills. The pill was so small it was impossible for my shaking fingers to grab hold. I had to lick the end of my finger in order to grasp it. There was no need for water to wash it down, the spit in my mouth did the job. Within ten minutes I felt normal again. This was all the proof I needed – I was well and truly hooked.

The children got themselves off to school that morning, a job they were to get well used doing over the coming years. As my mental state deteriorated they were also to become adept at making breakfast, dinner and supper while their mother lay in a drug-induced stupor, or else paraded the streets in great agitation. Halcion is an insidious drug, it works in a subtle yet dangerous way. It tricks the brain into thinking it is doing you good yet it destroys you in the process. The word 'halcyon' conjures up images of tranquil summer days, days spent lying in hayfields being gently caressed by the warm summer sun, while the troubles of everyday living are thrown by the wayside. When you take your first Halcion pill, this is exactly how you feel.

But what happens when the sun goes down and the chilly night air makes you shiver and the brightness turns into the shadowy outlines of clouds forming in the sky? You try to seek out other ways of brightening up your day, perhaps a drink or two, a warm cup of tea and a chat by the fireside with old friends. What happens when you realise you have lost most of those friends, the outward easy-going person they once knew has now turned into a lonely neurotic, one who invents illnesses to get attention. Only it is more than a need for attention – it is a cry for help. You don't want to admit you look like shit or that the sound of your voice is like verbal Mogadon because your life is dictated by a drug.

I'll tell you what happens – you take another pill to bring back the sun, to chase away the clouds of darkness, to release the shackles of fear and loneliness. That's when you make the stupid phone calls, make the hasty decision to visit someone before the effect wears off. Show the outside world your happy face, pretend your mental strength is natural and not supplemented by chemicals. When a person has a physical illness, family and friends are only too willing to help with everyday chores. If my body had been subjected to the surgeon's knife or I had filled buckets with the sweat of a fevered brow, all my Florence Nightingale friends would have been wearing down a path to the front door.

But when the old grey matter between the ears needs attention and you take on the demeanour of a fart in a trance you soon know who your friends are. Some people are of no help whatsoever, being too full of their own problems or too busy wallowing in the sound of their own voices. Others pretend to be caring, when in reality they are just being plain nosey. Some make polite conversation when it is quite obvious they're in a hurry to get away from you. I have become adept at knowing when my presence is welcome and when it is not, an expertise no doubt picked up from watching how people related to my mother – they always seemed to be in a hurry to escape from her, backing off as they spoke.

But most hurtful of all are those who are quick to be judgemental. I have overheard so-called friends pass judgement on me while they thought my far-away look meant I was on the world but not in it. Furthermore, they were unable to see that behind my seemingly normal outer shell – my pride made me look after my appearance, even dress in brightly coloured clothes – I was falling apart inside. It really hurt to hear their comments. "There doesn't seem to be much wrong with her. If only she had the worries I have – a few youngsters round her feet and a man out of work." "Aye, sure I know that, livin' in a bought house and not a worry in the world. It's a good kick up the ass she needs. Sure she's stuck up, always walking on her own."

Did they not stop to wonder why I was on my own? Could they not have realised they only reinforced my sense of aloneness by talking behind my back. My heart has always ruled my head; had my head ruled it I could have closed myself off from them or given them a piece of my mind. Not all my friends turned their backs, thank God. I will be forever grateful to those who didn't.

One person who had never turned his back was Elvis. Of course, he had never known me, but I think I knew him. According to all the stories that were circulating at the time, he too had lived on prescribed drugs, only in larger quantity. I could now understand his reasoning, why he wanted this fact kept quiet – no-one loves a junkie. In my own way I felt an empathy with him. I wasn't destroying my life for the love of it – I was trying to block out reality. The Halcion drug was building up that shattered wall of glass bit by bit. The bad thing about the wall of glass was that while it protected me from the outside world, that outside world could not get at me to help. I am sure this is what happened to Elvis. Slowly the drug took over my life – I now could not live with it and neither could I live without it. The Agony Aunt who used to solve other people's problems over a cup of coffee, the girl/woman who threw parties at the drop of a hat to liven up the lives of others, the hostess who could rustle up a dinner for twelve without batting an eye, and the lady who held Tupperware parties, was now almost incapable of thinking.

John tried to reason with me; he had read various articles about the effects of Halcion on the mind. He became concerned for my welfare and tried in vain to convince me I wasn't the girl he knew any more. According to him I was uncaring towards the family and towards him, and that the person who once acted like a sister towards the children now acted like a consumptive on the verge of dying, or else paced the house like a caged animal. As my brain became more addled the more I blamed John for my predicament.

"Go on then, blame the Halcion! If it wasn't for it I would have committed suicide by now! You and your job – damn both you and the bloody terrorists! Stuff the children and to hell with the friggin' neighbours!"

John slapped me round the face for cursing and also to stop my hysterics. I was trying to scratch the skin from my face with my finger nails I felt so agitated. He held my hands by my side and I spat in his face as if evil spirits had entered my body. I kicked out with my feet like a wild woman and continued with my barrage of curse words. Our younger children were crying at the sight while the two older ones went out in search of sanity. This mad act was played out every other day until I was physically drained; the finale would see me rocking back and forth on the edge of the bed pleading with John to put me in a mental home.

John did go to the doctor to ask if it was the Halcion that was to blame for my behaviour. He let John see the advertisement for Halcion which had been provided by the manufacturers. It showed a woman laughing with the joy of getting a night's sleep safe in the knowledge that side effects were non-existent.

"It can only be her nerves, Mr Maher. No drug manufacturer would let a drug slip through the net that would cause those symptoms."

And so I was labelled – Valerie Maher the nutcase. Every ailment I took after that was put down to nerves. I am convinced that if I had been wheeled into the doctor's with my head tucked under my arm I would have been told to keep taking the tablets and have a lie down. I took a very bad back, and the hospital diagnosed osteoarthritis. A sciatica set in down my right leg – I could neither sit, walk or lie down with the pain. It was so bad I was admitted to hospital for treatment. As the doctor examined me I could tell by his demeanour he was not in the least concerned. "Bed rest" was the only comment he made as he walked off to his next patient, who by coincidence had been admitted for the same complaint. She was pampered and fussed over and wrapped in a warm duvet to relieve the pain. When I asked for the same treatment the ward Sister ate the gob off me. "Have you ever thought of getting your nerves seen to, Mrs Maher?" She obviously had read my notes and saw those four dreaded words: 'Suffers from bad nerves.' I signed myself out and spent months under physiotherapy to ease the pain.

The indignity of having even hospital staff turn their backs on me made me feel even worse. Who could I turn to for help? I became paranoid, refusing to even go out to the clothes line to hang out the washing in case a neighbour started up a conversation. If the door bell rang I hid upstairs; my mind became so tormented I even hid in the wardrobe to protect myself from the outside world. Meals consisted of take-aways from the chip shop when John came home from work, for my ability to cook had ceased.

John's final attempt to make me well again – by sending me on a three-week holiday to America to visit my brothers, in an effort to free my mind from the realities of his job and the constant reminders of a country in turmoil – fell apart at the seams. I came back a complete basket case and had to be admitted to the mental hospital. I spent six weeks in hiding from my family. I allowed no-one apart from John to visit me I felt so ashamed. In a world of so-called 'progress' it was still a stigma to have been in a mental hospital.

While in the mental hospital I was still prescribed Halcion to make me sleep, and yet the psychiatrists didn't seem to connect them with my condition. My childhood, plus my early marriage that had seen more than its fair share of ups and downs, and the worry of John's job were the cause of everything, according to the psychiatrists. A few weeks rest away from these pressures and all would be well. The fact that my circulation had decided to turn my legs and arms blue every other day accompanied by a loss of feeling in my lower body, should have been concern for further diagnosis, but nerves are a funny thing according to the medical world – the mind can play havoc with the body.

Maybe it was getting away from the pressures of family life, not having to hide every time the doorbell rang or for that matter trying to avoid friends and neighbours, but I did actually feel better after the six weeks' respite. Or it could also have been the sight of other patients suffering from schizophrenia or really black depression that brought me to my senses. A stay in a mental hospital can be quite sobering. If so-called comedians who crack jokes at the expense of schizophrenics were made to spend a week with one of these unfortunate souls they would think twice before using this condition as a source of amusement. The sight of these patients, some as young as fifteen, struggling tormentedly with their inner voices, voices which just won't let up, is harrowing. If those who belittle schizophrenia were to see the physical scars that are self-inflicted in vain attempts to gain peace of mind, they would think twice about using the word schizo in mirth.

The 'Funny Farm', as some ignoramuses refer to it, is not funny to those who have had the misfortune to avail themselves of its facilities. Few would make fun of a person who has undergone major surgery, or try to make themselves look invisible while in hospital visiting. Yet this is precisely what happens when people fear being identified as the relation of a 'fruit and nut case'. The Lord gave each of us a brain, and just like the rest of our body it needs to be taken care of. While we worry about taking bad hearts, appendicitis, kidney trouble – you name it – we forget that our brains too are delicate computers which sometimes get overloaded and crash out. Our heart, liver and kidneys can often be replaced by the skill of the surgeon, but not the brain.

Lord, how I wish the clock could be put back to the day I was prescribed those pills, especially if I had then the knowledge I have now. They would have been thrown on the fire and eight years of my life would not be a haze and a dreadful ordeal to recall. They say bought wit is the best of wit; my bought wit cost me my son's wedding, the birth of my first grandchild, plus not being able to kiss my daughter Heather goodbye and good luck when she left home to work abroad. Good memories that should have been cherished.

These are only three of the important events that took place in my life during the time my brain was on another planet. The lesser events are nothing other than a faint recollection brought to the fore by photographs. The bad experiences will be imprinted on my mind forever. I have learnt to put them to the back of my mind in little storage compartments. Now and then I bring them out for a quick dust down, and each time they are dusted a small part of the horror falls away.

The art of living after my first hospital experience soon disappeared in a drug-induced cloud when all the old feelings of fear came creeping back. Coping without the help of my small blue companions was now a thing of the past, I felt so vulnerable in the house we lived in. The invisible wall of glass had now spread to the walls of the family home – they too appeared to be made of glass. There was nowhere to hide without being spied upon, so I kept on the move, pacing round and round in circles. Through the living room, into the dining room, then through to the kitchen and into the hallway . . . round and round until my head ached.

My heart beat to the rhythm of every footstep as I told myself: 'Keep on the move from room to room, girl, that way you're not a sitting target.' The tablets had made me paranoid and were going down my throat every six hours in a bid to try and keep my brain focused on the goings-on in the outside world. Bloody sleeping pills to keep me alert – this was 'Halcion'.

One pill heightened the senses, two made me sleep. In a bid to hide away from the world we moved house yet again, this time to a bungalow situated in its own grounds – grass hedges seven feet high and surrounded by trees. Being an older house its walls were thicker, it felt more secure – for a while. The gardens were beautiful, the previous occupants had landscaped them – rose bushes, Japanese maple trees, magnolias with clematis and quince heavy with fruit clinging to the outer walls. It was beautiful both inside and out. A lot of people would have given their right arm to live in it, a far cry from our small two up two down house on the Falls Road with its crumbling walls and outside loo.

Yet for all its beauty I would have sacrificed everything for the peace of mind I had in Balaclava Street, the sight of Mrs O'Brien in her wraparound pinny going through her snuff-sniffing ritual, the sound of Brendan asking me if I wanted a wee drap a tea, the fusty smell of Annie and Minnie's Dickensian shop and the warm feeling of friendly neighbours gathering together in times of need, when a hard day's work and a bit of 'craic' round the fireside before going to bed was the nearest you got to a sleeping pill.

John had worked hard and long hours to pay for the luxury of this home. He didn't smoke or drink and any money he brought home in his pay packet soon disappeared paying bills and the mortgage. The way some of our friends acted you would have thought we had been given the flaming thing. My search for privacy plunged me deeper into the nightmare.

Moving up in the world home-wise brings a new set of neighbours. In this case they were settled, middle-aged and childless. Four of our children were still living at home – Kevin had moved out while at university to spread his wings. Parents might find their children hard to cope with on occasion, but childless middle-aged Homo sapiens tend to look upon them as tiresome, irritable, obnoxious little brats. Some go to the extreme of almost denying them air to breathe. In my twilight world for the mentally bewildered, complaints about my children annoying these selfish specimens of humanity simply by playing in their own back garden were taken to heart. Instead of ignoring them or for that matter telling them simply to 'Go to hell' I took to sitting by the fireside crying in self-pity, continuously shouting at them and pleading with them to stay quiet. £40,000 was a hell of a price to pay to become a recluse in order to appease crotchety old maids and house-proud pensioners.

Stephen, the second eldest, being no longer a teenager, had given up the practice of kicking ball or climbing trees in the garden, and managed to escape the wrath of both myself and the neighbours, while the three youngest took to playing away from home. I was now left alone to stew in my self-made prison of bricks and pills. Elvis came back into my world in a big way – pop a pill, listen to Elvis. It was ironic that the very thing that attributed to his death should now be bringing us together again after so many years.

His gospel music and ballads soothed my troubled mind. Elvis had an uncanny knack of singing the words a person wanted to hear, be it words of love, words of hurt to suit a breaking heart, or words of healing in his gospel songs. He had come back to help me cope; he was now bringing back happy memories of my teenage years with all his old songs. Even though his 'Heartbreak Hotel' was now my own home, his 'Teddy Bear' was helping block out the harsh realities of life in a troubled land by transporting me back to the Plaza Ballroom in the late Fifties when Violet and I used to rock-'n'-roll until we almost dropped with healthy exhaustion. No need for sleeping pills then, my head hardly had time to hit the pillow before I fell asleep, while Elvis's 'Love me tender' played softly in my subconscious and lulled me into a feeling of wellbeing without the aid of man-made hypnotics.

"Life begins at forty!" That's what the doctor had told me on one of my frequent visits to the surgery. I prayed her words would come true. How was life going to begin when I had now taken to lying in bed most of the day with the phone off the hook so as not to be disturbed? No-one came to the door any more, no-one was interested in a lifeless anorexic who listened to a dead singer in a bid to regain sanity. The day my memory went on hold completely almost gave me and the family heart failure.

My morning drug-induced stupor had been constantly interrupted by a voice loudly calling my name. The voice had no earthly body attached to it, yet it sounded familiar – it was my father's voice! I had now started to hallucinate and I was extremely scared to say the least. The fear of schizophrenia, the thought of voices maybe telling me to harm either myself or my family terrified me. Why my father's voice? The voice that used to put the fear of hell into my very soul. I later learned it was the fact that I despised myself for becoming such a hateful person and I was punishing myself for being so weak-willed with horrible thoughts. I had the urge to shred the skin on my face and body with razor blades, to mutilate myself as a means of punishment, to disfigure myself so that people would not recognise me in the street, so that I would then be left alone, for no-one would know what to say to a disfigured person.

For quite a while household gadgets had begun to scare me. The kettle had taken on a life of its own and resembled a cat ready to pounce if I went too near. The sound that came from the fridge was the growl of a bear. The washing machine was a black hole that would suck me in if the washing wasn't put in at the speed of light, while the television took on a life of its own and all the faces and sounds were real. I lived in Coronation Street, Albert Square and Brookside; all their troubles were my troubles, and that adds up to a hell of a lot of troubles.

I knew it was the 'Halcion', yet the fear of fear stopped me from telling either the doctor or John. I knew if they found out they would stop the tablets completely. Someone had told me that coming off a drug too suddenly could start epileptic fits and maybe death. No, I wasn't ready for that, anyway there just might be an easier way to stop – just don't panic, girl, that miracle cure may be round the corner.

I had just woken out of a fitful sleep with a jolt and sat bolt upright in bed. The bed itself seemed to have moved to the middle of the room – all in my imagination as I later found out. I can't remember every detail, but I can remember that it was horrifying.

The walls of the room were closing in on me. I felt weightless, floating on air. I tried to call for help but forgot how to speak, then the room seemed to disappear as a tunnel vision effect began to invade my eyes. I sat suspended in time for what felt like hours but in actual fact was only seconds. The tick of the clock beside the bed became almost deafening, and how I managed to make it out of bed still remains a mystery, but somehow I found myself in the hallway outside the bedroom door. I could see Heather sitting in the living room through the glass partition that separated it from the hall but couldn't call out her name. Not that I could have called her, I couldn't remember her name, I didn't even know who she was.

I fell against the wall and knocked a picture down, and this made Heather look round to see where the noise was coming from. "What's wrong, mum? Speak to me, please."

Heather had me by the shoulders, she was trying to shake me out of my trance. For a few seconds my mind cleared. I thought of John. He had to come home from work to help me. "Get John at work." Heather still remained a stranger to me, it was frightening.

Heather did not know his work phone number. She asked me for it. I didn't know it. I had forgotten where he worked, never mind the phone number. She put the phone in my lap but it might just as well have been an ornament the state my mind was in. The feeling was similar to the one I had gone through the night I tried to go without the Halcion, only ten times worse. Why, I wondered, am I going through all this even when *on* the pills!

I remember asking Heather the time. She looked at her watch – it was twelve fifty-five. I can recall this because that time stayed in my head for months. 'Valerie Maher – time for her ceased at twelve fifty-five precisely', a voice in my head kept repeating. However, my guardian angel must have been on duty that day for just then the front door opened and John came in. He had one night guard duty every seventh day, and on these occasions he would arrive home at lunch time for a few hours sleep. By divine intervention it happened to fall on that day.

Over the past years John's patience had worn very thin; he might as well have lost his wife for all the use I had become. The smell of home cooking greeting him after a day's work was nothing more than a memory. And the sound of loving words and sex were confined to actors on the television. The sight of me lying in a trance had long since ceased to alarm him, and words of sympathy such as 'What's wrong, love?' were now replaced by 'Not bloody again, go and lie down.'

I managed to ask, "Where am I, John?"

"Where in hell's gates do you think you are! You're in the flamin' Canary Islands!" John answered sarcastically, pulling me up and depositing me on the bed. He hit his forehead with the palm of his hand and asked God to give him strength, for he could take no more.

"Please John, help me, my brain has gone."

"Where in the name of Christ has it gone? Val, I can't take any more. Please pull yourself together for the sake of the children at least."

"What children?"

"Our children – Kevin, Stephen, Heather, Peter and Shauna. They need a mother, for God's sake, not a gibbering idiot." I felt nothing other than fear. I went hysterical and started ripping the nightdress off my back in an attempt to get John to believe me when I said my brain had ceased to function.

I asked the time again as I felt hours had passed since Heather had informed me it was twelve fifty-five. "It's five past one," John answered in a tired and frustrated voice. "Why?"

"Five past one in the morning – why is it still light?"

John was on the phone for the doctor within seconds – the penny had dropped, the woman was definitely away in the head. The doctor, a complete stranger to us, arrived within fifteen minutes and diagnosed the problem as a virus in the brain, and he prescribed of all things an extra Halcion to make me sleep.

"She should be alright after a few days, Mr Maher." He closed his black bag and departed.

The 'few days' lasted a month, a month spent prone either in bed or on the settee. It felt as if someone had pulled at a piece of cord attached to my body and wrenched out all my energy. I was admitted to the mental hospital for the second time. I received the same treatment as before – rest and more rest until my head cleared. Six more weeks of being questioned by psychiatrists. The same questions, the same diagnosis – stress and being of a nervous disposition.

Only I knew different – as sure as eggs are eggs it was the Halcion, but I was still too afraid to admit to the fact. My own supply had been brought to the hospital with me and I was doctoring myself to keep the withdrawal symptoms at bay. I had hoped the psychiatrists would find a miracle cure with another magic pill and release me from the hell of this one. But how can a cure be found for an illness the doctor did not know existed? In trying to fool myself I had also fooled them.

Once again at home I recoiled back into my shell, living life not only behind the walls of glass but trapped in a mist. Hours were spent on the telephone talking to the Samaritans, a handful of pills in one hand, the receiver in the other.

Suicide scared me, which probably saved my life. However, it wasn't just fear of the unknown which stayed my hand, but thoughts of my family. I feared how the children would cope with outsiders making snide remarks that they too could be insane just like their mother. I felt guilty that Heather and Shauna were now turning into young women and had no mother to confide in. And above all, I knew it would break John's heart if I were to take my own life, for even though I was no longer the girl he once knew, he still loved me and forever lived in the hope that my mental state would eventually return to that of the happy-go-lucky person who cared about other people's feelings. Poor John, he had now become both mother and father, as well as holding down a job.

How I cursed those pills – the sight of them brought the sweat to my brow. With every prescription the doctor gave me he might just as well have given me a few nails for my coffin. When and how could I get released from the hell of Halcion? I tried anti-depressants in the hope of weaning myself off. It was fruitless, they only made me ill. The fact of the matter being I wasn't depressed in the first place, I had been scared – there is a big difference. Psychoanalysis would have been far better than pills, it would have spared me years of hell. But one can't look back, the past is history, the only way is forward.

Three quarters of my day was spent on my knees praying, not in public but in private. Surely God will hear sometime; there were more deserving cases than myself in this world but maybe in between helping the sick and the dying he will throw a little of his precious time in my direction. To get nearer to God I took to walking the streets at night, and as soon as John came home from work he was hawked out again to keep me company. The roof over my head felt like an obstacle between God and myself. Out in the open there would be no obstacle, it would be only me and the heavens. I walked the streets praying, asking God for guidance, to remove the chains of addiction, I begged him to please help me, to give me back to my family.

When I had finally given up all hope of ever being set free, I decided there was no other way out for me than to take my own life. John possessed a legally-held gun for security reasons. As he lay asleep in bed I picked it up and silently made my way to the living room. As I sat with the gun in my hand I had no tears in my eyes, no morbid thoughts, just the promise of being set free, of releasing John and the children from the hell of trying to cope with their own lives without the added burden of a mad wife and mother.

I did not go into the children's bedrooms to kiss them goodbye, or for that matter take the time to write a last sentimental letter. I just didn't care any more. Call it self-pity if you like, for that's what it was. It must have been, for it takes guts to live, while I was choosing the coward's way out.

The silence of the night made me put on an Elvis record. I just wanted to hear his voice one last time. He had helped me live, perhaps now he could help me die. I didn't even look at the cover of the record, I just lifted the arm of the record player and dropped it at random on the record. God had been listening, he must have been, for of all the Elvis songs he picked one with a message to help me. A song I had never really listened to before.

The title of the song was 'Help Me (to help you forget)'.

Lord, help me walk another mile,
Just one more mile.
I'm tired of walking all alone.

Lord, help me smile another smile,
Just one more smile.
You know I just can't make it on my own.
I never thought I needed help before,
I thought that I could get by, by myself.
But now I know I just can't take it any more.
With a humble heart, on bended knee,
I'm beggin' you, please help me.

Come down from your golden throne,
To meet lonely me.
I need to feel the touch of your tender hand.
Remove the chains of darkness,
Let me see, Lord, let me see,
Just where I fit into your master plan.

The words were so appropriate to the way I felt, I just had to listen. In fact I played it again and again. The tears were streaming down my cheeks. Elvis was singing just for me again, it felt as he was in the room. I could almost feel his presence, I could hear his voice. He was telling me not to waste my life, to be strong. I put the gun down on the floor, and through floods of tears, tears of healing, I told myself I had to take one of three options.

One, to stay on the drug and go completely mad. Two, to take the coward's way out and commit suicide. Three, sign myself into the mental hospital, admit to the doctors it was the Halcion, go through hell to come off and hopefully come out the other side free.

I chose number three. Today I thank God, for it was worth the pain and suffering, but had I known then what I was in for I might not have gone through with it.

Chapter 16

MISTER SONGMAN

The cold November air had covered the windows of our car with a light blanket of condensation giving the inside an eerie and claustrophobic feel. Earlier in the day I had felt strangely elated at the thought of soon being set free from the hell of my Halcion addiction, but now I was not so sure. My elation had been short-lived, and now my mental state matched the feel of the interior of the car. The clouded windows were symbolic of the black clouds that were hanging over my head, clouds of doubt as to whether or not I would ever feel normal again. The long wait for John coming home from work at six o'clock in the evening to drive me to the hospital had felt like an eternity and I was beginning to have second thoughts. I had to quell the urge to jump out and run back into the house, to tell the children I had changed my mind about going into hospital once more. The excuse of 'I'm just going in for a few weeks to get my strength built up' did not in my opinion answer their suspicions. The frightened look on their faces had made my heart hurt with guilt, the tears in their eyes were proof enough. They knew their mother was not leaving them only a month before Christmas simply for a rest. Christmas meant the family coming together and mother at the helm cooking the turkey, icing the cake, wrapping presents, decorating the Christmas tree, and not arsing off to the mental hospital.

Surely by the time Christmas comes I will have won the battle of 'Valerie versus the little blue mind-benders'? They were not street drugs, I didn't stand in dark alleyways paying a seedy drug peddler for my fix, these were drugs that had been prescribed by trained doctors to help me sleep, to fight the fear of fear. There must be an instant cure for my addiction, surely no-one would expect a person on a prescribed drug to experience the horror of the withdrawal symptoms that heroin or cocaine addicts suffer. Anyway, it couldn't be as bad coming off Halcion as a street drug, the doctors and nurses will be more sympathetic. Yet, as my father would have said, "That's the biggest load of bollocks I've ever heard, you will get as much sympathy as a hen has a chance of peckin' delft" – and for once in his life he would have been right.

I smoked three cigarettes and cried a bucketful of tears in the ten minutes it took to drive me to the hospital. John sat silently at the wheel of the car, his face grey and expressionless. I couldn't have blamed him if he had thoughts of running away from the whole bloody scene. All he had been subjected to for the last eight years was abuse, the sound of weeping and wailing and the depressing sight of a wife either walking in circles, rocking on the edge of the bed or lying about like a consumptive.

What he hadn't been subjected to was my fumbling attempt at suicide, or having to listen to me talk for hours on the telephone to the Samaritans, or my calls to various drug centres around the British Isles in the hope they would tell me not to worry, that Halcion was harmless. Nor did he hear the voices in my head every time I tried to sleep or the sensation of ants crawling over my skin whenever I needed another pill. Neither did he realise I couldn't cook because of my fear of kitchen gadgets, or wash clothes because of my fear that the washing machine would swallow me if I got too near. I had concealed all these things from him in case he put me in a mental hospital and threw away the key.

I can understand visitors trying to act sane when visiting a mental hospital to a certain extent, the people I can't stand are those who sit and giggle and play the game of 'Which one's the nutcase'. It is strange, the ones who look the sanest are often the patients – they are not pretending anything. The reason I mention this is that when John and I walked into the reception area all heads turned and stared. Because of the overnight bag one of us had to be the patient, and I felt that bets were being placed to find out which one was signing in for the nightmare. My nightmare started as soon as I set foot in the psychiatrist's office.

"Sit!" The command made me jump to attention, and for a few seconds I waited for a dog to appear from behind the door and lie down at my feet.

"I said sit down, Mrs Mmmm... what is your name anyway?" He glanced at my file which sat on the desk before him, then pushed it aside as if it stank to high heaven.

"Maher, Valerie." I felt I should have had a number attached to my name and apologised. "Sorry, I thought you knew."

"I know quite a lot, but mind-reading is not one of my fortes." He gave a sickly smile, an excuse for an apology at being so sarcastic. "Now why do you want to come into hospital, hmmmm... Mrs Mateer?"

"Maher," I reminded him. "If you read the letter it will explain." I felt this would get me out of having to explain it all myself, and help me hold on to a small portion of my dignity. He gazed over the top of his glasses and gave me a Draconian stare, very reminiscent of my father. "Maher, I beg your pardon – it's a very unusual name."

'And you're a very unusual doctor', I thought. Not a good start, maybe things will get better.

He opened the letter my doctor had given me earlier and again peered over the top of his half spectacles. "So you're on Halcion, not the best of drugs to be on. What has you on these?" he asked in a very patronising manner.

'Not the best of drugs'? I felt like asking him if he knew of a better one, in the hope he would say 'yes', but held my tongue.

"For my nerves."

He almost choked over his next remark.

"For your nerves? But Halcion is a sleeping pill?"

"I know," I meekly replied, dreading his next question.

"How many do you take?."

"One 0.25mg every four hours."

He scratched his balding head, removed his glasses and rubbed his eyes with clenched fists.

"The dosage is one a night, Mrs Mateer, sorry Maher. How come you took six a day? If I took six Halcion in one day I would never wake up. And how in heaven's name did you manage to get your hands on so many of these pills?"

"I just kept getting repeat prescriptions." I felt terrible after voicing this last remark, as if I were putting the blame on my doctors, for this was not my intention.

"Did the doctors not know how many you were getting, Mrs Maher?"

"The doctors were busy, and anyway, I had been prescribed them by some of the doctors from the Contactors Bureau on the days my own doctors were off." Computers have taken over now and patients' notes can be called up at the touch of a button. But not then, and I am ashamed to say I took advantage of this, for my mind was unhinged with the effects of that Godforsaken drug.

This inquisition was making me panic and I jumped off the chair. "Sorry, I can't take this, I'm going to have to leave." In my panic I became confused and started to cry uncontrollably.

"Mrs Maher, sit down PLEASE, let's not get out of control." My chest tightened, I could hardly breathe, the urge to open the door of the surgery and run away was overpowering. The psychiatrist stood up and grabbing me firmly by the shoulders guided me back towards the seat. For a moment I thought he was going to be sympathetic to my dilemma – wrong again.

"Let's start all over again, this time from the very beginning."

I went over my life for the umpteenth time, baring my soul to a complete stranger, who, going by the attitude he was displaying, didn't really give a damn. I explained how one pill led to a second to do the same work and how it had come to the point where I now could not live with them nor could I live without them. He shook his head.

"Mrs Maher, there's no such thing as not being able to live without a sleeping pill."

"I need help, Doctor, please get me off them," I begged.

"That's up to you, it's not going to be easy, it's completely up to how much willpower you have."

Not very heartening, in fact it felt terrifying. Not the instant help I had imagined I would have received.

"Hop up on the couch there till I have a look at the rest of you. Strip down to your bra and pants."

He proceeded to turn me inside out. I felt naked, not only on the outside but on the inside as well. I looked round the surgery for a female nurse for support. I had the feeling this so-called psychiatrist was impervious to the feelings of the so-called 'weaker' species of human beings. There are two kinds of psychiatrists, ones who care and bastards. I had come across one of the latter.

After he had finished his prodding and poking I was told to dress and sit down again.

"We will reduce your dosage by two tablets for a start, then reduce one every week until you're completely off them."

"No other treatment?"

"No – no other treatment. We'll just reduce the dosage and keep an eye on you."

"You mean to say I will be in hospital until the very last pill is stopped?"

"Indubitably, my dear." I expected Sherlock Holmes to appear at any moment. "It will take at least six weeks, Mrs Maher. The psychiatrist in charge of your case will see you in a couple of days to report on your progress."

"But that's until after Christmas. What will the family do?"

"Persevere. Now, the nurse will show you to your bed."

After a curt 'goodnight' he showed me to the door. My dignity had been torn from my soul, I was after all being treated as if I were a street drug addict. I left the surgery in a state of disbelief. 'Christ, what have I let myself in for, I feel so unclean.' Where was the compassion I had expected, the tender loving care of the nursing profession? Those two words, 'No treatment', echoed round my brain, yet I knew there was no turning back.

I had admitted my weakness, I didn't know then the hidden dangers of the drug. Had I known I would have demanded that I be treated with another, safer drug to enable me to come off without the horrors that lurked round the corner. To those who say, "She did it herself, she overdosed on this drug of her own accord" I would like to point out that I had been told by various doctors to take a Halcion pill whenever I found myself in distress. This drug is short-acting, lasting only two hours in one's system, at the outside five to six hours, with supposedly no adverse side effects – or so it was advertised in medical journals. The makers of this drug are 99% to blame in my book, I give myself the other 1% for believing them. With my lack of knowledge about the medical profession, I took the advice of those who had, and ended up an unsuspecting victim. When I entered the hospital in late November 1987 the psychiatrists were by then aware of the dangers but the damage had been done.

The nurse who helped settle me into the ward searched my belongings in an effort to find any hidden drugs and then proceeded to watch as I stripped into my nightdress. My daytime clothes were then turned inside out and the hems of my coat and skirt were examined with expert fingers for signs of pills sewn into them. I almost expected her to rifle through my hair and stare down my earholes. Her Hitlerite attitude made me tremble and once again the urge to run up the ward, out the door and make a break for freedom, overwhelmed me – only I knew I had nowhere to run. John would have been notified of my escape and in his frustration would have led me straight back by the gills and told them to tie me to the bed.

I cannot express the fear I felt as I sat on the end of the bed stripped of not only my clothes but my pride. An old lady in the bed opposite started howling like a banshee, over and over, the howl becoming louder as the minutes ticked by, then she stopped. A few moments later she started reciting the Lord's Prayer at the top of her voice. Halfway through this she stopped, and the prayer was replaced by every curse word under the sun, before the howling started up again. Through the dimmed lights of the ward her small white almost bald crown and gaping toothless mouth reminded me of Oliver Plunket's head. The sides of the bed had been pulled up to stop her falling out. Not that there was much chance of this happening, for the bedclothes had been wrapped so tightly around her body in order to restrain her movements she resembled a moth trying to escape from its cocoon.

A nurse put her head around the ward door and tut-tutted, a second nurse joined her and chorused her verbal disapproval. "We're in for another night with Minnie. Thank God I had a good sleep today or the thought of spending another night listening to her antics would put me as mental as the patients!" She looked in my direction and added. "Pill time will not be long. I'm sure your wait is driving you crazy." There were sarcastic overtones to her remark which made me feel as low as one can get.

By the time 'pill time' arrived the old familiar withdrawal symptoms were beginning to surface. Minnie's howling added a new feeling to my already none too steady nerves – the feeling of committing murder in order to shut her up. I waited on tenderhooks until my name was called for my night-time medication. The medication is not brought to you in the mental hospital, you are subjected to the indignity of having to walk the length of the corridor to receive your pills and potions.

"VALERIE MAHER."

Again the feeling that a number should have been attached to the end of my name made me feel as if I were in jail. I thought of the terrorist prisoners lying in their cells and wondered if one of them could have been the person responsible for my predicament, and whether *he* was having nightmares. I responded to the call of my name, trying not to act all eager for fear of being labelled a junkie, and nonchalantly made my way to the treatment room. Halfway there my name boomed over the corridor again, only louder.

'VALERIE MAHER!'

I quickened my pace and stood at the door. "Do you want this or not?" A red-faced moustached male nurse handed me the small plastic container that held my medication, with a look that would have withered a freshly-opened rose. Normally at night I took two Halcion to get me over to sleep, but there was only one in the cup.

"I usually take two at night."

"Do you now? Well, you're down for one in the book, dear."

'Christ, why did I say that? It will make matters worse,' I thought, and mentally kicked myself for uttering the words. The one pill calmed me down slightly but sleep refused to come. By half past eleven my withdrawal symptoms resumed again. It would be nine o'clock in the morning before my next Halcion, and my insides fell apart at the seams. Minnie had not stopped howling, praying and cursing since I had arrived, though the other patients seemed impervious to the din. While I was in here to be weaned off a drug, they were being drugged for mental conditions such as schizophrenia and manic depression, and were fast asleep.

By one o'clock in the early morning my body and brain could take no more of Minnie's incessant ramblings. I came to within a hair's breadth of committing murder. One of the lesser-known side-effects of Halcion had taken hold – the ability to turn a docile nature into the very opposite.

I lifted the pillow from my bed, made my way towards Minnie's bed, and was toying with the idea of putting the pillow over her face, when the nurse walked in a few moments later, otherwise I would be in jail today for murder.

"Mrs Maher – what are you doing?"

"I'm going to smother that effin' woman, she's putting me friggin' mad!"

"NURSE FLANNIGAN! COME IN HERE QUICK!" The nurse screamed.

Nurse Flannigan came running into the ward and helped the nurse who had found me almost in the act of murder. They steered me back to my bed and for the first time since my arrival in hospital I was shown a little bit of tender loving care.

"Calm down, Mrs Maher, Minnie can't help getting on the way she does. She has senile dementia, she can't control herself."

I felt guilty. I cursed myself for becoming the person I now was and begged the nurses to forgive my actions. "Please believe me, I am not an aggressive person, I don't know what came over me."

"We understand, it's withdrawal, but our hands are tied we can't help you. The only thing we can do is move you to another ward."

The move to another ward did not help, for Minnie's howling echoed all over the hospital building, breaking the silence of the night. I paced the corridor like a caged animal, a short insight into what lay ahead. The dim night-time lights were suddenly replaced with the harsh lights that came on at 6.30 am. My nightdress was clinging to my body with sweat and I was shaking from head to foot. Nausea had set in, making me retch to such an extent it hurt, my stomach was cramping and I was bent over the toilet with tears streaming out of my eyes. My body craved the drug that had put me in this condition, the physical along with the mental craving had me confused.

When the night nurse ordered everyone to make their beds before the day staff came on I was so frightened to disobey I staggered up to the ward. At the sight of my bed I realised how agitated I must have been – it was wrecked. My co-ordination was up the left and no matter how much I tried the sheets would not fit into place. The pillows had also fallen onto the floor much to the annoyance of the staff nurse.

"Pick those up, please!" She stood beside the bed with a look of thunder on her face. "You put the pillows on the chair while making the bed." She made her disapproval known by thumping the chair with the palm of her hand, hurting herself in the process.

"Sorry." I seemed to be spending most of my time apologising.

"'Sorry' will not make the bed, Mrs Maher. And another thing, don't get back in after it's made."

She rubbed her hand on her backside to ease the pain she had inflicted on herself because of her temper. Had I have been my old self I'd have said, 'Up yours, missus, make the flamin' thing yourself or else shove it sideways where the sun don't shine.'

As I felt on the verge of death I decided to carry out her orders as a last two-fingered salute at life. She turned on her heels and stomped out of the ward in her bright red uniform, her fat backside wobbling behind her. The film 'One flew over the cuckoo's nest' suddenly came to mind and I nicknamed her Nurse Ratchet after the nurse in that movie. I mouthed the words, 'Why don't you do a frontal lobotomy on my brain, it might make your job easier.'

After six days of this treatment I signed myself out. Six days without sleep and 144 hours of living in what seemed like the jaws of Armageddon. John was none too pleased but I managed to convince him it was for the best. I would stick to the regime of four tablets per day at home in order to get Christmas over for the children. He agreed on one condition – he held on to the tablets. I had thirty Halcion tablets hidden about the house in case of emergencies. I worked it out that this would get me over the Christmas period, then I would let the hell start all over again. With hindsight it was a very foolhardy move, for it only made me worse.

My family doctor had no sympathy the following day as I sat in his office for a prescription of Halcion. The hospital had obviously been in touch to tell him what to prescribe, so I can't blame my doctor for being so strict. I sat with my little list of physical complaints that I had written down on a piece of notepaper, as my mind felt all jumbled and I didn't want to forget anything in case I had to go back cap in hand.

He grabbed the note from my hand and threw it in the wastepaper bin. He glared over his spectacles and tut-tutted. "I don't take shopping lists, thank you very much."

I'm not often stuck for an answer and had I been more alert, I would have replied, 'If that had been my shopping list I would most definitely not be suffering from diarrhoea, vomiting, spasms of cramp or extreme depression, I would have these ailments cured by now.' However, my brain had gone on vacation and what he saw before him was an empty shell.

"A week has passed since the hospital cut down on your pills. I am cutting the dose by a further 0.25mg per day. That leaves you with three a day for a week, I then want you to cut down by a further 0.25mg every week. In three week's time I want to see you off them completely."

He curtly threw the prescription in my direction and pressed the buzzer for his next patient. In other words, he had no time for simpering wrecks with the imagination of a hypochondriac. I looked at John hoping he would stand up for me, and tell the doctor it was too quick a drop. Instead John agreed with him as if it was as easy as coming off Smarties. I silently cursed him for taking the doctor's side, not realising he wouldn't have known what I was going through. I collected my prescribed forty-two Halcion, and no medication for my other ailments. Exactly three weeks supply of pills that could have fitted into a thimble, not one more, not one less – three weeks to break an eight year hell. I mentally added the thirty I had hidden with the forty-two prescribed and realised it meant eighteen pills per week – a drop of twenty four. Less than three pills per day – I would have been better off in hospital, after all.

That Christmas was the worst experience in my life. You cannot escape the trappings of Christmas – and the Christmas tree lights and decorations gave me a phobia that still exists to this day. Every Christmas I am reminded of the nightmare and breathe a sigh of relief when the decorations come down. Elvis's song 'Blue Christmas' would have been too colourful, it was more of a monochrome yuletide. Everything appeared to be in black and white to match my mood. In fact you could rule out the white, my day being spent under a black cloud that hung over my head like the fall-out dust of an atom bomb. My bedroom became my place of refuge, visitors were forbidden and even the children's friends were barred from calling at the house.

The only voice I wanted to hear was Elvis's, yet sometimes even that was too much and I sat in complete silence. I played all his songs that had meaning for the way I felt. Elvis had a song for all moods – it's amazing, but he was the only singer I know who had that ability. I listened to his gospel music whenever I felt the urge to extinguish what little flame of life flickered in my tormented mind. While at a very low ebb I made arrangements for my own funeral service should I pop my clogs. 'How great thou art' would start the funeral service, followed by 'Without him' in the middle. I pictured my coffin being borne shoulder high to the song 'Life' as I left the church feet first and cried my lamps out at the thought of how sad the congregation would feel. Self-pity can really make the tears fall, though as tears are a healer I suppose I can thank Elvis for this little bit of therapeutic medicine.

When I die, I still want those instructions carried out. My family has been informed and God help the person who fails to comply. I will be waiting either up there or down there to wring their flaming neck!

The nights were the worst: the silence, the loneliness, the fear, the pain – they are all magnified at night. The days were none too pleasant either. They say daylight is supposed to make things appear normal – not in my case. I listened to the words of 'Mr Songman', my favourite Elvis record, day in and day out, the words helping me over some very bad times.

> *Here's another dime for you,*
> *Mr Songman.*
> *Sing the loneliness of broken dreams away,*
> *If you can.*
> *Yes, it's only me and you,*
> *Mr Songman.*
> *Take away the night, sing away the hurt,*
> *Mr Songman.*

In your ivory-covered palace,
Safe behind your walls of glass;
You keep staring back at me,
Like a memory from the past.

Won't you sing me away to a summer's night,
Let me hold you in my arms again;
I know memory is not reliving,
But at least it's not the end.

I always had a dime for Elvis, to sing the loneliness and hurt away. I knew now what he must have been going through, having to live his life on medication – no-one destroys their life for the love of it, there is always a reason. Loneliness is not confined to those who live on their own, you can still feel lonely in a crowd as Elvis did. When he sang of being 'safe behind your walls of glass' perhaps he was trying to convey his inner feelings. In his home 'Graceland' he was alone with those feelings. Could it be that his memories were staring back at him? Memories of happier times that haunted him? He often asked 'Why am I Elvis Presley?' What the public see from the outside is not always what a person feels himself to be on the inside. And before you say 'No-one forced him to be famous', remember his generosity towards others. He spread his wealth around to the point where he died almost broke. He once said, 'Never criticise what you don't understand, son. You never walked in that man's shoes.' He walked barefoot and ended up riding saddle-back, a rags to riches story. But contrary to popular belief he preferred to give rather than take, and almost ended with a riches to rags epitaph on his gravestone. He helped the needy and the handicapped while the rich got richer on his heavy work schedule. He didn't boast about it, he did it without publicity or as an excuse to cover up his failings. He knew the feeling of poverty only too well, and of being labelled an outcast.

Sometimes I wouldn't have blamed him if he had faked his own death in order to get away from the pressures of living and the strain of not being able to break down that glass wall. I know it's ridiculous to even imagine him alive but one can always dream. A person cannot spend their life in a permanent state of agitation, living from one pill to the next, sitting alone and praying, without cracking up completely, which I did on 30 December 1987. That date is also imprinted on my mind. It will remain there forever because it was the last day I spent with my husband and children under the influence of 'Halcion'.

I knew I had reached the end of that long lonely highway, and that my brain had not only gone walkabout but had taken a wrong turning and got lost, when I threw a cup of boiling hot coffee over

Heather for absolutely nothing at all. The daughter I had worried so much over as a child, the child I feared would never live. She never told anyone I did it, a sign she understood – and this hurt. Her seventeenth birthday was only two weeks away, she would be leaving home to work in England the following week and she couldn't even talk to me about her plans for her future. This was the straw that broke the camel's back.

I went into hospital for the last time, to get better even if it meant being restrained in a straight-jacket. I also knew I was going to look a right mess coming off, and I did not want my children to suffer any more so I forbade John to let them visit me.

"What will I tell them?" John asked impatiently, as he had begun to run out of excuses on behalf of his wreck of a wife.

"Just tell them the truth," I answered, feeling beaten and battered mentally.

Nothing had changed in the hospital, they knew I would be back and let me know, in no uncertain terms, that if I signed myself out again they would wash their hands off me. The full horrors of coming off Halcion hit me like a bolt of lightning. Not having had sleep for a month had weakened me no end. I tried to sleep, but gave up after the hallucinations started in earnest. I was buried alive, thousands of maggots were eating into my flesh, and the more I picked the more took their place. My mouth and eyes were full of the white writhing creatures and the smell of decay filled my senses. I tried to scream but no sound would come – they were crawling down my throat. A skeleton's hand pulled at my arm.

"Wake up, Mrs Maher, wake up!"

I opened my eyes to see a nurse shaking me by the shoulder, only she was not a nurse, she was a skeleton with a gaping mouth.

"Get away from me! I don't want to die! Get those maggots off me!" I had found my voice at last.

"Mrs Maher, you're dreaming, pull yourself together!"

"What time is it?"

I was hoping she would say six thirty in the morning, then I would know the night was over.

"It's half past twelve, Mrs Maher."

I had got into bed at midnight after outstaying my welcome in the television lounge by an hour, where the night nurse had given me a Medussa look and turned off the television in disgust.

I cried out in horror. 'God, no! Not again! Not another long dark lonely night! Please God, don't let the horrors start, please give my mind rest!' I made up my mind not to fall asleep again to avoid the nightmares, but I now started to have waking dreams, hallucinating while awake. During the day the sounds of hospital life kept my mind partly occupied, helping to stave off the worst horrors of withdrawal. Night time has a different sound to it and a mental hospital is not quiet at night. Minnie started her nocturnal howling and cursing at exactly 1 a.m. God help her, I do not wish to be unkind towards her illness, but there were times when her life was still in mortal danger of being snuffed out by smothering.

Some of the night staff were very inconsiderate towards those trying to sleep. As we were not allowed bed rest during the day they could at least have given us peace at night. Instead, they played games right beside patient's beds, and the male staff from the men's end joined the female staff for games of Trivial Pursuits at two o'clock in the morning. The male patients would have told them to 'fuck off', but the women were too frightened to say anything and had to suffer in silence. In normal circumstances this is hard to bear, but when you are in the grip of withdrawal as I was, it was unbearable. In an effort to let them know they were annoying us and keeping the patients awake I started answering their questions for them.

"What is square and yet it is round?" a male nurse shouted just beside my lughole. In a temper I shouted back "An effin' boxing ring!" I still had some of my humour left plus a little bit of brain power. All went quiet for a few seconds and I prayed they had taken the hint. Not on your nelly, it made matters worse and they talked even louder out of spite.

There seems to be an unwritten rule in some mental hospitals – 'Don't report staff for being a nuisance.' I broke this rule and paid dearly for it. I wasn't nasty, I just asked them to please try and be a trifle quieter in their games; I knew the nights were long but please would they try to keep their voices down. One of the male nurses waited for his chance to get back at me, a nasty piece of work who had as much compassion as I had hairs on my chest – and that was none.

A very nasty hallucination, where the walls of the ward had opened up revealing rats the size of cats and spiders too hideous for even Stephen King to have imagined, had made me extremely agitated. In my dread of being eaten alive by these monsters I had run up the corridor in a bid for freedom, trying to find a friendly face to talk me round. Who should be standing at the end of the corridor but the unsympathetic excuse for a nurse who had earlier boasted to the staff how merry he got when he took Valium along with his drink. I suspected he had said this deliberately to annoy me, for he had often made snide remarks about drug addicts when he knew I was within earshot.

"And where do you think you're going at two in the morning?"

"I have to get out of here, I'm going mad!"

"Is that so, Mrs Maher? Well, you're in the right place for it, maybe you would like a bit of help."

He grabbed my right arm, twisted it up my back and ran me back along the corridor, whispering menacingly in my ear, "One more complaint from you and it's up to the lock-up ward with the rest of the headcases!"

My back hurt and my leg ached from the back condition I suffered from, yet I was too scared to report him in case he made my life even harder.

I am glad to say that not all the staff treated patients in this way, indeed the majority were very understanding – but then it only takes one bad apple. The days of imagining that everyone working in the medical profession is there because they care about others seem long gone. It is only too obvious that for some it is only a job and to hell with tender loving care.

Four weeks passed and I thought I would never get better. They could not reduce my intake of Halcion because of my mental state. A girl who had come over from England in an attempt to come off heroin could not understand how a prescribed drug could make a person's withdrawal worse than the street drug she had been taking. Then again, you get help coming off heroin – you are given a substitute drug to help you through the worst part of withdrawal.

Those four weeks were a living hell, not being able to eat, yet retching continuously. I had to force Complan down my throat so as to put a lining on my stomach, the constant diarrhoea making my stomach cramp day in and day out. The sweat I lost would have filled a bath and I had to bathe four or five times daily to keep my body odour at bay. The poisons in my body were leaking through my pores, I smelt like a French onion seller who had been rubbed down with garlic. You soon know who your friends are when you pong to high heaven, and I did not have many of these left.

I felt constantly confused, even getting washed and dressed in the morning was a battle between my brain and my hands. My co-ordination was completely up the left. In an effort to clean my teeth I often tried to use my hair brush, but in trying to comb my hair I was more like a three year old, the comb refusing to make contact with my head because my hands could not determine right from left. It took an hour to get dressed as I tried to work out where each garment went. I found myself trying to put my trousers over my head, and my legs down the sleeves of my sweater. At times I was convinced I had pre-senile dementia I felt so confused and forgetful.

These were the minor symptoms, the major symptoms were trying to control the continuous shaking and trembling plus the feelings of unreality. I tried to exercise my brain, in an attempt to stop it seizing up altogether, by listening to the radio. Each song they played became a brain teaser: 'What year did that one come out?' If I got the year right it meant my mind was still active. I prayed for them to play an Elvis song to brighten my day, anything other than 'Jailhouse Rock', as I felt trapped in a jail as it was. They did play an Elvis song and you've guessed it – they played 'Jailhouse

Rock'. It was the first time since the age of thirteen that I turned Elvis off.

Things were indeed in a bad way when I turned my back on Elvis. Don't get me wrong, I did not put Elvis Presley in front of my family. He did not have to listen or look at me as did my family; their hearts were at breaking point and they needed a rest from me. Elvis on the other hand had never known 'I' existed, whereas I knew 'he' still existed for me. I could moan at him, tell him my problems without fear of him telling me to get lost.

In an attempt to get me on the road to recovery, John tried every trick in the book. He took me out in the car at night for drives. We drove round and round in ever-decreasing circles as I had now become completely agoraphobic. The thought of maybe getting caught up in a bomb scare and not getting back in time for my medication had me at panic stations and I would not let him go near built-up areas. Yet I could not sit in the visiting room of the hospital, my nerves were so jangled. The haunted look of a fugitive was permanently imprinted on my face. I would sit perched on a window ledge near the exit door and count the minutes until my name was called for my little blue pill. I couldn't go out, yet I couldn't go in.

As a last resort John asked a faith healer to come and visit me. We had passed the stage where religious beliefs, whether Catholic or Protestant, mattered. We didn't care if the man was Hindu or Moslem, Catholic or Protestant. He could have been a flaming witch-doctor with bones through his nose and shrunken heads dangling from a string around his neck, just as long as had the power to heal. The faith healer was a kindly man, but I'm afraid kindness did not help. My faith in God was diminishing by the hour and at one point I would have sold my soul to the devil for a night's sleep. In fact I took on the look of a 'She Devil'. If my head had started to turn round in circles while I spat out green bile John would not have turned a hair. I had come to the end of the road.

The psychiatrists must have realised the futility of trying to get me off the Halcion whenever I wouldn't let them out of my sight and followed them about as they made their ward rounds. They had no other choice but to prescribe me another drug to wean me off. Accordingly, 60mg of Valium was prescribed daily and the Halcion was discontinued completely. They took a hell of a risk prescribing this amount of Valium, proving even then they were aware of the dangers of Halcion. For all they knew I could have become addicted to the replacement drug, but as Valium is a slow release drug it took away the physical symptoms of withdrawal, permitting me to sleep in peace for the first time in months. The relief was like the weight of the world being lifted from my shoulders. To be free from the hallucinations, the sweats, the shakes, the feelings of unreality was a gift from God.

I knew I was getting better when my sense of humour started to return. I could once again laugh at the silly mistakes John made when describing objects, a legacy from his mother. On one occasion a nurse brought in the shell of a sea anemone to show to her colleagues. John sometimes imagines he is a bit of an expert on nature, and duly informed everyone that the object was a 'living orgasm' instead of 'organism'. I let him talk on about the mysteries of the deep and how miraculous nature was by inventing these 'living orgasms'. Everyone else had cottoned on to his faux pas and were making jokes about "keeping a safe distance" between themselves and these 'living orgasms' in case they got pregnant. For all the jesting, poor John did not realise his mistake, until I told him to try whistling Dixie through his ass for an encore. The penny dropped, and for the first time in eight years I laughed until my belly ached. Memories of the home bakery in Victoria Street came flooding back: Violet and myself were rolling about with uncontrollable laughter; the naked man in the pith helmet was racing up the street; I could smell the Plaza ballroom, the cheap perfume, the Brylcreem and the body odour of happy dancers as they jived the night away to Elvis, Eddie Cochrane and the Big Bopper. I felt alive and wanted to punch the air with my fist. I refrained in case the doctors decided to keep me in the mental hospital for the duration.

Until then I had given up all hope of ever feeling the sun shine on my face, or seeing the colours of trees and flowers, or watching my children grow into adults or being able to hold my grandchildren. I had almost given up on God. I knew he had more deserving cases than myself, but I had become a victim of someone else's mistake and I often asked God, 'Why me?' Since then I have read newspaper articles detailing the horror stories of other people trapped in the same hell, some of whom are languishing in jail for committing murder under the influence of this terrible drug. They should be set free, and the makers put away in their place.

As it turned out I was able to come off the Valium gradually and my life is almost back to normal. I do have flashbacks, especially at Christmas, or when I see a snowdrop, as snowdrops were growing in my garden when I left my children just after the Christmas of 1987. The sight of a snowdrop reminds me of their pale faces as I left them crying for their mother, a mother who was nothing more than an empty shell. One single snowdrop grew in my garden in January of this year and as I plucked it out, for a few seconds I was back in the mental hospital fighting for sanity. Perhaps the seed was blown by the wind to remind me not to forget those who are still suffering the anguish and hell that is 'Halcion.'

To those people I would say never give up hope and keep

praying, fight for your rights whatever it takes. Make your doctor or psychiatrist listen to your pleas for help, don't sit back and let your brain be taken over. Demand alternative treatment, you have nothing to lose and everything to gain. You have not been a victim of your own making, you have been a pawn in the game of lining the pockets of scurrilous manufacturers who don't care who they destroy as long as they make a rich picking. And don't blame the doctors who prescribed the drug, they were victims as well.

I find the hardest part of the whole affair is the ignorance of others, those who imagine they are smart by making cocky remarks. It's not the first person who has tried to make out I'm a hypochondriac of the first degree. I am not allowed to be ill without snide remarks like 'The chemists have run out of tablets, Val?' or 'Are the aule nerves away with it again?' Even if I complain of a migraine it's: 'Oh you suffer from those *as well.*' 'As well' as what?

I take life one day at a time now. You don't realise what life means to you until you almost lose it – everyday is precious to me now. When you step out of the shadows you feel sunshine, and colours take on new life. I forgot that the trees have so many shades of green, that the morning chorus sounds so beautiful. That doctor was almost right when she told me 'Life begins at forty' – she was only five years out.

John retired from his job shortly after I came off the Halcion, but he also regained the wife he thought he had lost. The veil of darkness had now lifted, and my cup is again half full and not half empty. The walls of glass had started to shatter. I could see at last, even if only through the cracks.

Chapter 17

MY WISH CAME TRUE

The road to recovery, or should I say sanity, did not come overnight. The effects of the Halcion lingered in the recesses of my brain, now and then being revealed in spurts of forgetfulness and quite a few periods of extreme tiredness. I had to rest a lot, not to try and hurry up nature's healing through impatience and anger. Impatience and anger do nothing other than eat away at your soul. I should have been content with at least being able to sleep without relentless nightmares and bodyless voices invading my ears.

I could at last let my father rest in peace. I no longer had to shout out: 'Go away! Just because you died in anger don't try to take your revenge out on me! Call out God's name – he should be your strength, not me!'

God did become *my* strength and I prayed every hour on the hour. I know I did not look well, and I still kept a distance between myself and my neighbours as I did not want to explain why I looked so sickly. For a long time I felt ashamed, as if it was my fault for being so weak-willed. We moved house once again. Friends had even recommended we purchase a caravan and park it wherever I took a fancy. I seriously toyed with the idea, for the thought of living in some remote part of the countryside with only cows and sheep for company beckoned to me, just as a moth is drawn to a light. Indeed, I felt just as fragile as a moth.

We moved into a newly-built house in the spring of 1988 – a new house and a new beginning. Wanting so much to make a fresh start, to leave behind all that reminded me of the bungalow and its memories, we purchased new furniture, curtains, carpets, lamps, and even pots, pans, kettle and electrical appliances – the local furniture and electricity store must have thought Christmas had arrived early. I think the neighbours were convinced we had dropped in from another planet. In a way we, or should I say 'I', *had* been on another planet, it was about time I came down to earth.

The move cost us dearly, every penny John had saved and more, but it was worth it. At last my children's friends could call at the door and gain entrance. If I was caught napping on the settee a migraine could always be invented as an excuse. The faith healer who had visited me in hospital came to see me. His cheerful presence was most welcome, and we talked and prayed together. Again, religious persuasion did not matter, we knew his beliefs and he did not question ours. There is no fighting beyond the grave, we leave our hatred behind – God is too busy trying to keep the Devil at bay on earth to worry about what goes on behind the Pearly Gates.

Gradually my strength improved and I found myself upright more often than on my back sleeping. The sound of my children's choice of music sometimes irritated me, the monotonous thump, thump, thump of bass guitars and drums in the background almost had me at screaming point. Until that day one of my daughters informed me 'Old fogies like you don't understand the young ones and their music'. For a minute I agreed, then I remembered saying the same thing to my parents when my ear was glued to Radio Luxembourg on a Sunday evening, especially a Sunday in May of 1956.

"I don't what!" My temper gave me a strength I had long ago thought had disappeared. The get up and go that I had assumed had got up and went, came surging back to me.

"Alright," I informed them, "I will prove to you I do understand." I matched them record for record. For every one of their choice I played Elvis. They laughed and poked fun that Elvis was dead, no more, extinct, to all those people under the age of being eligible for bus passes.

"Hang on," I answered, "My bus pass is years away, don't you dare run my Elvis down." 'My Elvis' – I had to laugh; after all these years I still thought of him as being put on this earth only for me.

The idea of again starting to have some sort of a social life after ten years entered my mind, a visit to a theatre would be a start. Too soon for mixing socially, the confines of a small theatre without the added burden of having to make conversation beckoned me like that fragile moth to the light.

"Let's go to the Arts Theatre this Sunday." John had been looking up the entertainment section of the *Belfast Telegraph* and noticed that an Elvis impersonator called Frank Chisum was performing.

"Never heard of him," I answered. Anyway, no-one could copy Elvis, especially someone called 'Frank Chisum'!

"Sounds more like an undertaker than an Elvis impersonator," I laughed. Well at least it *had* made me laugh, an emotion I had been in short supply of for a hell of a while. "Ah well, might as well go for the hell of it – book the tickets." I thought to myself: 'One thing's for sure – he won't be over-booked.' Famous last words.

Sunday night found John and I queuing outside the theatre. "Are you sure we're at the right place?" I asked John, as I surveyed the crowd, for some of the people waiting weren't even born when Elvis died.

"Well his name's on the board," answered John, with as much enthusiasm as a turkey at Christmas. When the lights dimmed in the theatre, the familiar sound of Elvis's signature tune echoed through a building which was bursting at the seams with people of all ages. 'Also Spake Zarathustra' – then more commonly known as the opening theme of the film '2001, A Space Odyssey' – boomed out of the amplifiers which straddled the stage. A deep foreboding American voice gave a short history of Elvis's life before announcing: 'And now we have Frank Chisum as Elvis!'

A spotlight hovered over the entrance to the stage and I had to stifle the urge to giggle at someone with the bare-faced cheek to try and imitate the King.

I spent the next two hours transfixed to my seat. Elvis had indeed been brought back from the grave, albeit a little smaller in stature but nevertheless a very good likeness. The jumpsuits and American Army outfit had been very carefully copied, right down to the cape Frank donned as he performed Elvis's 'American Trilogy' crescendo at the end of his performance.

As we left the theatre we were handed a photograph of Frank with his manager's telephone number printed on it. I put it in my handbag and thought no more about it. What you are about to read next may make you have second thoughts as to whether or not my sanity had indeed started to return or whether my sanity had taken a turn for the worse.

Cleaning out the ashes of the fireplace is not the most inspirational of jobs. More a housewife's nightmare than a time to be startled by bodyless voices. The voice was saying, 'Give Frank Chisum's manager a call.' I shook my head and prayed my mind was not once more playing tricks. The voice persisted: 'Ring him, ring him.' 'What the hell for?' I thought, as I carried on with my Cinderella task. 'You have to make it known that Elvis Presley still lives on in spirit.' Talk about an 'out of body' experience! The hairs on my head stood on end and I could feel an invisible hand push me toward the telephone.

I sat on the telephone seat feeling betwixt and bewildered, yet somehow excited – a curious mixture of feelings. I got up again and went on with the cleaning, and called myself for all the stupid cows ever to be let loose. The voice still bantered in my ear: 'Call Frank's manager.' The photograph that had been handed to me in the foyer of the Arts Theatre was tucked away out of sight in my handbag – or should I say nose-bag for a horse, for I always carry an extra large handbag filled with everything but the kitchen sink. 'Be prepared' was always my motto, even down to an extra pair of knickers – well, one does not know when one might be knocked down and carted off to the nearest hospital.

I dialled Frank's manager, who was then Charlie McBrien. He answered the phone and I had to make up a story pronto.

"Er... Mr McBrien."

"Call me Charlie, my dear. Mr McBrien makes me feel old." My knees almost buckled beneath me, as I asked very sheepishly if I could interview Frank Chisum regarding a book I was in the process of writing. I could feel my nose grow as I had no intentions then of writing a letter never mind a book. The words just tumbled out on their own without any coaxing.

"No problem, call Frank on the telephone, number blah, blah, blah, he will make arrangements."

"Thank you. Mr McBrien."

"Charlie, if you don't mind."

"Er... Charlie." I hung up and made myself a cup of coffee to calm my nerves. What the hell's gate's do I do now, I thought. Well, I told him I was writing a book, so write a book I must do, but on what? The answer came to me immediately – write a book on how Elvis influenced the singers of today. On the following Monday I rang Frank and in a rather timid voice asked for an interview. He agreed to meet me that night before his act.

He remarked that my voice sounded very nervous. I'm almost sure he twigged on that I was not a professional journalist or writer. John bought me a small tape recorder so that I would look the part, and I jotted down some questions on a journalist's note pad. Armed with my aide mémoire John and I drove to my appointment. God was tortured that night as I prayed for confidence to guide me in my hour of need.

My image of Frank Chisum, star of stage, was shattered as soon as I walked into his dressing room. There he stood stripped to the waist, his face covered in shaving cream.

"Take a seat there, rest your backside." His broad Omagh brogue took me by surprise – in my naivety I had imagined a slow Memphis drawl. "Fuck me, that's one awful bloody night, it's pissin' out there. We got lost twice comin' here. Went to the effin' wrong gig, nearly stood in for Roly Daniels we did. By the way, excuse the dressing room, it doubles for the men's toilet. Mind you, I've got dressed in worse conditions."

I soon felt at ease, or maybe this was his way of making me feel at ease. Frank is an avid Elvis fan, but as he says he "has no illusions – there is, or was, only one Elvis and always will be." He is also eager to give you his personal opinions about Elvis, mostly positive.

I was soon to find out that Frank also has a temper, and over the years we have had our little tiffs. However, I must thank him for introducing me to Graeme Lowry and Tom Mahony, his PR man and personal friend. Tom and his wife Anne have become very good friends of John and I.

At the end of the interview, which was more of a friendly chat, Frank gave me Graeme's telephone number, plus a quick summary of Graeme's writing experience as well as the illness that had so cruelly cut short his career. A brain tumour had been diagnosed just when he had received his degree in journalism. At the time I didn't quite realise the seriousness of Graeme's plight.

The following day I telephoned Graeme; his voice sounded far too young for my image of a journalist. Only after our first meeting did I realise it was not his age that was responsible for his 'young' voice but his gentle nature. This, coupled with the effects of chemotherapy, made him look, as well as sound, extremely fragile.

I was not prepared for the sight of Graeme standing at his open door in a wee black woolly hat, which did little to disguise the harshness of his illness. His pale, almost translucent, complexion lit up as he smiled from ear to ear – it is imprinted on my mind forever. As my eyes brimmed with tears I had to quell the urge to hug him. What age did Frank say – twenty-three? I pictured my own son who was around that age, a strapping big lad full of health, and thought to myself: 'Life is so unfair.' Here was I, standing with my bits and pieces about how Elvis had helped me overcome a bad life experience, with the cheek to ask for help with my writing from someone who, even though he was only half my age, had to watch his own life slip away before him. Talk about a humbling experience.

His wife Celine, to whom he had been married for less than a year, busied herself making coffee as we talked over my plans. By the end of my visit his enthusiasm had convinced me to begin writing my book on Elvis. In fact he said he felt excited and invigorated by the challenge. God help him, he did not live to see the challenge bear fruition. He had an inner strength that shone through his feeble exterior, a strength that only those who appreciate the simple things in life radiate.

As I left his house he warned me, "By the time your book is into its third chapter you will be sorry you didn't take up knitting instead." I shook him by the hand and was taken aback by how gentle his handshake was, almost childlike. I wondered if it was a side effect of his illness until I gazed down at his hand. He had the hands of a writer – artistic and refined.

After a few months I was not only sorry I had taken up writing, I was sorry I had gone to the Arts Theatre to see Frank Chisum. But my brain finally began to function, and I decided that now I'd started I would finish. As the weeks passed my confidence increased and I interviewed various artists about the influence Elvis had on their lives. Not all, I am sorry to say, were enthusiastic, others were darn right rude, including some who should have reacted better having made a living out of singing some of Elvis's songs.

"Elvis would not have made it if he had not have had the good looks." This remark was often made by those whose own looks left much to be desired. My answer was: "well, I fell for Elvis's voice long before I knew what he looked like, so answer that." That usually left them speechless. Others had the gift of the gab and I was left gobsmacked. My confidence took a right battering at times. Graeme would have none of my moaning and told me, "No-one is better than you. Go for it. Just imagine them sitting on the toilet with their trousers round their ankles when you talk to them." It worked.

Only for Graeme I would have thrown in the towel – he was my guiding light. Not all of the singers I talked to were nasty pieces of work. Brendan Bowyer, once better known as the singer with 'The Royal Showband' – later to be called 'The Big 8' – knew Elvis personally. We shared a few funny stories concerning him and Elvis, one of which went as follows.

When Brendan was singing on stage in Las Vegas he often sang a medley of Elvis's songs. It just so happened to be an Elvis song he was in the middle of singing, when out of the corner of his eye he spotted this 'eejit' – to use his very words – jump out of the wings and dance like Elvis as Brendan sang his heart out. Well, with the lights and the sweat pouring from his brow he thought someone was taking the Mickey. He told this 'eejit' to get off the stage as he was ruining his act. The audience laughed and clapped and poor Brendan thought he had seen the last of Las Vegas for the duration. Gone were six months of his yearly income to some crackpot who wanted to hog the limelight. He was telling him to take a hike out of the corner of his mouth, and just about ready to clock him on the gob, when, to his surprise, the 'eejit' turned out to be Elvis himself, just having a bit of a laugh!

Boy, did Brendan feel bad – he couldn't apologise enough, but old El boy just broke up. He later asked Brendan if he could record one of *his* songs – 'Kiss me quick'. That's how that song is on one of his albums. Brendan and his wife attended many a party held by Elvis, and Elvis was often in the audience listening to Brendan perform. He has nothing bad to say about Elvis and he made one of my dreams come true by sending me a photograph of him and the man himself taken on the set of the film 'Spin Out'. I treasure it, and would not part with it for the world.

As time passed I realised the memory of Elvis had an effect on so many people, I would have been interviewing singers until I was blue in the face. Then it dawned on me that I myself had been inspired by Elvis to the point were I could almost say he saved my life. I changed the purpose of the book and decided to write my own story. From that moment I have felt as if Elvis Presley was my guiding angel. Writing is a very lonely occupation, not to mention frustrating. Apart from penning the occasional article for fan magazines and newspapers which took up no more than two A4 sheets of paper, my literary talents were limited. The daunting task of completing a manuscript three inches thick gave me nightmares. My temper is at the norm quite manageable, but, as John can confirm, when I lose it, I could frighten the Devil. The only aspect of my temper tantrums he couldn't stand was when I would have to take to my bed with exhaustion after rushing round the house like a whirling dervish, ranting and raving about other people's inconsideration for the plight of a budding writer. How dare publishers return my part-manuscripts, and who the hell does Frank Chisum think he is refusing to speak to me when I needed help on matters concerning Elvis! Jumped up little fart, there should have been a law against people like him! Sorry Frank, you understand how I felt!

Looking back it made me more determined to prove myself. I think Frank knew this as we often laugh about it now. The last time I spoke to Frank he ended our conversation with the words: "I am proud of you, Valerie, I didn't think you could do it you were so nervous, but by Christ you proved me wrong. Stay in there, girl, don't let the bastards get you down." Even if I never see you again, Frank, at least your words will stay engraved in my mind.

If I thought the first experience of being pushed by unseen hands was uncanny, nothing would or could beat my next encounter with the unexplainable. I had gone to bed early after a hard day at the typewriter, my brain filled with doubt as to who would be in the least bit concerned about reading the life story of an unknown housewife. Yet I had to let my story be known, I had to keep my promise to Elvis, I could not let him down. During my battle against the after-effects of the 'Halcion' I had practised self-hypnosis as a way of relaxing. One of the many ways of getting into a relaxed state of mind is to think of walking down steps into a beautiful garden. In my mind's eye I pictured the steps and proceeded to descend a step with each breath. But this time a figure emerged slowly from the bright sunshine that bathed the flowers and trees in its soft warm glow. This had never happened before when I went into my relaxed state and I tried to shake the vision from my mind. I sighed with frustration at having seemingly lost my ability to relax. And all the while the figure just came nearer and nearer.

Oh hell! I thought I might as well go with the flow. As the figure got even closer I realised it was Elvis who had intruded into my beautiful garden. An overwhelming feeling of happiness flooded over me. He looked young and handsome and in his prime. He was wearing a red shirt and I could make out every detail, right down to the stitching that caught the sleeves in above the elbows and again at the wrists. I remember thinking it an unusual shirt – indeed, more befitting an assistant in a bookie's shop. He gently kissed me on the lips, not a passionate kiss but a kiss that said 'You are my friend'. I could feel his soft lips on mine and I felt serene and content, not as some might think filled with the urge to engage in passionate activity. If this had happened in real life I most likely would have floored him and pinned him to the ground.

Just as gently as he had appeared he started to disappear back into the garden, saying as he did so: "Thank you, Valerie, you will finish your book, and it will be published. You will also visit me and place five red roses in a part of 'Graceland' where I often found solace."

I tried to conjure up his image again, but he did not return. All of a sudden I became fully alert. I was crying, not with sadness but with joy. I felt as if I had actually met him in person. I told John what had happened and he gave me a look usually kept for the benefit of the mentally bewildered.

Visiting 'Graceland' was most definitely not on my agenda. For a start I would have had to grow wings as our bank statement was not so much a statement as a plea from the heart from a bank manager now probably regretting being so overgenerous with his overdraft allowance. We had just got over the Christmas holidays by the skin of our teeth on borrowed money; in fact the 'hole in the wall' had refused me ten pounds earlier on that very day.

"You will visit me and place five red roses in a part of 'Graceland' where I often found solace." What did those words mean, and why *five* red roses? I had convinced myself that the vision had been a dream, but what on earth did those words mean? I was to find out sooner than I thought.

In February John had an insurance policy paid out. It came as a surprise for it had matured a year earlier than expected. Just enough to pay for a holiday to Memphis and clear our overdraft. We packed our cases, sunglasses, camera, camcorder and my tape recorder in case I got talking to anyone who knew Elvis and didn't want to forget any interesting stories about old 'El' boy. If I got them on tape they would be caught for posterity and be proof to my friends and family I was not ready for the twilight home for the over-imaginative. After a tiresome car trip to Dublin we checked into the Airport Hotel for a good night's sleep before our flight the next morning. Some sleep we were to get! A rock band started to play in the function room below us. Being a light sleeper I asked the manager for a change of room. John, however, being a heavy sleeper, had already conked out and has never remembered being led into a bedroom two floors up by the manager and myself. He woke the following morning minus his partial bottom dentures and thought he had swallowed them. He thought this hilarious while I went berserk at the very idea of him visiting Graceland with hardly a bar in his grate. I gazed hopelessly at the gop standing in the nude – all sixteen stone of him – and the urge to decapitate him was almost overwhelming.

"You can't go! I hope you realise this! Why did you have to go and loose your teeth, of all things?"

To make matters worse he started to act Elvis by singing 'All shook Up' in the noddy. "Well, bless my soul, what's wrong with me? I'm itching like a man who's caught VD."

It was not a pleasant sight.

"That's sacrilege!" I screamed.

"If Elvis was alive he would look just like me at this minute, Val – do you realise that?"

"Piss off and find your teeth, ye gabshite! This is neither the time nor place for levity. Do you not realise the seriousness of this journey – it is nothing short of a pilgrimage!"

"Hang on a minute, I'm not in the same room as I was in last night!"

· "Oh, you realise that now, do you?" I answered sarcastically. "Well, maybe your teeth are, so get huntin' or you go straight back to Antrim."

As we checked out a voice on the intercom asked: "If anyone finds a pair of teet', will they please leave them at the front desk, tank you very much,' in a broad Dublin accent. The offending teeth were later found under the bed by the cleaning lady. How they got there was a mystery. The journey I had yearned for all these years had started.

Delta Airlines winged us on our way to a wish come true, even though it was tinged with sadness. There would be no Elvis, just memories. Well, at least I could dream. As the plane touched down in Memphis on a humid May evening the realisation of at last visiting his home hit me with a jolt. The night-time arrival prevented us from seeing inside 'Graceland' until the following day. We drove up 'Elvis Presley Boulevard' in the darkness. The taxi driver stopped at the famous 'Music Gates' at the end of the driveway to his home, and my heart almost stopped beating as I took in the sight before me. The house beckoned with its twinkling lights. To my right I could see the 'Lisa Marie' – his private jet plane. The 'TCB' insignia on the tail teased me the same way his name on the cinema hoarding had teased me when I first went to see him in 'Love me tender'.

231

I remember thinking 'I am here! I am here at last!' I fell into a fitful sleep with Elvis's song 'My wish came true' ringing in my ears. 'Graceland' opens early in the morning so that visitors can visit the graves, before the doors to the mansion itself are opened, but for some unknown reason I wanted to see inside before visiting the site where Elvis had been laid to rest. In the building facing 'Graceland', where you buy the tickets, a stall of red roses sits to the left of the doors that lead you on to the tour bus. My first reaction was to purchase a single red rose for Elvis, to place on his grave, but I remembered the request 'Elvis' had made when he asked me to leave five red roses at the place where he had found solace. I glanced at a glass-fronted display case beside the stall, and inside lay five single roses wrapped in heart-covered cellophane, each one tied with a red ribbon. The music from the loudspeakers was playing 'Mama loved the roses'.

The hairs on the nape of my neck stood on end, and, as if someone else had control of my voice, I asked for five roses. I remembered his mother had been buried beside him – maybe he wanted me to place one on her grave for him. Clutching my small bouquet of roses we boarded the tour bus, its passengers surprisingly quiet as we wound our way up the driveway that led to his home. People of all races and creeds united with one thought: *how* did Elvis live, would his home shed any light on the private life of the man?

We alighted at the steps leading up to the front door. I recognised the stone lions that flanked the steps from photographs, and the familiar white pillars that had made it look so majestic in books. When the front door opened we filed in under the scrutiny of an army of eagle-eyed guards. As the door closed behind me I felt like an intruder, as if the owner did not approve of my visit. A young girl – too young to have remembered Elvis when he was alive – gave the visitors a quick and somewhat indifferent tour of his dining room which was situated to the left of the entrance hall, while the guards did not miss a movement of those present. Before I go any further I will advise those who are thinking of visiting 'Graceland' to keep in mind that the furnishings are very Seventies in style. Some might even think they are in very bad taste, with their bright crimsons, electric blues, citric yellows and lots and lots of mirrors that reflect what you see in the rooms on the walls and ceilings. 'You did indeed live 'Behind Walls of Glass', my old son, you even chose the title of my book,' was my first reaction, as I looked at the empty rooms that were once filled with the hustle and bustle of minders and hangers-on.

Keep this in mind and you won't be disappointed. The fact that no camera flash is allowed, or video recording, spoilt the tour. One is hastened through so quickly a lot of detail is missed, the privilege of catching it on film called for another two visits to take it all in.

We passed through, or should I say looked over dividing ropes at the living room, pool room, jungle room and television room before catching a glimpse of where he played his last game of squash and where he practised rifle shooting. I had warned John of the fact that I would probably break down in tears with the emotion, but he was understanding. "Cry a bucket if it makes you feel better," he answered. But no tears would come, I just wanted out for some reason. Still clutching my roses we made our way to the garden of remembrance, the only place I felt strangely drawn to.

Elvis's grave is situated beside the swimming pool, where he lies beside his father, mother, and Aunt Minnie May. A small brass plaque has been placed in remembrance of his twin brother, Jesse Garon, who died at birth. Five names – five red roses! I cried for the first time, the tears slowly trickling down my cheeks, a single tear landing on one of the roses. It resembled a diamond as it glittered in the Memphis sunshine, a precious stone fit for a king. I took this rose and placed it on his grave, then placed the others on the other four. I said a prayer and thought 'You deserve the rest, Elvis, how on earth did you live with the ever-present gaze of strangers watching your every move?' Then it suddenly dawned on me – a peaceful garden beside the swimming pool! 'This is where you used to walk in peace – your place of solace.' I had carried out his wishes and I too felt tranquil. Had I not entered the house, this moment would be imprinted on my mind for ever.

I talked to George Klein and Richard Davis, Elvis's stand-in for film stunts. They told me a few amusing stories about how Elvis loved to play tricks, in fact he had a very humorous side to his nature, a side seldom seen by the public.

A year later I had the privilege of meeting Charlie Hodge, Elvis's long time friend and part of his band. He was the one who draped the scarves round his neck on stage before giving them away to fans. I suppose a hint of Elvis's sweat or aftershave was quite a thrill to his fans. The best way of describing Charlie is as a bit of a wag, the joker of the pack who kept everyone amused. After I left him I could understand why – he had me in stitches with his stories. He agreed with my assertion that Elvis could not have performed on stage if he was as drugged as some people made him out to be.

Elvis gave his closest friends a gold TCB or TLC necklace or a green sapphire and diamond ring. They were very proud in showing these two pieces of jewellery to all and sundry. They usually made a big thing about it on such occasions. As I own a gold TLC necklace and green sapphire and diamond ring I had a field day pretending Elvis had given them to me. I let it go on for a while and watched their faces as they tried to find out how and where he had given them to me. Boy, did they look surprised. It was on one of these occasions Charlie realised he was not the only joker in town!

The Memphis heat weakens the body, and after a few days of sightseeing and shopping for souvenirs, my physical strength was spent and we moved on. A few days in Nashville and then home. The following year I met Patsy Andersen, Fans Relations Manager, at an Elvis convention in Dublin. She had brought a suit that belonged to Elvis to put on show for the event. Patsy and I had a long talk about how Elvis had helped me overcome my problems over the years. She was not surprised as she had heard similar tales from various other people and did not doubt my story. Later that night I saw the suit that she had brought over with her from 'Graceland'. A white leather sleeveless jacket studded with gold stones, and black trousers with the same studs to complete the ensemble. Out of curiosity I asked her what shirt he wore under it.

In a slow Memphis drawl she answered: "He wore this suit on private occasions; he had this red shirt with sleeves gathered in at the elbow and wrist to go with it. He always wore red when he felt happy."

The blood drained from my face.

"Why, whatever's wrong, you look really faint all of a sudden?" she asked with a worried look on her face.

"You wouldn't believe it if I told you."

With a look of concern she answered, "Sure I will, Valerie." After I had relayed the story she too looked quite pale. My vision had come true down to the last detail. I never had the same experience again. I have tried but it is as if he had just made that one visit to show me the way.

Patsy Andersen did give me an invitation to call for coffee at 'Graceland' any time I was over. I can imagine what the guard on the gate would say if I told him I had been invited for coffee – it is unprintable! Still, someday I might try it. It would make my day if he let me through those big music gates to direct me to the kitchen.

My final wish – to sit on the steps of 'Graceland' at one minute to twelve in the evening on my own with Elvis singing 'It's midnight' in the background.

Then again, I should be content at having a second bash at life, for not everyone gets that privilege.

Postscript

Graeme Lowry died on 14 September 1993 at twenty seven years of age, just as I was completing the first draft of this book.

He would not have wanted me to feel sad, he would have told me to hold a party, to down a bottle of the grape and get plastered. "Play aule Elvis and dance till ye drop. Life is for living, and when your number's up, go out fighting – for I did."

I now have a guiding spirit on each shoulder. One whose face smiles not only from the lips but from the eyes, a sign that a person is genuine, generous and sincere. He's wearing a duncher cap, a tweed jacket and corduroy trousers.

The other: a man in a jumpsuit that glitters with multi-coloured stones and a lop-sided smile on his face. He too once had a dream. He is telling me "to follow that dream" wherever that dream will lead.

God bless you both, redeem your souls and fly. The light of that candle will show you the way to the peace you so richly deserve.